GODSTRUCK

Also by Kelsey Osgood

How to Disappear Completely: On Modern Anorexia

GODSTRUCK

*Seven Women's
Unexpected Journeys to
Religious Conversion*

Kelsey Osgood

VIKING

VIKING

An imprint of Penguin Random House LLC

1745 Broadway, New York, NY 10019

penguinrandomhouse.com

Designed by Alexis Farabaugh

LIBRARY OF CONGRESS CATALOGING-IN-PUBLICATION DATA

Names: Osgood, Kelsey, author.
Title: Godstruck : seven women's unexpected journeys to
religious conversion / Kelsey Osgood.
Description: [New York] : Viking, [2025]
Identifiers: LCCN 2024042395 (print) | LCCN 2024042396 (ebook) |
ISBN 9780593834671 (hardcover) | ISBN 9780593511411 (ebook)
Subjects: LCSH: Converts—United States—Biography. |
Religious biography—United States. | Women—Religious life—United States.
Classification: LCC BL639 .O84 2025 (print) | LCC BL639 (ebook) |
DDC 248.2/4092520973—dc23/eng/20250103
LC record available at https://lccn.loc.gov/2024042395
LC ebook record available at https://lccn.loc.gov/2024042396

Printed in the United States of America
1st Printing

Some names and identifying characteristics have been
changed to protect the privacy of the individuals involved.

The authorized representative in the EU for product safety and compliance is
Penguin Random House Ireland, Morrison Chambers, 32 Nassau Street,
Dublin D02 YH68, Ireland, https://eu-contact.penguin.ie.

For my subjects
And for Matt, Isaiah, Solomon, and Caleb

Some nights, going in to kiss her girls in their sleep, she will stop and look and feel before these many beasts of Gytha's something akin to what she felt as a child when the nuns sang their most beautiful, most awesome psalms, a slow internal pouring of ecstasy. Awe. If only she had time to examine this feeling, Wulfhild thinks ruefully; but she does not have time, she never has time, her children call, the business of the abbey calls, the hungers and fatigues of her body call. She will come closer to god when she is old, in a garden among the flowers and the birds, she tells herself; yes, some day she will sit in silence until she knows god, she thinks, lying down in her bed to sleep. Just not now.

LAUREN GROFF, *MATRIX*

Rabbi Barukh's grandson Yehiel was once playing hide-and-seek with another boy. He hid himself well and waited for his playmate to find him. When he had waited for a long time, he came out of his hiding-place, but the other was nowhere to be seen. Now Yehiel realized that he had not looked for him from the very beginning. This made him cry, and crying he ran to his grandfather and complained of his faithless friend. Then tears brimmed in Rabbi Barukh's eyes and he said: "God says the same thing: 'I hide, but no one wants to seek me.'"

MARTIN BUBER, *TALES OF THE HASIDIM*

Contents

Introduction

In May 2015, I stood in the basement of a nondescript building on the side of a city highway, the warm water of a mikvah, a Jewish ritual bath, lightly lapping my shoulders, my eyes swollen from spending most of the morning in tears. I wasn't sad, just overwhelmed. At the threshold of the door, three rabbis—their gazes averted to avoid seeing me unclothed—asked me, via a series of yes-or-no questions, to confirm my loyalty to the Jewish people. After answering them, I dunked under the water—the rabbis turned around then, although of course I couldn't see them, to ensure every last strand of hair was submerged—and then emerged, finally a Jew.

The mikvah is the final step in the process of converting to Judaism, and for me it came at the end of three years of study and lifestyle changes (no more Christmas trees, no driving on Saturdays) and a lifetime of seeking. I was a young person whose inner life had been—and still is, in so many ways—dominated by existential restlessness, and Judaism was a way to both validate that restlessness and channel it. I also happened to believe it was true.

Introduction

It was certainly not a transformation anyone who had known me for long saw coming. I was raised in a broadly nonreligious milieu, in a nuclear family that was (and is) best described as secularized American Christian: appreciates giving gifts on holidays but is either apathetic toward or opposed to God, depending on the individual. One of my favorite extended family members was my maternal grandfather, a self-described agnostic and misanthrope who enjoyed skewering our (few) religious family members at gatherings. For much of my early life, I went far beyond my peers in my distaste for religion, declaring God definitively Not Real in the third grade. I thought it painfully obvious that to be religious meant to be unintelligent—and intelligent was the only thing I really wanted to be. Later, I went to college in New York City, where I spent my time intoxicated by postmodern thought (and, well, intoxicants), interning at high-profile fashion magazines and nursing fantasies of a bohemian future. But years into a typical wild-and-woolly urban twenties experience, I found myself drawn to a Judaism that was mystical, conservative, and rigorous, and so, in direct contrast to most of my peers—and to the statistical trends that show Americans, and in particular young Americans, rapidly secularizing—I pursued it.

In one sense, my decision to convert can be viewed as a deeply conventional one: I signed on to a system that broadly supports traditional values about family, gender, community, and a host of other things. But in another way, for those same exact reasons, it might also be considered a wildly countercultural move. We're at a curious tipping point: what was once the epitome of conformity (dressing modestly, advocating for traditional family structures, and, yes, believing in God) now suddenly, in certain contexts, looks transgressive. Who in our glorious age of "progress" would choose to look *backward* for truth, rather than take advantage of the freedoms we now consider our birthright?

Almost every study on the matter in recent years has shown that the percentage of Americans who describe themselves as not religious is growing. The Pew Research Center, a think tank that often collects data about religious affiliation and spiritual trends, found that between 2007 and 2021, the percentage of Americans who identified as having no religion at all rose from 16 percent to 29 percent, while those who identified as Christian dropped from 78 percent to 63 percent. "The secularizing shifts evident in American society so far in the 21st century," the researchers wrote, "show no signs of slowing." There's some reason to believe this movement is particularly pronounced among young women, with some data showing that Gen Z women are far more likely to identify as nones (34 percent) than Gen X or millennials (23 percent).

Coverage of "the rise of the nones," as it's often framed, in mainstream media tends to be conveyed in a tone simultaneously self-satisfied and resigned: *Well, of course! We live in a world with science and medicine and technology and progressive values; why would we keep these ancient bugaboos around?* Many people I've spoken to who have backgrounds similar to my own—which is to say, secular liberal ones—interpret the collective loss of religion as a validation of their own worldviews, though they often inherited those with a passivity similar to the kind that's often decried in religious people. Yet despite the broad consensus that Nietzsche might have been right to declare God dead, there remains a wistfulness, sometimes conscious and sometimes less so, over the fact that, in losing our religion, we've found it harder to access a lot of its benefits, like effective community bonding mechanisms, access to the transcendent, wisdom that feel timeless and unblemished by corporate values, a sense of our place in the span of history, a connection to the physical earth, a sense of mystery and wonder, and so on. Though, as with so many things, it's hard to tease out what's correlation and what's causation, the religious life seems to be salutary too:

people of faith—especially those who attend services—report greater levels of happiness and less loneliness than their secular peers, they give more in charity, and some research suggests they are less likely to develop substance abuse problems or die of cardiovascular disease or cancer. Among the secular, there is often a frantic attempt to capture these benefits (remember "atheist church," briefly thought to be ascendant in the 2010s?), but few have been successful. "We used to know how to do these things," a convert to Judaism I once met said, sighing.

Though the data overwhelmingly supports the idea of secularization, there are snippets of evidence here and there that interest in, if not outright embrace of, religion remains. According to one study conducted by the Pew Center, around 50 percent of American adults have changed faiths at least once since the age of eighteen, though it's unclear how many of those were out of genuine spiritual conviction and how many were for practical purposes, like marriage. In 2021, *Tablet* magazine asked seventy-nine rabbis about their experiences with conversion, and found that thirty-six, or nearly half, said they were doing more conversions than ever before; interestingly, they all also said these were rarely for the sake of a Jewish romantic partner. In mid-2023, a handful of videos were posted on YouTube in which an array of thinkers attempted to answer the same question: Why were so many young Britons converting to Islam? There's also evidence that when younger people are interested in religion, they tend to be interested in more conservative iterations of it, which doesn't quite match with our stereotypes about youth: young Catholics discerning a religious vocation drawn toward orders that require full habits decades after such rules were relaxed by the Vatican; young Jews choosing the strictures of Orthodoxy over the big tent, God-optional liberal strains.

But this isn't a work that tries to justify itself with numbers. Whenever I encounter, in some article or essay, a series of statistics clearly inserted to convince you that what you are reading about is Objectively Important and Actionable, my shoulders sag a little. "More than four in ten workers do not take all their allotted time off." "The percentage of high-school students who report 'persistent feelings of sadness or hopelessness' shot up from 26 percent in 2009 to 44 percent in 2021." "A caress feels best when it is delivered with a small amount of force and a speed of about 1 inch per second." (These are all real, by the way.) We are bombarded with so much information that has the imprimatur of big data these days; we feel we are supposed to take something about how to be a human in the world from such tidbits, but what? One of the things I've relished about adopting a religious worldview is that it's a refuge from this kind of dry didactic framework, and I feel relatively inoculated from the particularly modern impulse to treat my life as a mathematical exercise with an eye toward optimization.

A common refrain these days from religious semi-apologists is that secularization isn't the only story; religion isn't dying out, they say, but rather morphing into something more personalized and less institutional. This looks like lots of things: astrology enthusiasts, bespoke spiritual rituals for corporate entities, mindfulness meditation apps, #digitalsabbaths, gratitude lists, randomly staring at lit candles. I believe that this is happening—that it is, in other words, *sociologically* true—but I am skeptical that this will help fill the void at the heart of contemporary Western culture (and there *is*, undeniably, a void). For one, personalized religion does not and cannot offer the communal benefits that established faiths do. But more than that, I believe strongly that part of the reason people are so weary these days is because hyperindividualism has created a situation in which the individual has become the sole arbiter of mythos and meaning. As the philosopher Charles Taylor writes, "Modern Westerners have a clear boundary between mind and world, even mind and body. Moral and other meanings are 'in the mind.' They cannot reside outside, and thus the boundary is firm." Elsewhere, he puts it this way: "[The modern] self can see itself as invulnerable, as master of the meanings of *things* for *it*." (Emphasis mine.) In Taylor's view, the modern self is historically unique in being able to conceive of itself as "invulnerable," because it believes the mind to be the locus of control (think of the contemporary exhortation to change your perspective on something you don't like: a medieval person would not consider a psychological shift as fundamentally altering the nature of an event). But of course, the modern self is not invulnerable, and it does not create meaning ex nihilo, unless you take a very humancentric view of earthly happenings. I think many people recognize somewhere deep down that we shouldn't be in charge, that we aren't in total control, and that the act of submitting the self to something else is a talent we've forfeited, and we suffer from that. To that end, if this book is anything, it's a nudge to reconsider *organized* religion—an argument I make with some trepidation, given its reputational deficit.

By far, the biggest question I got asked while I was working on this book was why I was focusing on women. There are a few answers to this, but first among them is that most religious converts are women, a fact that might be surprising to people. I always assumed that a woman would be less likely or willing to become religious, because most traditional religions are patriarchal in nature, and therefore a female convert would have more to lose, both practically and spiritually. It *is* true that many religions are patriarchal in many ways; I tend to think this is not a great thing, and I recognize that many women have suffered as a result of it over the course of history. This is a meaty dichotomy to unpack, and I thought it would be interesting to let women who've made this move themselves—myself included—talk about why the assumption that secular liberalism equals freedom equals happiness might be flawed, even for those who were supposed to be some of its primary beneficiaries.

In an essay entitled "The Lonely Man of Faith," Rabbi Joseph Soloveitchik, a very influential figure in Modern Orthodox Judaism, examines the religious man's plight through the two Adam figures in the alternative accounts of creation in Genesis. Adam the First is a paragon of action; he fashions himself after God in the latter's creative "mastery" of his surroundings (flags planted on mountaintops, spaceships built to orbit the earth, that kind of thing). Adam the Second, in contrast, is called to introspection, humility, and submission to the divine will. Soloveitchik suggests that the modern religious person experiences a kind of multilayered loneliness: not only is he "ontologically lonely" as a result of constantly trying to synthesize these two paradigms internally, and because of God's inherent elusiveness, but he is rendered more so by living in an era that negates the values of the second Adam. "What can a man of faith like myself," he asks, "living by a doctrine which has no technical potential, by a law which cannot be tested in the laboratory, steadfast in his loyalty to an eschatological vision whose fulfillment cannot be predicted with any degree of probability, let alone certainty, even by the most complex, advanced mathematical calculations—what can such a man say to a functional, utilitarian society which is *saeculum*-oriented and whose practical reasons of the mind have long ago supplanted the sensitive reasons of the heart?" Soloveitchik asked this question in 1965, and I maintain it's just as relevant today. What, indeed, can such a person say?

Well, let's see.

GODSTRUCK

1.

ANGELA, TO THE INNER LIGHT OF QUAKERISM

*Are you open to new light, from whatever
source it may come? Do you approach
new ideas with discernment?*

—QUAKER FAITH AND PRACTICE, FIFTH EDITION

I would not say that, of all my friends, Angela seemed to be the *least* likely to undergo a conversion experience, but that is largely because virtually all of my nonreligious friends seemed to me equally unlikely to seek God. But still, a highly educated younger millennial, a writer for various prestigious media outlets, interested in AI and science and the impact of data on self-conception, and a queer-identifying Asian immigrant with no familial religious background: of all the bad bets, she seemed like a particularly bad one. And yet somehow there she was, in March 2021, sitting at the Brooklyn Meeting of the Religious Society of Friends, more commonly known as the Quakers, listening for God's voice above the din of city traffic outside.

I met Angela for the first time in 2015, a few weeks after I got married and mere days before I left for a two-year stint in England, for my husband's job. She'd read a recent published essay of mine and asked a mutual friend to introduce us. We met at a small, nondescript coffee shop with dizzyingly high walls near the hotel where I was staying, my apartment having already been emptied of our belongings. We talked mostly, if I remember correctly, about work: my first book had been published in late 2013, and she had just left a reporting job to freelance.

I can't remember if it was love at first sight exactly, but it was certainly love at first correspondence: over the ensuing years, we exchanged probably thousands of emails, on everything from publishing industry gossip to what single object we'd write an entire book on if given the chance (her: fitness trackers; me: candles) to whether we should put much stock in studies that claim to measure a certain culture's happiness, given the subjectivity inherent in defining "happiness." We've always enjoyed probing at timely, thorny philosophical questions, particularly bioethical ones: If it were possible to do so, would it be wrong to engineer a synthetic fetus to harvest its tissues for medical treatments? What are the potential moral issues with assisted suicide? Should scientists be allowed to perform medical research on pregnant women provided they consent to be experimented on? You know, casual conversation.

Quite early on in our dialogues, I noticed that Angela seemed unusually at ease when I expressed an opinion different to hers, a skill I don't always feel I share. Ours was a prolonged conversation that we both seemed to instinctively agree was predicated on the idea that intellectual debate was paramount. But like the average mortal, I'd bristle slightly, if only internally, at the mere apparition of conflict. (Probably some of this was because I felt that Angela was so intelligent that, if she disagreed with me, then it must be me who was wrong.)

Angela, though, always seemed unfazed. There was a particularly adroit thing she would do when I knew our views didn't align: she'd home in on one aspect of the argument she did or *could* agree with and voice that point of accord or use it to ask a broader question that took the discussion to a less detailed and more theoretical place. Once, when I made an argument about choice that I felt pretty confident she wouldn't agree with, she responded sanguinely: "It's an interesting question, how much control people should have over their lives." Even in the moment, I remember being impressed. I don't need to repeat banalities about our current discourse, marked as it is by intransigence and tribalism and smugness, to underline how rare and valuable such intellectual flexibility is. Was this gift natural, I wondered, or honed over time?

＊

Angela was born in Huangshi, China, in 1991 and spent her early years about two hours away, in Wuhan, a humid industrial city that straddles the Yangtze River in eastern central China. When she was two years old, her parents departed for the United States to pursue master's degrees, but Angela was denied her own visa three times, so she remained behind in China with relatives. Over the ensuing three years, she did not see her mom or dad once. "My parents would call—but not often, because international long distance was expensive—and I would say hello and sound all cheery bright," she wrote later in an essay about the experience. "When I hung up, I would tell my relatives that my parents were lying to me again and they were never coming back." The relatives she lived with in China viewed her as an extra burden in their lives, which were already laden with hardships. Though for years she downplayed the impact of this parental separation, she later wondered if it hadn't helped to shape her personality more than she assumed: she recalls people describing her as a lighthearted toddler who then grew into a cerebral, reserved child and adolescent.

When she was five, she finally joined her parents where they had settled, in Ohio. A few months later, the family moved again to Sunnyvale, California, a city in the Bay Area just outside San Jose, which real estate flyers called "the heart of Silicon Valley." This was in the middle of the nineties dot-com boom, when the area exploded in growth and a steady stream of workers, largely from India and China, moved in. Angela attended the same high school as did Steve Jobs and Steve Wozniak years earlier, and for a brief, hilarious period of time as a preteen, helped her mom run an online store that sold safety products like stun guns, knives, and bear repellent, doing everything from customer relations to fiddling with the SEO to processing orders. The adults she knew largely worked for companies like IBM and Apple (her father worked for Intel). But she didn't feel saturated in start-up culture as a kid, or starry-eyed about it; for years, her most indelible memories of her hometown were traversing the creek behind her friend's house or practicing color guard on the school fields.

Angela's family was not religious, so her "default" (her word) was to follow suit. They celebrated Christmas in a "purely consumerist" fashion: the first Christmas she lived in the United States, her parents asked her whether she preferred to get gifts from them or from Santa Claus. (By the following year, they'd realized it wasn't normal to ask your child this; from then on, all her gifts came from Santa.) "Religion wasn't something we ever talked about. It wasn't an organizing principle in a positive or negative fashion," she explained, although—given her largely secular, liberal milieu—she did pick up on other assumptions about it, like that religious people were "backward, homophobic," and, crucially, not smart. "At least as a child, I definitely at some point absorbed the idea that religion was the opposite of rationality and progress."

Her high school years coincided with the rise of the New Atheists—writers like Richard Dawkins, Sam Harris, Christopher Hitchens, and

Daniel Dennett (the self-proclaimed "Four Horsemen"), who not only didn't identify as believers but, very often, argued that religion should be viewed as an entirely malevolent force and abolished entirely. A boy Angela had a crush on in high school was a big Dawkins fan, so she read Dawkins's book *The God Delusion* so she could have an excuse to chat with him. She initially admired Dawkins's zeal: "There was something about [the New Atheists'] conviction and the force of their contempt that was appealing to me," she said. "In high school, I think people like being snarky and they like tearing things down. And this was very much that. It appealed to me on aesthetic grounds maybe even more so than intellectual or spiritual grounds."

Ultimately, though, she didn't end up seeing atheism, any more than religion, as a driving force behind her identity. "I was essentially already an atheist, just an apathetic one. I wouldn't have called myself an agnostic if I had to choose. I would have said atheist, but it wasn't something that mattered to me." Later, she'd move even further from the label: "It never felt necessary to label myself that way in the same way it wouldn't feel necessary to define myself as a 'non–figure skater.' Yes, I'm technically a non–figure skater, but I would literally never describe myself that way."

Though Angela was never enamored with computers or the industry that surrounded her in California, there was one adjacent topic she latched on to: data. It has always been very important to her to "understand the world accurately," she told me, and though she also loved literature—she'd go on to major in comparative lit in college, focusing on Russian literature—the humanities still seemed too "fuzzy and subjective." She doesn't remember exactly when her predilection for data and evidence took root, but she recalls her revelation that, when she'd ignore her mother's Eastern medical cures as a kid, nothing catastrophic would happen. As she grew older, she developed "a horror of anything that didn't come armed with five citations."

She felt so compelled by the idea of better living through data that for two years in her twenties she wrote a column called DATA on the subject for the online magazine *Catapult*. In one essay in the series, she wrote how, at the end of every year, she used to make specific predictions about what the coming months had in store for her, down to the probability that she'd sleep with an acquaintance or actually go through with running a marathon; in another, she relayed how a boyfriend once told her that there was an "eighty to ninety percent chance" he was in love with her, which she found (inexplicably, to me) charming.

To the mathematically uninclined like myself, the ability to parse data in this way is intimidating and impressive, but Angela herself recognized a certain anxiety behind the endeavor. "I want to believe that the key to a better life is inside me waiting to be unlocked; that the right answer is accessible if I just strain to listen. But I've learned to distrust 'intuition' as a guide," she wrote in one installment on fitness-related data, like the kind garnered from Fitbit. "So many of my instincts seem skewed, so many of my thoughts shaped by forces that hinder me. Too often have I believed that simply feeling something strongly is proof that it's true. . . . Numbers, for me, are grounding. They provide evidence [of phenomena] that I have trouble feeling."

This preference for a "clear picture, even if it said something unpleasant or painful," as she put it, found its natural expression in rationality, which Angela became interested in during college. Rationality is a way of reasoning or of trying to understand the world that often heavily privileges empirical and quantitative knowledge, including applying probability and statistics to almost any issue, in the hopes that a person can demolish their cognitive bias and see the world as it really is. (It has only a tentative connection to the seventeenth- and eighteenth-century philosophy associated with thinkers like Descartes and Spinoza; many rationalists like to use "rationality" instead of "rationalism" in order to distinguish the two.) The rationalist community is usually said to have arisen in the mid-2000s on various websites and forums with names like Overcoming Bias and LessWrong. ("It is extremely appealing to me to be less wrong," Angela told me, which seems as close to a universal desire as might exist.) Today, most rationalists' involvement with the movement remains largely digital, but in San Francisco, there are some group homes and even summer camps for young people organized by rationalist principles.

Rationalists are passionate about allowing for heterodox—even contrarian—thinking, and they are insistent upon free speech. Their areas of interest largely cluster around artificial intelligence, animal rights, futurism, neuroscience, transhumanism, and the effective altruism movement, which is based on the idea that using "evidence and reason" can help determine how to live more ethically and be more efficient in giving to charity (as I was writing this, the FTX scandal broke, perhaps forever linking effective altruism and the cryptocurrency fraudster Sam Bankman-Fried in the minds of the public). Generally speaking, rationalists are apathetic toward, or even outright dismissive of, less overtly "useful" human endeavors like art and literature.

Not surprisingly, rationalists are not often religious, though they have their own canonical texts—books on ethics, pop psychology, and economics like *Superintelligence*; *Thinking, Fast and Slow*; and *Famine, Affluence, and Morality*, among many others—and luminaries, like AI researcher Eliezer Yudkowsky, economist Robin Hanson, and psychiatrist Scott Siskind, the latter of whom maintained the voluminous blog *Slate Star Codex*, now the Substack Astral Codex Ten. A FAQ page on the site LessWrong defines rationality in a series of neat and tidy bullet points:

- Rationality is thinking in ways which systematically arrive at truth.

- Rationality is thinking in ways which cause you to systematically achieve your goals.

- Rationality is trying to do better on purpose.

- Rationality is reasoning well even in the face of massive uncertainty.

- Rationality is making good decisions even when it's hard.

- Rationality is being self-aware, understanding how your own mind works, and applying this knowledge to thinking better.

Angela's interest in rationality peaked right after college, when she moved to New York to take a job at a newspaper. She had some friends who were rationalists, and she'd do the reading that was recommended on various rationality blogs and go to the occasional meetup, but she didn't post anything in the forums, and her social circle wasn't relegated solely to members of the community. Still, she felt like there was "more resonance" for her with rationality than with atheism, because she didn't share Dawkins's aim of eradicating religion, whereas she *did* feel that she shared the "epistemic values" of the rationalists, specifically to see more clearly (even if what you see is "ugly"), to be more self-aware, to always reach for empiricism and hard evidence when you can.

Of course, we all want those things, or at least many of us do. But what if your attempts to arrive at the truth in a "systematic" way prove dispiriting or untenable or, sometimes, simply boring? What if you wonder about the malleability of such terms as "truth" and "good" and "self-aware"? What if you feel that maybe—as I do when confronted with rationalist doctrine—the idea that one could ever overcome self-delusion is *itself* a delusion? What if you can't neatly discard the unknowable, like the prospect of a supernatural reality, or the seemingly trivial, like the concept of "art for art's sake"? What if your rationality brings you somewhere totally inexplicable and, by your own previous standards, ludicrous: an embrace of the seemingly irrational?

Knowledge is often skeptical of belief, seeing in it something narcotizing, beguiling, casuistic, and belief returns in kind, as if the former's hard edge will puncture the latter's airy softness. My own Jewish faith has an ambivalent relationship to the role of the intellect in spiritual formation: on the one hand, it is a deeply scholarly tradition, one in which study is a good deed that trumps even honoring one's parents, but on the other hand, many Jewish thinkers have worried that intellectualism detracts from a purer love of God. The founder of the mystical eighteenth-century Jewish renewal movement, Hasidism, the Ba'al Shem Tov, once suggested that a person who came to faith via "reason and philosophical thought" had an advantage over someone who just inherited it and hadn't thought it through; but on the flip side, "if confronted with the arguments that tear down the logical structure of his faith, he can be tempted away." Various denominations of Christianity have their own feelings about the intellect (Catholic, generally pro; Anabaptist, generally less so); the Quran, meanwhile, is riddled with references to the intellect, including some very choice words for those who neglect to use it, calling them, in one instance, "the meanest beasts in God's sight."

The tug-of-war between faith and intellect is a dilemma Leo Tolstoy—novelist, mystic, and, to some, irredeemable crank—would have readily understood. Born in 1828 into an upper-class family, Tolstoy was raised Russian Orthodox in the way that all the landed gentry were, which is to say by that same default Angela's family was not-religious. In his teenage years, he cast off the pesky flies of ritualized belief—everyone went to services but snickered throughout, anyway—and spent his time mired in debauchery: "Lying, thieving, promiscuity of all kinds, drunkenness, violence, murder . . . there was no crime I didn't commit." In his brief but impactful spiritual memoir, *A Confession*, he describes, as a young man, replacing a belief in God with a belief in self-perfection, which soon morphed into a cruel, interpersonal competition, "a desire to be better not in my own eyes or before God but in the eyes of other people. And very soon this determination to be better than others became a wish to be more powerful than others: more famous, more important, wealthier."

After years of trying to find a pursuit that didn't make him feel jaded—he joined the army, explored the artistic scene, and organized schools for peasant children—he married and had a large family (thirteen children, eight of whom survived to adulthood). By the time he was fifty, he had achieved a level of fame few writers could ever dream of; with the success of *War and Peace* and *Anna Karenina*, he was so well known that he was sometimes called Russia's second tsar. Though, technically speaking, he wouldn't have needed to work at all if he hadn't wanted to: from his parents, he had inherited an estate that came with over five thousand acres and a few hundred serfs and, therefore, a guaranteed income. All things considered, Tolstoy was in good shape.

But as he approached his fiftieth birthday, existential questions began to trouble him—first sporadically, then relentlessly. "Why do I live?" he wondered. "Why do I wish for anything, or do anything? . . .

[I]s there any meaning in my life that will not be annihilated by the inevitability of death which awaits me?" When he found he could not answer these questions, he was plunged into a dark depression. "Life had grown hateful to me," he wrote, "and some insuperable force was leading me to seek deliverance from it by whatever means. . . . The thought of suicide now came to me as naturally as thoughts of improving my life had previously come to me."

With what will he had left, he began a furious self-directed study, taking advantage of his many connections to search "all branches of knowledge" for answers to his questions, but he found nothing to pacify him. Of all the subjects, he saved his most venomous barbs for certain scientific disciplines: "If we turn to those branches of knowledge that attempt to provide solutions to the questions of life, to physiology, psychology, biology and sociology, we encounter a startling poverty of thought, extreme lack of clarity and a completely unjustified pretension to resolve questions beyond their scope, together with continual contradiction between one thinker and another (or even within their own selves)." He recognized the intricacy and beauty in the harder sciences, like physics and astronomy, but decided their "precision and clarity are inversely proportionate to their applicability to questions concerning life."

Eventually, he came to the conclusion that while the intellectual and financial elite were morally bankrupt, average folks appeared on the whole far happier. What was it that the masses had that he did not? It was simple: they had faith. All of a sudden, he saw that he had been attempting to resolve his dilemma incorrectly, by utilizing rational thinking rather than by actually *abandoning* it. He saw that the powers of his logic were insufficient when dealing with the "unusual nature of religious knowledge," and that the goal was not to find a comprehensive and totally comprehensible structure of thought, but to "be brought to the inevitably inexplicable." Though he'd found a key that fit into the lock, this epiphany wasn't entirely happy, because it meant abandoning everything he knew about his identity and position in the world. "According to rational knowledge life is an evil and people know it . . . [but] according to faith it follows that in order to comprehend the meaning of life I must renounce my reason, the very thing for which meaning was necessary."

As difficult as it originally seemed, renouncing his reason and embracing God was, in the end, exactly what Tolstoy did. He embarked on a program of study similar to his earlier one, but this time on various religious faiths, with a special focus on Christianity. When he felt pessimistic about the prospect of finding God, he reverted to debating himself, eventually determining that the fact that he'd been saved from mental anguish (or worse) was itself proof of God's existence (though he claims throughout the text to be abandoning rationality entirely, he often resorts to deliberating methodically in order to reach the most reliable conclusion, which is a rational *process* regardless of the end result).

Though he tried to reenter the Russian Orthodox church, he ended up "revolted" by what he saw as its empty theatrics and its propensity to maintain the structural divisions in Russian society. He ultimately fashioned his own, rather eccentric Christianity: he gave up meat, smoking, and alcohol, and began exclusively wearing peasant tunics and making his own shoes (which, by all accounts excepting his own, were nearly unwearable). He railed publicly against authoritarianism—not a super-safe move in czarist Russia—and corresponded with Gandhi on the subject of pacifism; eventually, he amassed a ragtag band of disciples (although he had mixed feelings about being a guru) who set up international communes in his name, and he renounced the rights to his literary works to his wife. But despite the strengths and virtues (as I see them, anyway) of his new spiritual direction, it must also be said that Tolstoy's life became increasingly more chaotic after his makeshift conversion: his marriage, always on shaky ground, was overtaken by bitterness; despite all his ranting against private property, he never succeeded in giving away his estate; and though he continued to write, none of his postconversion fiction ever soared to the heights of his early novels.

The first note Angela sent me after we met at that coffee shop in 2015 was a list of links to articles by and about Leah Libresco (now, since her marriage, Leah Libresco Sargeant), an atheist blogger who'd been in the rationalist scene and then made waves when she'd announced she was converting to Catholicism in 2012. (I no longer remember how Leah came up in conversation: I knew nothing of rationality then, and Angela was years away from exploring Quakerism.) Angela and Leah didn't know each other personally, though they might have crossed paths at a rationalist event once, around 2013, Angela thinks, and she recognized Leah—though not a Tolstoy-level celebrity, Leah's conversion caused something of a stir even beyond the relatively small world of rationality. In many ways, Leah reminded Angela of herself: educated, data driven, skeptical. "When you see someone with a similar background or similar beliefs converting and being transformed by it, I think you naturally wonder why," she told me. When she thought about Leah over the ensuing years, she often asked herself: *What is it that she's found?*

Unlike Tolstoy, Leah didn't see her embrace of Catholicism after a lifetime of atheism as a result of her abandoning her reason; she saw it as the inevitable *telos* of her reason. Growing up on suburban Long Island, she knew almost no one who was religious. Her school classmates were mostly secular Jews; the town was so thoroughly a-religious that in a class on European history in high school, one of the students raised their hand to ask if Lutherans still existed. Leah was a self-described nerd who adored math, Harry Potter, and debate. Her parents were both teachers, and both made it clear that religion wasn't true. Because she only encountered the topic in news reports about Evangelicals trying to interfere in politics, she eventually came to believe that not only was it untrue, it was also, as the New Atheists claimed, a destructive, illiberal force.

Certainly she didn't feel religion was necessary to develop a moral compass; in fact, she herself was an extremely staunch moralist without it. Her devotion to moral action was so great that she found herself happy when a classmate she was nice to was mean in return, because it meant she hadn't been friendly to them for self-serving reasons. A big fan of musicals, Leah's favorite character in the Broadway play *Les Misérables* was Javert, the policeman who doggedly pursues the hero, Jean Valjean, and eventually takes his own life. Though Javert was ostensibly the villain, young Leah thought his devotion to the law as great equalizer was noble. "I wanted to grow up to be just that tall, stable, ramrod-straight, inviolate, and wholly consecrated to duty," she writes in her memoir *Arriving at Amen: Seven Catholic Prayers That Even I Can Offer*. Years later, she described her lifelong certainty that morality was "objective, human-independent, something we uncover like archaeologists, not something we build like architects." But how she was certain of that, she wasn't yet able to articulate.

While a student at Yale University, Leah met practicing Christians for the first time. Like her, many participated in the Political Union, a debate society where participants could only argue positions they themselves held, and earned points by changing people's minds. Later, she ended up dating a serious Catholic boy. In many ways she felt more like the Christian students than those who, like her, described themselves as atheists, because the Christians were interested in aspiring toward a verifiable, transcendent morality, just as she was. In hopes of arguing more effectively against her Christian peers, she read their luminaries, like G. K. Chesterton and C. S. Lewis, whose *Mere Christianity* made many of the same points she did about an external morality, albeit through the lens of faith.

"Consequently, this Rule of Right and Wrong, or Law of Human Nature, or whatever you call it, must somehow or other be a real thing—a thing that is really there, not made up by ourselves," Lewis writes. "And yet it is not a fact in the ordinary sense, in the same way as our actual behavior is a fact. It begins to look as if we shall have to admit that there is more than one kind of reality; that, in this particular case, there is something above and beyond the ordinary facts of men's behavior, and yet quite definitely real—a real law, which none of us made, but which we find pressing on us." She once described reading Lewis's argument as a kind of intellectual homecoming, though she didn't quite see how deism automatically flowed from it. Still, she was starting to feel that, contrary to her high school impressions of Evangelicalism, Christianity was largely admirable in that it was a system that made sense within itself, even if that didn't necessarily make it objectively *true*.

Her nonreligious peers told her that even though her devotion to an ethical conduct of behavior was admirable, that didn't mean her ethics weren't *arbitrary*. She rejected this notion with "every fiber of [her] being," and yet couldn't point to anything outside herself that reflected this belief "the way the seeds of a sunflower incarnate the Fibonacci sequence." At the time, she was becoming somewhat well known in the atheist blogosphere, writing articles for her Patheos page (which she dubbed "Unequally Yoked: A Geeky Atheist Picks Fights with Her Catholic Boyfriend") and the *Huffington Post* with titles like "Dalai Lama Wrong on Religious Tolerance" and "Go Ahead, Tell Me What's Wrong with Homosexuality," but she found it frustrating that atheists seemed to be more concerned about pointing out what they *didn't* believe than in figuring what *was* true, or determining how to use atheism as a guide to living a more ethical life. She saw this as part of her mission as a human, so she read books from "her" side too, in hopes of being able to hand one over to a Christian counterpart and say, "See this? *This* is what I believe." It took her awhile, but finally she found a text that resonated: *After Virtue*, by the Scottish philosopher Alasdair MacIntyre, who says the only hope for humanity is a return to classical Aristotelian ethics. When she triumphantly gave the book to a religious friend she'd been sparring with, though, she was met with irritating news. "You do know MacIntyre converted to Catholicism, right?"

After college, Leah moved to Washington, D.C., and went to work as a statistician, but she returned to New Haven for Political Union alma mater debates annually. Each time, she was bothered by the fact that if an uneducated observer were to listen to all the speeches, they'd undoubtedly assume, based on her arguments, that Leah belonged with the Catholics or Orthodox Christians. At her second reunion, she pulled aside a Lutheran friend. "Whenever I come back for these things, I have the urge to convert," she told him. He offered to hash out the issue with her. Having firmly declared herself a virtue ethicist, she felt sure that morality was a thing that existed independent to her; if it weren't, then people wouldn't behave as if it were real. Even those who claimed it was developed entirely by men for the preservation of society—learned "on the job," so to speak, rather than intuited and felt—cleaved to it in sometimes petty or irrational or self-negating ways, like resisting the urge to steal at the merest hint of desire for something or refusing to desert their troops at the height of battle even to save their own lives. And yet Leah couldn't prove that morality was something you could locate in nature, the same way you could look at two stones and partake of the Platonic number *two*. If one couldn't access morality through nature, her Lutheran friend asked her, then how was it everyone seemed to have innate access to it?

"I don't know," Leah said. "I've got bupkis."

"Your best guess."

"I haven't got one."

"You must have some idea."

"I don't know. I've got nothing," she replied. "I guess morality just loves me or something."

Leah asked her friend to be quiet, so she could digest what she'd just said. If morality "loved" her, it must be something like an active agent with its own goals and desires. It must be something like God.

A few months after Leah's return to D.C., she penned a blog post explaining that she was pursuing a Catholic conversion. The story got so much traction that she was interviewed on CNN and (less surprisingly) Catholic television. Her Christian friends were obviously supportive, her atheist ones perplexed. At one point she stumbled across a post on LessWrong written by a friend of hers with the subject line "Thwarting a Catholic Conversion?" The poster wrote that he was "devastated" to hear that Leah had aligned herself with a church that would question her identity—Leah had previously come out as bisexual—and would just prefer that she "grok the math that makes religious hypotheses so unlikely as to not be worth your time." What were the best argumentative tactics to use when approaching her? (Responses to his post varied, but mostly pushed back: "As long as she stays fundamentally the same person, I don't see what the big deal is," one person wrote. Another suggested, "Hating people for being wrong is a seductive and tricky thing and can lead to unproductive situations. Limited but generous forgiveness and acceptance are optimal strategies in an imperfect world with imperfect communications channels and fallible actors.") In fact, Leah preferred this friend's approach to the rather blasé acceptance of some others she knew: at least he saw her conversion as a matter of real consequence! (Her least favorite response was "Whatever makes you happy.")

Though Leah had been posting on LessWrong for some time before her conversion, she actually became more involved in the rationalist community *after* she'd officially converted, even moving to the Bay Area for a year to be an instructor at the Center for Applied Rationality, a community hub in Berkeley that runs workshops on rationalist thought, among other endeavors. Today, she still reads LessWrong and posts there on occasion, and also belongs to a Discord chat group about rationalist parenting. The things that originally attracted her to rationality still feel vital; for example, though they don't prioritize donating to AI research, she and her husband do use the effective altruist framework when making decisions about giving to charity. "[The San Francisco Rationalist community] really takes seriously that it's likely you should change your mind about something, and you should not be surprised or ashamed when that happens. That's a much healthier space to find truth."

Everyone says they want to have an open mind, in other words, but unless you're in an environment that really allows for fluctuation, you're unlikely to really accept it's possible. "It's not something that you can say and commit to; you really have to see it *lived*." Though religion would appear on its surface to demand more of a submissive belief than rationality, there are similarities between the two, including the goal of continually perfecting yourself, of taking your one life very, very seriously. In the latter, you are perfecting your rationality, in the former, your conscience, but in both, the movement is always upward, toward the Good.

Angela began investigating Christianity in earnest around 2015, a few years after she graduated from college, when a writer she knew from Twitter posted a message about being baptized a Christian after having previously been an atheist. This writer, like Leah, reminded Angela of herself, and Angela, curious about her transformation, messaged her privately. The writer invited her to participate in a Listserv she'd started, where a number of women journalists and writers discussed Christianity. (Most of the women were Protestant Christians of some flavor, though there was at least one practicing Catholic.)

Of all the discussions that took place, Angela liked the ones about prayer the most. "At some points, people would ask for prayer requests, and I just felt there was something so communal about it. It felt like a way to give people agency and for people to come through and even just a way to share the troubles in your life. It was a prescriptive, acceptable way to do that that felt very natural," she said. (Leah Libresco Sargeant had a similar experience after joining a Catholic Facebook group: "Without the possibility of asking me to pray for them, my secular friends are less likely to share with me their deepest troubles, not wanting to burden me with a problem I can do nothing about," she wrote in her memoir. "In Catholic circles, technically no problem falls into this category.")

Around this time, Angela started attending services on occasion at various churches around New York City, including at least one at Saint John the Divine, the majestic Episcopal cathedral near Columbia University's campus on the Upper West Side. She found herself drawn to the aesthetics of Catholicism—the dark, ghostly undertones of the Mass, the ornate, gothic imagery—but worried about the church's historic abuse of power and its homophobia. Though she didn't necessarily worry about her own identity proving a barrier to Catholicism: Angela herself is asexual, a deceivingly simplistic term that describes people who do not experience sexual attraction. "I had never experienced 'just attraction,' a physical impulse—only emotional desire that manifested physically," she'd later write in her book, *Ace: What Asexuality Reveals About Desire, Society, and the Meaning of Sex.* But the ancient, eerie patina of Catholicism still sometimes seduced: She'd find herself walking through the Cloisters, an abbey-like space constructed of four European cloisters subsequently relocated to upper Manhattan that houses a large collection of medieval art; or listening to the haunting melodies of Saint Hildegard of Bingen, a twelfth-century Benedictine nun and mystic, and feel that if she could only become a Christian, these things would in some way *belong* to her, would be imbued with a profound depth of meaning that was, at present, unreachable.

She'd already recognized that in times of distress, when she felt useless or defective or alone, she'd turn to religious ideas. ("I have a vague memory of one day feeling like no one liked me, or if they did at any moment they could not like me—which is probably literally true because people are fickle—and then having the random thought that Jesus liked me, which was so weird!") So she knew she was moving toward a kind of theism, or maybe possessed a kind of latent theism, but certain things about Christianity just seemed untenable, particularly the idea of Heaven, which seemed too good to be true, and hell, which she found "comedically terrible." (They still feel untenable: while she identifies as a theist, she still doesn't identify as a Christian, because she can't get on board with the more supernatural elements.)

She never considered investigating other faiths: it seemed that to pursue Judaism or Islam would be "appropriative"—she'd be self-conscious about her minority status in worship spaces, and worry she'd be pilfering from the cultural history of another group. Though becoming a Buddhist wouldn't present that problem, its theology wasn't appealing to her. "Buddhism seemed more individualistic and about personal enlightenment, or at least that's what I think I'd focus on if I were Buddhist. But I don't just want enlightenment; I want religion to help me improve the world." These years of seeking weren't marked, as Tolstoy's were, by emotional agony. "It was not a dark night of the soul. I was not breaking down. It was not existential crisis," she told me. "But there was a feeling that this was not going to go away."

Late one night in the summer of 2019, Angela was hanging out with her friend Josephine, who mentioned offhand that her mother was now a Buddhist but had previously been a Quaker. Angela didn't know what Quakers were—she assumed they were like the Amish, probably because, like many Americans, she associated them with the guy from the oatmeal box, with his vaguely colonial hat and dark jacket—so she asked. Josephine told her they were "mystical yet grounded," and the description struck Angela immediately as exactly what she was looking for.

The Quakers, sometimes called the Religious Society of Friends, are a denomination of Christianity officially founded in 1652 in northwest England, though the movement had been coalescing for some years prior. A number of spirited radicals contributed to its early growth, but credit for its establishment is usually placed squarely on the shoulders of a man named George Fox. The son of a Leicestershire weaver, Fox describes himself in his journals as a religiously serious, even dour, child: "In my very young years I had a gravity and stayedness of mind and spirit not usual in children; insomuch that when I saw old men behave lightly and wantonly towards each other, I had a dislike thereof raised in my heart, and said within myself, 'If ever I come to be a man, surely I shall not do so, nor be so wanton.'" (It must be said that for a person fixated on simplicity and equality, Fox wasn't above ego: he somehow manages to be the hero of every story in his own retellings.)

Fox left his hometown in his late teens and began aimlessly wandering through the countryside on his way to London, beset by "temptations and depression" all the way. He sought spiritual relief from priests, but was dissatisfied with their remedies, which included taking tobacco and reciting psalms; he recoiled from scenes of drunkenness and folly. Particularly in London, his critical eye also landed frequently on professorial types, whom he describes as "chained under darkness and sin." (In his cold appraisal of intellectuals, Tolstoy is quite similar to Fox, and in fact the idiosyncratic Christianity Tolstoy devised was much like Quakerism in many ways: focused on aesthetic simplicity, pacifism, and the eradication of societal hierarchies.)

It was out of these tormented wanderings that some of Fox's most salient, lasting spiritual ideas coalesced. This was the time of the English Civil War, and the countryside was dotted with troops, among whom some of the most provocative religious ideas were percolating. Fox was inspired by the beliefs of certain groups of Dissenters, particularly their insistence on strict separation between church and state. At the time, it was de rigueur for Anglican priests to attend Oxford or Cambridge, something that Fox and other critics believed completely wrong. In an echo of Martin Luther's criticisms a century earlier, Fox and other reformers considered spirituality the birthright of all people, not only the educated, wealthy, or otherwise specially designated, but no one went quite as far as Fox did when it came to decrying the idea of an intermediary with the divine. To him, because everyone had the "inner light" of Christ within them—he pointed to Jeremiah for confirmation: "And they shall teach no more every man his neighbor, and every man his brother, saying Know the Lord: for they all know me, from the least of them unto the greatest of them"—there was no need for preachers of any kind, not even ones drawn from the common people.

Fox could be rabid in his anticlericalism, going so far as to refuse to use the word "church," instead mocking them as "steeple-houses" that held no greater spiritual import than any other edifice. His insistence on spiritual equality meant that Quakers have throughout their history often been at the forefront of social justice issues: women were permitted to preach and wrote a significant number of early Quaker pamphlets, and the group played an outsize role in the abolition movement, the treatment of the mentally ill, and prison reform—particularly in the United States, where Quakers began settling in the mid-seventeenth century. They were also known in their early history for a host of quirky practices, including the refusal to swear oaths, eschewing brightly colored clothing, addressing each other as "thee" and "thou," and looking askance at art of all kinds, in keeping with the biblical prohibition against "graven images," understood to be either particularly aimed at icons and idols or, more broadly, against representations of things in nature of any kind.

Over the centuries, three distinct streams of Quakerism began to form. Today, the largest contingent is Evangelical, who are mostly based in Africa and tend to be more theologically and culturally conservative (and, obviously, evangelistic). Their worship looks much more stereotypically Christian than that of other Quaker groups, with boisterous music and sermons. Liberal Friends dominate in Europe and in parts of the United States, as well as some other regions, and prioritize individual revelation over theological certainty. They can hold views that would be blatantly heretical for other Christians: some see Jesus as a divine figure, others view him as a particularly astute philosopher who was nevertheless wholly human and mortal; they tend to be liberal on social matters where other, louder Christians are more conservative, like sexuality and abortion; they can be openly agnostic or even atheist. In their founding, they distinguished themselves from their Evangelical and other counterparts by asserting the belief that experience trumped scripture, faith should be relevant to the age in which it exists, and in each subsequent era we know more of God, a belief known as progressivism. Liberal Quakers tend to emphasize the "noncreedal" aspects of their faith—the idea that no specific belief is mandated—and to tie this noncreedalism back to George Fox's idea that no man should act as spiritual authority to another. As the Quaker academic "Ben" Pink Dandelion put it in a speech to a Friends General Conference meeting in Virginia in 2009, "From a rational place, the basis of liberal religion, we have come to be clear that any claims we make about God will necessarily be 'perhaps' kinds of statements. We operate an 'absolute perhaps' and it sets us apart from other spiritualities . . . total finders or zealots of any persuasion will be in tension with the group." Conservative Friends, who are mostly American, fall somewhere between these two poles: they tend to be more orthodox in their Christian beliefs than Liberals, but generally feel that revelation comes first and is upheld by scripture, not the other way around. What unites these strikingly different theologies are a set of core beliefs: in pacifism, in the ability of all to commune with God, and in a universal spiritual equality.

Presented with these branches in any context, Angela would have opted to attend a Liberal meeting, which was convenient because it was the only option available to her in New York. Soon after her conversation with Josephine, she found herself standing outside the Brooklyn Friends Meeting House one Sunday morning, just before the Meeting for Worship was about to begin. Constructed in 1857, the Meeting House is a charming redbrick building with enormous upper-floor windows that sits on a particularly drab wide avenue in downtown Brooklyn, an architectural oasis amid the dingy government buildings and converted offices. People who know anything about Quakers—there aren't many, given that it's a fairly tiny religious group—usually know that they worship in silence, which is one of just a handful of things Angela knew about them when she sat down on the creaky benches and prepared to be still and quiet for an hour.

The silent worship was something Fox borrowed from another group of English Dissenters called the Seekers, and was in keeping with his desire to do away with outward sacraments of all kinds. At a Liberal Quaker meeting, there is no hymn singing, no communion, no baptism, no spoken prayers, no sermon (the Meeting Houses, similarly, are unadorned: no crosses, no iconography, little visual stimuli of any kind). "Walk into a Quaker Meeting for Worship the first time and nothing seems to be going on," an explanatory pamphlet offered at the Brooklyn Meeting House begins. But this is misleading, the writer continues. "At the center of Meeting for Worship is a core belief: the divine spirit—call it the 'indwelling Christ' as some Friends do, or God, or the Great Spirit—it is present with every worshipper, to teach, lead, and reveal truth. . . . In a Meeting for Worship, therefore, our task is to 'mind the light': to put aside our thinking and feelings and pay attention to our inner teacher. We have to distinguish between the insights that come from the divine and those that come from our ego."

Sitting in a room with strangers silently can be surprisingly moving, even if it's hard to clear your mind of thoughts if you struggle with meditating, as Angela does. (The Quaker aversion to "thinking" might be a bit overblown, though: up to two thirds of Liberal Friends say "thinking" best describes what they do during meetings.) At some meetings, people might feel called to sing, or recite poetry, or speak; often, though, the entire hour is spent silently. (On podcasts and You-Tube, you can find clips of Quakers worshipping with only the backdrop of a ticking clock or a crackling iron stove.) At the end, people will rise to request that the community hold certain people in the light: maybe a friend of theirs enduring hardship, or a nonspecific group, like those suffering from illness.

"I just remember finding it really peaceful and low pressure," Angela said of that first worship service. At other churches, when she'd listen to the sermons, she'd find herself slipping out of spiritual mode and becoming, instead, more "cognitively engaged," maybe arguing in her mind with the main thesis of the speech or expounding upon it. And she often wondered about the obligation to *feel* something at some particularly pivotal moment in the service—like, say, the way one might during a Catholic Communion, when the wafer is placed upon the tongue—which then just made her worry whether her internal state didn't match up with what she assumed she was *supposed* to be feeling. Though it appears (and is!) more easygoing than other faiths, Quakerism—stripped bare of all flashy song-and-dance numbers, devoid of the "stream of chatter" she felt characterized other worship—actually required a different kind of discipline: the commitment to locate God inside of you, with little to no outside reinforcement.

After that first Sunday, Angela didn't feel ready to convert just yet (the Quaker term for conversion is to "become Quaker by convincement"). But she felt sure she would return to meetings. It wasn't just the sense of obligation that she knew would draw her back, nor was the calming worship service alone enough of a balm. "The sense of values, sacrifice, the lineage, the mysticism, all of that does matter, but I think at the core there is that sense that without some belief in religion and forgiveness and redemption and moral value, my value just wildly oscillates depending on what the world thinks of me," she told me. She felt it was important to locate her own worth, and more importantly, other people's worth, somewhere else, in something steady and fixed and separate. "Religion seemed the truest way to get to everyone having equal value, and Quakerism is especially good for that."

✳

What *is* a human being's value? Philosophers, theologians, biologists, and others have argued over this question for centuries. Today, a few "anthropologies" prevail. If your inclination is to say that a human being is a creature capable of rational thought, you might be a "sentiocentrist" like Peter Singer, a patron saint of rationality and perhaps the world's most famous working philosopher. Singer and other "radical utilitarians" argue that dignity springs from consciousness, as well as self-awareness, a desire for the future, and other hallmarks of advanced thinking.

Seems reasonable enough. But sentiocentrism leaves the door open for conclusions that the average person might find dubious or terrifying or both. For instance, if sentience is the hallmark of dignity, then a less sentient being, like an infant—human babies being particularly pathetic compared to the infants of other species—or a cognitively disabled person, would have less dignity than a comparatively intelligent creature, like a chimp or a cow (Singer is a passionate proponent of vegetarianism). By this metric, killing a chimpanzee is worse than killing a human infant, who is not yet self-aware, and who has no sense of what it means to suffer or to miss out on life. Similarly, an adult with diminished cognitive capacities might consider suicide, or perhaps is even obligated to do so, under the utilitarian view: "In the cases of those who will be demented, it is a rational duty to die physically before dying morally," the philosopher Dennis R. Cooley wrote. "The moral agent should select self-inflicted death before she becomes incompetent because she owes it to herself as a moral agent." The baby and the "demented" are, to use the anthropological term for it, "contested humans"; we uncontested beings bestow their worth on them rather than acknowledging their inherent and equal worth and dignity.

Another view is that of biological anthropology, whose best-known proponent is probably Richard Dawkins of New Atheist fame. To these folks, a human is defined by a particular genetic code. For sure, the contemplation of such an intricate, invisible design as DNA can incite its own kind of awe. "When I say that human beings are just gene machines, one shouldn't put too much emphasis on the word 'just,'" Dawkins chastened on the PBS program *Faith and Reason*. "There is a very great deal of complication, and indeed beauty in being a gene machine." But of course, every living creature has its own genetic code—why would a human's be *more* "beautiful" or interesting than that of a fly or a salmon, despite the latter's inability to logically reason, as per utilitarianism? To many enthusiasts, it wouldn't: the human is simply another biological entity. "In the last ten years we have come to realize humans are more like worms than we ever imagined," the biologist Bruce Alberts once proclaimed. In some sense, the biological definition, too, is a satisfying answer.

But again, there are pitfalls. For example, if we say that human life is largely determined by genes, we might be pledging fealty to a narrative that limits the possibilities for self-determination and change. Such a view also neglects the nonmaterial endeavors of humans, the ones that *do* distinguish us from other living creatures: Why do we create art? Why do we love stories? Why do we philosophize, or blush, or dance? (Why, perhaps, do we even ask what our nature is at *all*, as these academics do, and as, at least as far as we know, no other living beings do?) Finally, if we view humans as machines—however elegant those machines are—with no sacral properties whatsoever, we might end up feeling there is no moral issue with tinkering with them. After all, a machine should function at peak level, so to that end, there's no problem with manipulating genes so as to create the "best" model possible. There are some possibilities here that seem wonderful: Who wouldn't want to eliminate genetic diseases like Tay-Sachs or Canavan disease? But darker things lurk just aside exciting ones: a past in which the pursuit of genetic perfection meant it was acceptable to brutally experiment on racial minorities and the cognitively impaired, and a future, too, in which medicine rushes in where angels fear to tread, maybe alleviating pain but changing the human experience beyond recognition.

The average individual likely doesn't spend much time engaging in intellectual exercises like these. Most probably don't consider human value a question at all. People's lives are inherently worthwhile: What else is there to talk about? But even this assumption raises some questions: If there *is* worth, where does it come from? How is it measured? One approach is to insist that human equality, as the writers of the American Declaration of Independence did, is "self-evident." But there's a problem here: namely, that it is not self-evident at all. You don't even have to resort to a bleak sentiocentrism or reductive biological anthropology to run into walls: some people are more charitable, some are kinder, some are better parents—surely these people are "better" than their counterparts, who don't give money, are jerks, or are mean to their children? Some people are considered more physically attractive by greater swaths of the population; some are born into wealthy families. If you're born into a culture that values money, let's say, you might be inclined to assign a greater worth to a wealthier person; if your society is particularly lookist, you might think the person more conventionally beautiful is "better" than someone who is not.

The predominant feeling today is that these latter two means of measuring worth would be morally bankrupt, but there are other instances where we may reinforce a hierarchy of humanity without even realizing it, or without considering the slippery-slope effect of doing so. An experiment: You're presented with two people. For control's sake, let's say they're around the same age and they come from roughly the same socioeconomic background. One, however, is a pediatrician who parachutes into war zones to treat the injuries of children, and the other is unemployed by choice, treats lovers poorly, refuses to volunteer for good causes—oh, and doesn't share your political views. You might be tempted to deem the latter person "worse" than the former, on the basis that they don't contribute meaningfully to society. So perhaps "contribute meaningfully to society" is your yardstick: totally fair! Except then, might you not be unwittingly devaluing the lives of those who don't do so for reasons beyond their control: those contested humans again, with their sad, lifeless limbs; their soft, infantile skulls; their papery old skin and decaying memories? Might "contribute" in this context just be a softer way of saying "participates in the economy" or "earns money" or "is professionally successful"?

We all know what it would look like if we tried to make everyone exactly equal in ways that we could measure: it would look dystopian. In Kurt Vonnegut's classic short story "Harrison Bergeron," a dictatorial government weighs down the strong and athletic with heavy bags, forces the pretty to wear hideous face masks, and inserts a radio receiver into the ear of the intelligent, so their thoughts will be periodically interrupted by booming, horrendous noises. The titular character is a teenage rebel who is ultimately shot dead by the ruling party, but the story mostly takes place in the living room of his parents, Hazel and George, neither of whom feel compelled to question the equality orthodoxy—except for one pivotal moment, when Hazel wonders whether they could just remove some of the bird shot out of the canvas bags George is required to wear around his neck to ensure he isn't allowed to exhibit too much physical strength. He looks so tired; couldn't he just rest awhile, if it was only her who could see? "'If I tried to get away with it,' said George, 'then other people'd get away with it—and pretty soon we'd be right back to the dark ages again, with everybody competing against everybody else. You wouldn't like that, would you?'" he asks his wife. Of course, there are gentler correctives that create a more even playing field in certain regards, like enforcing equitable taxation policies so that no one is grotesquely richer than another. But when it comes to other aspects of humanity, it seems clear that we can never fully ensure that everyone has the same number and quality of advantages, is viewed the same way, or is valued as much as everyone else.

Personally, I don't remember thinking too much as a child about where human value sprang from. I had a *lot* of existential concerns—moral relativism was a big sticking point for me—but how you determine the worth of an individual didn't keep me up at night. Probably my lodestar, if I'd been forced to articulate it, would have been something along the lines of "public accomplishment," a cousin to "contributes meaningfully": the more successful a person is in their chosen field, the more valuable they are. (As I grew up in a wealthy suburb, I undoubtedly equated success with wealth, though this association lessened as I aged.) When pressed to articulate what defined my own personal worth, I would likely have been at a loss. I knew I was valued by others for certain traits that, clustered together, amounted to my "personality": I was smart (though far from an overachiever, academically; I preferred to watch TV rather than study), sarcastic, funny, and opinionated. But these traits didn't really seem quantifiable enough, to me, to be the bedrock of my worth.

As a preteen, I became anorexic, which seemed a much easier means of appraisal than just being liked for being wry, though obviously a self-defeating one: the more weight I lost, the fewer calories I ate, the "better" I was. Though it took awhile, eventually I realized that, of course, this was wrong. There was a kind of vague idea espoused over the course of my treatment that we patients should learn to love ourselves, implying some inherent value in each of us, but *why* one should do this, or *how* one should cultivate such love, wasn't really directly addressed: it was just a thoughtless imperative. (To those who might wonder why I'd even raise this objection, consider that the idea that one would be morally obligated to love *all* people is a pretty hard case to make, so why should you *have* to love yourself simply because you exist? It makes your life easier if you can cohabit with yourself, sure, but that doesn't mean it's nonnegotiable.)

In my midtwenties, when I began to pursue writing more seriously as a career, I transferred all my anxieties about achievement and value from my body over onto my vocation without fully comprehending I was doing this. The more I wrote, the more prestigious my bylines, the louder the praise, the more value I understood myself to have. Writing as a means of evaluating my identity felt far less brutal and masochistic than anorexia, because I could talk about writing as art, as higher calling, as being in service of nonconformism and radical independence and blah blah blah. There was, indeed, this brief, glorious period of time, right when my first book came out, when I felt like I had finally confirmed that I was a person of value. Not only had I written a *book*—tangible proof of my own existence!—it was relatively well received. I got a wave of nice press, I participated in discussions with fancy-pants New York intellectuals, I was interviewed for magazine profiles and on podcasts and once, awkwardly, on a short-lived web-based television show run by a bigwig in media. I had an identity: I was a *writer*, and I was good at it!

In retrospect, my happiness at this time wasn't derived from having found a *true* value system; it was because, for that moment, I was succeeding within a particular value system that was, like the others that had come before it, socially reinforced but ultimately arbitrary. I know this, because shortly after I met Angela and moved to London, I entered a period in which writing work at first slowed to a trickle and then, like a parched riverhead, entirely dried up. Did I happily retreat into solitary days spent with only words of poetry for comfort? Did I rant about editors and critics being the worthless enemies of true vision, like, oh, I don't know, Flaubert would have? Did I toil away endlessly at a behemoth manuscript, unbothered by the prospect that no one would ever see it?

Reader, I did not. My self-esteem plummeted in tandem with the frequency of my bylines; I felt weepy when faced with a calendar devoid of any obligations at all. I felt so utterly without purpose that I found myself waiting at the exit to the grocery store for awkwardly long periods of time, so momentarily comforted was I at the chance to hold open the door for a stranger. The arrival of my first child, for a time, only served to make things worse: now I had no job at all, I was only a *housewife*, which on the hierarchy of "contributes meaningfully" in my mind wasn't particularly high, because in the educated, liberal, urban milieu I'd been marinating in for the past decade-plus, value was highly correlated with white-collar job performance.

There was another option available to me aside from seeing my value solely in my weight, or in the trappings of intellectual life. This option didn't inadvertently debase others with its metrics, or harbor all sorts of icky suspicions about dependency and weakness, or rob me of my sense of control, or incentivize me to keep striving toward some aim that, upon further reflection, turned out to be just as meaningless as the previous one. That option was to view myself, somewhat unfashionably, as created in the image of a divine maker—in Hebrew, b'tzelem Elokim—worthy not because of the things I had done or would do, but because of an essence that couldn't be degraded or extinguished. (Yes, I had converted shortly before I moved to England, but it took quite awhile to detox from the East Coast variety of America's individualistic, aspirational paradigm.) For those of an Abrahamic faith, this does not mean that humans actually look like God, who is formless and featureless—although this is less true for Christians, who obviously believe that God came to earth in human form—but rather that God created humans out of love, to be seen as special and worthy, and with a spark of His own powers in them: the power to create, to rest, to be merciful, to love, to take care.

According to the German philosopher Karl Jaspers, this idea of a universal human worth arose during the Axial Age, a period of energetic religious and philosophical change in disparate parts of the globe, including China, India, Israel and the Levant, and Greece, which lasted from around 500 to 300 BCE.* Movements as different as Taoism, monotheism, Hinduism, and philosophical rationality moved away

---

* Historians quibble with some of the details of the Axial Age, although it remains an influential and largely accepted idea in academia and elsewhere.

from the previously held exclusive view of religion—I have my god who takes care of me and mine, and you have yours, and to appeal to a different group's god would be to have your pleas go unanswered—and instead "extended the moral boundaries of communities to include those ordinarily treated as outsiders," as the sociologist Don Grant has summarized. "Not all of these movements promoted a belief in the supernatural, but all of them recognized a transcendent element at the core of every human being that can only be encountered through acts of compassion." Jaspers put it more succinctly: "The step into universality was taken in every sense."

Despite Jaspers's positivity, the theological viewpoint is often held up to scrutiny, and quite fairly, too, because some who claim to hold it behave in ways diametrically opposed (to pick just one example, some Christians in the United States seem utterly hardened to the suffering of refugees). And yet the possibilities of its core kindness remain: even into our modern era, some of the most eloquent voices on human rights have been those steeped in the spiritual. The Catholic convert Dorothy Day, for instance, cofounded the Catholic Worker Movement, a pacifist organ that agitated on behalf of the poor; the rabbi Abraham Joshua Heschel was a close confidant and supporter of Reverend Martin Luther King's, and a passionate advocate on behalf of Jews living in the then-Soviet Union, who were brutally oppressed. For her part, Angela never forgot that Pierce Butler, the lone dissenter in the *Buck v. Bell* Supreme Court case, which ruled that a young woman deemed "feeble-minded" could be forcibly sterilized (and by extension, so could anyone else the state declared unfit), was a devout Catholic. (Because he did not write an opinion, we will never know how much his religion influenced his decision, though his fellow justice Oliver Wendell Holmes once stated he suspected it had.) And while theological anthropology's opposing viewpoints tend to have the aura of sophistication and intelligence and hypermodern ideas of mercy and tolerance, surprisingly, often the opposite is true: according to research conducted by sociologist John Evans, proponents of utilitarianism are more likely to sanction buying organs from poor people, ending the life of an elderly person because they are a drain on resources, and torturing people if there's a possibility it could save other lives; adherents to the biological viewpoint share these opinions, excepting torture.

To believe that something took the time and effort to create you is, of course, to believe that this entity loves you. For a person like Angela, this solved a number of problems. Unlike for me, the specific question of human value *had* occurred to her at a tender age, although she describes her early interest as based more in rigidity and resentment than in generosity. "I was really concerned with fairness. It really bothered me if I felt that people had unearned power or unearned authority," she said.

As she got older, the question of worth persisted, and although softened, still retained a hard, meritocratic edge to it. "I think I was self-aware enough long ago to notice that I *did* judge people who I thought were worth less than me, and I didn't like that about myself. I wouldn't have put it this way, but I think part of me wanted to appeal to something higher to help me, to anchor me in why that was wrong." Of course, if you're worried that you're devaluing others, then of course you must also, in some way, worry that you will be devalued yourself, remain unloved, left alone. A few months after first attending a Quaker meeting, Angela was meditating to a video of a flickering candle on YouTube ("I kid you not") when a thought popped into her head: there was no way she could ever get to the idea of being unequivocally loved—despite your flaws, your disabilities, your quirks, your deeply human failures—without religion. "Ever since then I haven't thought of myself as an atheist," she told me. "It's kind of like the Gordian knot, where I was trying to solve it intellectually, thinking about utilitarianism or something. And then the idea of spiritual equality came and just cut through that and said, There's that of God in everyone, we are all spiritually equal, let's try to act like it. And that felt really powerful."

Powerful, but also slightly embarrassing, she admitted, and "daddy-esque." Wasn't it immature to want to be cared for interminably? Didn't it reflect a desire to be a kind of permanent child? Maybe. But maybe it's also an unassailable part of human nature, to want to be known and cherished and, yes, tended to. Once, when I was in college and very ill with anorexia, I was working on a paper for a class on Shakespeare when I mistakenly hit a button that deleted the entirety of the text; panicking, I asked the professor, who happened to be the father of an acquaintance of mine from summer camp, if I could hand it in late. When I arrived at his office at the crack of dawn the next morning, he must have sensed something was wrong with me that went beyond technological mishaps—probably I looked exhausted and drained of color, maybe I mentioned, cryptically, something about "health problems"—and he launched into what I felt at the time was a non sequitur. "Everyone wants to be taken care of, deep down," he said to me. "Even adults."

This registered as rather revelatory, because I had thought that the entire point of growing up was to shed your reliance on others. (Such a vision of being loved doesn't preclude tough love either: I think of the oft-repeated Midrashic idea that says every blade of grass has its own angel that whispers to it, encouraging it to grow, which actually, in proper translation, has the angel smacking it instead.) When the shame of this desire surges, perhaps we should consider that we might not only be hearkening back to our infancy when we yearn for such care, but also fast-forwarding to our future, when we will be just as feeble and vulnerable as we were when we were babies, but less immediately endearing in our form, diminished from a plump, new sweetness to a figure withered and angular and infirm. Perhaps that is the true dependency that terrifies and repulses us, and which we must learn to see as just as dignified as the freshness of our beginnings or the strength of middle life, or even the particular grim beauty of youthful illness. "When your hair turns gray, I will still carry you," God tells the prophet Isaiah to relay to the people. "I made you, I will bear you, I will carry you, and I will rescue you."

Angela attended Meeting for Worship throughout the fall of 2019 and into the early winter of 2020, until the coronavirus pandemic reached New York City. Like much of the country—indeed, the world—the Brooklyn Friends Meeting immediately shifted online, but Angela found the Zoom meetings underwhelming. Being in a community with people who share your values was "calming," she said, but something about being in that community in a disembodied way just felt eerie. She stopped going for a while, but during that time, "I still felt like I was talking to God or thinking of myself as a Quaker or trying to find a theology." And the caesura actually ended up putting to rest some of her concerns about her involvement. She'd always worried, for example, that she was expecting some kind of big emotional climax from spirituality, one that she would become dependent upon if she got it, like a peak experience addict. "I think I tend to distrust those big feelings, even as part of me is drawn to them and crave them," she told me, but because Quakerism had gradually become part of the architecture of her mind even when its (rather minimal) trappings weren't there, she felt reassured that she wasn't looking to it because she was expecting it to provide her with periodic highs.

Still, there are aspects of faith that Angela continues to struggle with. She's less attracted to the ornate symbolism of denominations like Catholicism than she used to be—a later trip to the Vatican left a bad taste in her mouth—but she's still a little sad that there isn't a rich tradition of Quaker art. When the seventeenth-century British composer Solomon Eccles became a Friend, he first sold all his music and instruments, then, reconsidering, bought them back and burned them, lest they tempt others to "vanity" (George Fox's descriptor for music). Likely very few Liberal Quakers today would refuse to go to the symphony or a museum, but with a history like that, it makes sense that there isn't much of a canon. There are only a handful of notable Quaker writers and artists, like Judi Dench, Bonnie Raitt, and James Turrell, the minimalist artist whose work is heavily influenced by light. Indeed, some of Turrell's famous "skyspaces"—essentially holes cut into ceilings that prompt the viewer to gaze upward and enter into a silent, worshipful state—have been installed in Quaker meeting houses. "In a way, it's not that far from making something that is visual ministry," he's said.

And even though there isn't a huge corpus of Quaker art, Angela has found Quaker ideas in other work that help her feel that artistic leanings and her Quaker values are compatible, like in Walt Whitman's *Leaves of Grass* ("I celebrate myself, and sing myself," the opening poem "Song of Myself" begins, "And what I assume you shall assume / For every atom belonging to me as good belongs to you"), or Ralph Waldo Emerson's famous essay "Nature," a call to arms for people to encounter God themselves, in the natural world and in their own era, and not simply to build on the "sepulchres of the fathers." "I become a transparent eye-ball; I am nothing; I see all," Angela's favorite part goes. "The currents of the Universal Being circulate through me; I am part or particle of God." (Neither Whitman nor Emerson were Quakers, but both were very influenced by its theology. Once, when a relative asked Emerson if he were a Swedenborgian, he replied, "I am more of a Quaker than anything else. I believe in the 'still, small voice,' and that voice is Christ within us.")

Maybe that was what one should aspire to be, amid so much of the anger and chaos that defines modern life: something that bears witness and filters. Even her much-admired Saint Hildegard's work teems with Quakeresque sentiment: "For when God gazed into the face of the human being whom he formed / he beheld all his works / in that same human form, entire."

On occasion, she still craves something a little more ritual heavy, more dogmatic, even. "Sometimes I struggle with the fact that there's so *much* space," she told me. "Of course, I go to meeting for worship, and I do that regularly. You don't have to be falling on your knees until you don't feel anything even there. So that's one of the appeals of it. But I do struggle with it because sometimes I do wish there was more I could do to cement my connection to the community."

The guiding principles of simplicity, peace, integrity, community, equality, and stewardship—what Quakers call "SPICES"—are useful directives, but vague ones, open to such wide interpretation that one can get lost, or potentially convince themselves that anything goes, as long as the intention is there. But this is anathema to a person like Angela, who craves a way to translate ethical principles into action. Many Quakers are vegetarians, so she's cut down on her meat consumption, although it feels a little culturally insensitive, given that her native Chinese cuisine is fairly meat based. She's never been a big drinker, but she now drinks even less, as a nod to the still widely held Quaker testimony of abstemiousness. And she's more conscious of climate change: "Of course, I care about the climate as everyone does, but because that kind of environmental stewardship is really pretty deeply ingrained in Quakerism, I think I just pay more attention," she said.

Simplicity is a tougher embrace. Angela would never dress truly Plainly, though that hardly matters considering most Quakers don't. Still, her penchant for a little flair every now and again is somewhat at odds with the idea of eschewing unnecessary adornments. On the day I met her at a meeting for worship, she was wearing a dramatic, brightly patterned dress and big dangly earrings. "Not very Plain," she said with a smile, shrugging. (I mentioned noticing a young man with a dyed mohawk in attendance, though, which probably qualified as even less simple.)

Like Leah Libresco Sargeant, and unlike Tolstoy, say, Angela never felt she had to "fully reject" rationality in order to embrace faith—though she concedes that religion and rationality aren't natural bedfellows, because the latter is interested only in what can be proven, and you cannot, as of yet, prove the existence of God. And her relationship to both the subculture and that kind of harder knowledge—data, statistics, facts, whatever—*has* changed somewhat. "If you'd asked me ten years ago, I would have said that I just don't want to believe something that has a fairly high likelihood of not being real," she said. "And now that doesn't seem like a relevant question."

Applying logical reasoning to questions of faith now feels like "it would be a category mistake": "I think I would say that we all need to have different viewpoints and ways of evaluating the world and that we need to be flexible with them. You do not evaluate your coworker in the same way that you evaluate your child, and I don't evaluate faith in the same way I evaluate other claims." She invoked the paleontologist and evolutionary biologist Stephen Jay Gould's idea of "nonoverlapping magisteria," from his 1997 essay of the same title. (*Magisteria* here, from the Latin, connotes realms of teaching or expertise, rather than the oft-assumed "majesty.") "I believe, with all my heart, in a respectful, even loving concordant between our magisteria," Gould wrote. "If religion can no longer dictate the nature of factual conclusions properly under the magisterium of science, then scientists cannot claim higher insight into moral truth from any superior knowledge of the world's empirical constitution." But these magisteria, despite being different, don't have to be in active conflict; rather, they can be, as Angela puts it, "complementary." If she was sick, she would go see a doctor, not sit at home and pray to be healed, but if she wanted to evaluate the moral or spiritual worth of something, she would turn to her faith, rather than try "to find some kind of evidence-based answer."

Ever the cautious, self-probing type, Angela continued attending Meeting for Worship while remaining unsure she would formally join (the official process is to submit a letter requesting membership and then meet with a "clearness committee," who then make a recommendation for admission). So many things remained in flux: whether she still secretly harbored the desire to sit in an incense-filled cathedral surrounded by iconography; whether she was drawn to Quakerism for its own singular beauties and wouldn't be just as well off as a Unitarian or a Buddhist dabbler; whether she even believed in God, even though that wouldn't preclude her from becoming a Liberal Friend. "It's not like sometimes I believe in God and sometimes I don't; it's more like I always believe in God a little (or at least want to) and always don't believe in him, all at the same time," she told me. And yet she had the distinct sense of inching ever closer to her faith, of realizing that somehow, over the past two years, in a very real way she had *become* Quaker, deep down, without having fully grasped the shift. "I think at some point it just felt like I couldn't imagine not making this part of my life," she said. "It's been long enough that I can trust the feeling I had at the beginning that this was right for me."

2.

SARA, TO THE ECSTATIC HEALING OF EVANGELICALISM

Afflicted and close to death from my
youth up, / I suffer your terrors; I am helpless.

—PSALM 88

It was around midafternoon, April 15, 2013, almost three hours after the winners had crossed the finish line of the Boston Marathon, when Sara Gentile, then a junior at nearby Emerson College, was walking on Newbury Street, parallel to Boylston, the main drag of the race. Sara's plan was to cut over near the finish line to meet up with some friends who were gathering to cheer on classmates who were running, but before she'd left campus, she'd stopped momentarily to pet her friend's cute little Corgi. "I think me petting the dog is what honestly saved my life, because I would have been at the finish line two minutes earlier," she told me years later, sipping English Breakfast tea in the obscenely pleasant courtyard of a boutique Los Angeles hotel. "I see a lot of protection in that."

There was a building separating Sara and the finish line on the next street over when the first bomb went off. "I knew something was very wrong. I thought, *That was not a firework.*" *Was that a gun?* she wondered. But it seemed too loud to be a single shot. *Maybe multiple guns?* She turned on her heels and began running away from the noise. She was about to turn onto a side street toward Boylston when the second bomb went off ahead of her. This time, she saw the air turn ashen; a metallic smell wafted around her, and the screaming seemed to be coming from everywhere. The ground shook. She changed directions again, sprinting away from the site—toward where, she wasn't sure; having no idea what was happening, she had no real way of knowing where would be safe. Two frantic thoughts came to her: *God, if I believed in you, I bet I would be praying right now, but I don't, so I'm not,* and *Call your mom before the cell towers go out.*

In something between a panic and a daze, Sara began moving in the direction of her apartment. The city was a maelstrom of ambulances and sirens; people with blood splattered on their clothing stumbled by her on the street. At one point, she overheard someone say that the bombs had been planted in trash cans, so she found herself avoiding every corner with a bin. The most indelible image from that day remains for her a trio she saw on a street corner, a grandfather, a father, and a young boy, possibly three or four, in a stroller.

"What's going on?" the little boy asked.

"We're just going to go home so we can make sure we're safe," the adults answered him.

"That's the memory that makes me the most upset," Sara told me later. "These three generations of men with their young son. . . . Oh gosh, it makes me so emotional."

Compared to some she knew, Sara was lucky. One of her friends was working in a restaurant right next to where the second bomb went off and spent the afternoon pulling shocked people, their skin slick with blood, off the street; another was saved from certain death when shrapnel from the explosive mostly hit the laptop bag she was carrying (she still had to endure multiple procedures over the ensuing years to remove residual shrapnel embedded in her skin; to this day, her pores appear black). In total, eight students from her university were physically injured at the marathon, not to mention the many other spectators who were hurt and the three people who were killed.

In the days that followed the bombing, Sara did feel like there was "beauty in the communal feelings" of grieving and recovery at school, but she struggled when it came to her own turmoil. She felt it was only right that everyone prioritize the experiences of those who had been physically hurt or those who had witnessed more carnage than she had, but she felt she lacked an outlet for her pain, which only led to her drinking more alcohol and secretly stuffing herself with food until she was uncomfortable. Sometimes she caught herself wishing she *had* been physically injured so she would bear some literal and identifiable mark of her suffering, but then she'd lambaste herself for having such a selfish thought. This messy admixture of feelings was something she was comfortable discussing with friends, because most of them could relate in some way: people who had been running felt guilty for inviting their friends and then putting them in harm's way, students who had stayed on campus and knew no one who'd been affected were still spooked that something like that had happened so close to school. But the discussions didn't last: "It felt like a few weeks later everyone moved on, and I didn't."

Sara's panic attacks began almost immediately after the bombings. They could be triggered by any number of commonplace things: loud sounds, like a door slamming closed, the smell of candles (birthday candles in particular set her off), the sight of a trash can. She lived about twenty minutes away from the main area of campus, but she was afraid both to walk—too many garbage cans, too many men with backpacks—and to take the subway. She was on edge all the time, often vacillating between wanting to isolate but feeling more afraid when she was alone. The fear "was taking over my whole life," she said.

The campus health department referred her to a PTSD expert near school, a prim older woman with whom she did a few sessions of EMDR, a type of therapy that involves mentally replaying a traumatic event while tapping yourself on strategic points on the body, which is thought to desensitize people to distressing memories. She went for one or two sessions, but then didn't return. "I think I was too traumatized to actually *sit* in my trauma," she said. One of the last things she told her therapist was that she felt like she should go to church. "Well, why don't you?" the counselor asked. A school friend named Jillian, who had graduated a year earlier and was living in Brooklyn, suggested Sara reach out to a guy she knew who was attending nondenominational Christian services in the area, so Sara sent him a Facebook message to coordinate. Shortly before she and I met in real life, more than ten years after their exchange, Sara had looked up her messages with this guy, and was struck by how obviously anxious she seemed. "I sound so lost," she said. "It's a different voice than mine."

Nearly a century after the formalization of psychology as a branch of science, we still are no nearer to a definitive answer as to why some people are more resilient than others, so Sara can't know precisely why she continued to struggle long after most of her classmates seemed to recover. Her childhood offers few clues: it was, by her own account, nice and fine and good. She was raised in a suburban town in central

New Jersey, about halfway between Philadelphia and New York City. Her home life was happy; she had a close relationship with her parents and with her younger brother. She enjoyed all the trappings of a classic American suburban childhood: art projects, soccer, ample books to read, trips to the Jersey Shore in the summertime. An unusually driven child, she knew at an early age what she wanted to be when she grew up, which wouldn't be so noteworthy if her chosen métier wasn't an atypical one for a kid. "I knew that since the fifth grade I wanted to be a TV producer and then also work with young people, like teenagers and high schoolers," she said (how exactly she landed on this specific combination, she couldn't quite remember). Though she was a quiet child, she was also "always an advocate," standing up for the friend who didn't get picked for a team in gym class or speaking out on behalf of anyone getting bullied.

Her mom's side of the family is Irish, and her dad's is Italian, so naturally the family was Catholic. But the affiliation was much more cultural than theological. When Sara was young, the whole family went to Mass every Sunday, and the Gentile siblings faithfully attended catechism classes, but her parents never talked about God outside of church, and their faith didn't really seem to dictate their life choices, which Sara found occasionally perplexing. "I definitely had a lot of questions. I didn't really feel like there were a lot of places to have them answered, and I felt like I was just being told a lot, but without really getting to digest it for myself," she said. Still, it was a decidedly "neutral" experience—"I liked the music, art, and architecture"—that left little impression on her: to this day, she remembers almost nothing of her Catholic education aside from some prayers, the names of a few saints, and the fact that you aren't supposed to have sex outside of marriage. Right after her younger brother was confirmed at fourteen, the family's church attendance dwindled and eventually ceased altogether.

When she was fifteen, Sara started complaining to her mom that she was feeling "off," though she couldn't define her symptoms: "I just kept saying *I'm not feeling well.* I felt so tired." The two went to the pediatrician, who referred Sara to an endocrinologist. Everyone anticipated something manageable and banal like low-grade anemia, so they were shocked when the blood test revealed she had type 1 diabetes (later in life, she'd also be diagnosed with celiac disease and pernicious anemia). Because her pancreas couldn't produce insulin on its own, Sara would be reliant upon insulin injections for the rest of her life, or until some cure was developed. Overnight, she went from a relatively carefree teen to one tasked with maintaining a delicate equilibrium in her body. When we had lunch together, she modeled for me the relentless decision-making process required of a diabetic faced with a simple meal: "Okay, when did I last eat? What am I going to have now? Oh, I'm having potatoes. I need to give myself some insulin first because potatoes are going to spike my blood sugar. If I want to exercise later, I need to exercise probably three hours from now to make sure there's no more insulin in my system."

She was a quick student of the logistics of it all, but looking back, she laments that there was virtually no discussion of the emotional impact of her diagnosis. To be told not only that you have an incurable illness, but also that it's largely your responsibility to treat it, and too little or too much of the medicine you administer to yourself could kill you: it felt at times like far too heavy a mental load to carry. She hated getting woozy in public when her blood sugar was low, or having to leave class to go to the nurse and fetch her injection kit. "There were a few times in high school where I just had complete breakdowns," she said. Managing her symptoms was exhausting. To compound the stress, at the end of middle school, Sara had started to have the negative thoughts about her body and about food so common to pubescent girls.

All the girls on her soccer team were rail thin, and she "always had a butt," so she started alternately avoiding junk food and sneaking handfuls of chocolate chips on evenings when the rest of her family were ensconced on the couch watching TV, opening the plastic bags ever so quietly so no one would hear her. Diabetes just served to further enmesh food with rebellion and success and stress management for her.

Sara went to college to study TV production, just like she'd always wanted to do. Until the bombing, her college experience was in many ways analogous to mine: a disorienting mix of fun debauchery and simmering, inexplicable loneliness. Worn out by the culture of binge drinking, missing her family, still constantly fatigued and bloated and depressed—and still years away from being formally diagnosed with celiac disease, which is common in diabetics and which Sara feels was at the root of some of these issues—she finally dragged herself to see a counselor on campus. Maybe out of some lingering Catholic guilt, or maybe because something was "stirring" in her, she made a spontaneous announcement to the counselor that surprised her: "Oh, I think the answer is not here with you. I think the answer is in church."

"What do you think is holding you back from going?" the counselor asked.

She brushed aside the question as ludicrous: she was a freewheeling college student at an extremely progressive school, who hadn't been to church in years! "I get to make my own choices now," she thought. "So I'm not going to church. I'm going to parties."

By the time she made that identical observation to her EMDR therapist after the marathon, though, she was desperate enough to begin church-hopping with a few other Emerson students. The free-flowing nondenominational services she attended contrasted sharply with the rigidly structured Catholic Mass of her youth, and she loved their alt-rock-inflected melodies, particularly at the congregation right near the famed Berklee School of Music, where the music students would provide the soundtrack to their Sunday morning prayers. At one service, the pastor taught a lesson in which he used a marathon as an extended metaphor for holiness in marriage, and she didn't feel any rising panic at all. On occasion, she'd also go to a women's Bible study group near campus, where she mostly just wondered how the other attendees had become so conversant with scripture. *How do they know who Paul is?* she asked herself. *How do they understand what they're reading?* Above all, she was interested in the man at the center of all this, the one these women seemed to know so intimately, as if he were a friend and confidant rather than a historical figure. "*Who is this Jesus?*"

As her curiosity about Christianity grew, though, her psychic health plummeted ever downward. Panic filled her days; at night, she still dreamed of the bombings. To cope with feeling constantly on edge, she started drinking in class, disguising the alcohol by carrying it in coffee cups; for the first time, she went to class stoned. She was eating more in secret, gulping down pints of Ben & Jerry's ice cream alone and then stuffing the empty containers into the bottom of the trash can so her roommate wouldn't see them. She felt like a zombie with food, like she was being controlled by something outside of herself. While she was binging, she'd lose track of how much she was consuming and stop giving herself insulin entirely because she was afraid of inadvertently "stacking," a term for giving yourself successive doses so as to quickly lower your blood sugar, which can lead to hypoglycemic episodes that can cause fainting, seizures, or even death. She felt a "heaviness" with her always, but she was able to convince herself she wasn't completely out of control, because she was careful never to black out from drinking (a loss of consciousness, she knew, could have deadly ramifications for her when it came to her blood sugar).

For her last semester of school, she moved to Emerson's Los Angeles campus, on Sunset Boulevard, smack-dab in the middle of Hollywood, where she was able to get an internship in the production department of a large television network. But the panic followed her there, and she spent most of her nights out at clubs, spending profligately on drinks and then sleeping late into the morning. Once again, Jillian (who'd also spent her last semester in Los Angeles) suggested a church that just happened to be within walking distance of school—certainly a small miracle for someone living in famously sprawling L.A. It was called Reality (its name comes from the epistle of Paul to the Colossians: "These are shadows of things to come; the reality belongs to Christ"). At the time, Reality's leader was a man named Tim Chaddick, a former drug-taking, rock 'n' roll bad boy—with the tattooed sleeves to match—whose story of finding Jesus Sara found "authentic and also moving and relatable." She threw herself into church life, becoming a part of a Reality-organized "small group," a kind of ready-made cadre of Christian friends with whom she'd study Bible, celebrate engagements and birthdays, organize impromptu brunches, and convene on holidays. She began taking a "discipleship" class, a kind of "theology 101" program for new churchgoers. As she tore through the Bible, she kept a notebook with an ever-growing list of questions about what the words meant for her own life (in response to a New Testament commandment to be "sober-minded," she asked, "Does that mean I can't drink at all? Or does that mean something different?")

"I don't know what I was thinking or why I was putting myself into Christian community," she told me. She'd always planned to move back to New York to work in film there and be close to her family, but she was now feeling a pull to stay put. "I think I need to finish this with God," she remembers thinking. "Whatever's happening here, I don't think we're done yet." Her family was crushed, but they understood when she explained that she was planning to stay in Los Angeles for the professional connections—not entirely untrue, but also not the main motivation.

It was around this time that she began to pray, sometimes during services, which met in a high school auditorium, speaking quietly to God in her head and heart. Sometimes she did this on her knees on carpets the church laid out for people, her hands raised toward the stage; other times, she found herself talking aloud to God in her car while she sat in endless traffic. For reasons she can't pinpoint even now, she began training for a half-marathon, even though she'd always hated the running part of sports and still felt scarred by the bombings. While sweating through her daily miles in the streets of her neighborhood or the hills of Griffith Park, she listened to worship music and "spent time with Jesus," a kind of kinetic prayer. She landed on a refrain to express her strongest wish at the time: *God, I'm starting to believe with my mind, but I'm not feeling you in my heart.* It wasn't like anyone *told* her she had to do both; she just sensed a "disconnect" that she didn't want. *Change that like a light switch*, she asked repeatedly. *Help me to believe in you in my heart.*

On September 14, 2014, Sara dragged herself, hungover, into the auditorium, just as she had done nearly every Sunday for the previous nine months. She felt that day like she did every day back then: "open, bleeding." She sat alone, in a spot almost directly in the middle of the audience. By this point, she was living with roommates in an apartment in the Valley and working as a production assistant on a home renovation show; from the outside, her life looked exactly as fifth-grade Sara would have hoped, but she still felt stuck in a cycle of panic, binge drinking, binge eating, striving for professional success, never feeling good enough, always hiding, always running away. That Sunday, Pastor Tim gave a sermon about the introduction to Paul's letter to Titus,

a short passage that, at first blush, looks like little more than a nice
epistolary greeting:

> Paul, a servant of God and an apostle of Jesus Christ, for
> the sake of the faith of God's elect and their knowledge of
> the truth, which accords with godliness, in hope of eternal
> life, which God, who never lies, promised before the ages
> began and at the proper time manifested in his word
> through the preaching with which I have been entrusted by
> the command of God our Savior;
>
> To Titus, my true child in a common faith:
>
> Grace and peace from God the Father and Christ Jesus
> our Savior.

In hope of eternal life. Pastor Tim explained that what Paul was actually doing here was acknowledging that, in Jesus, one is given an entirely new life. Because Jesus died for humanity already, anyone can
have access to this new life, and everyone owes him for this opportunity. Surely some would find this unduly burdensome—"Jesus died for
somebody's sins, but not mine," Patti Smith famously and bitterly
crooned—but for Sara, it was transformative: it felt like an enormous
gift. Agreeing to let Jesus into her heart, to follow his teachings, seemed
small and eminently doable in the face of such precious, momentous
selflessness. *Yes, yes, yes,* she felt herself saying.

"In that moment of saying yes, he spoke to me," she told me. "*Sara,
I'm showing you your heart.* And I saw this image of my heart. And
around my heart were these brick walls. And God was like, *you put
these walls up,*" Sara said, lifting her hands to outline the shape of the
fortress around her heart. "But he was like, *I love you so much that I'm*

going to break these down for you." And at that moment, the walls crumbled immediately, and a complete sense of "peace and joy and hope" flooded into her. *Yes, I want new life in you. Yes, I believe in Jesus. Yes, tear down these walls.* In this silent moment of acceptance, she envisioned the anxiety and fear of PTSD as chains wrapped around her arms, and she saw the chains being cut off, her limbs freed. She realized she was sobbing uncontrollably, and continued to sob as the sermon gave way to open worship time; she was vaguely aware of the hand of the person behind her patting her gently on the back. For the first time in years—maybe ever—she took a very deep breath, and when she told me the story, she inhaled deeply again, as if to remind herself she could still do it.

After that September Sunday, Sara stopped panicking at the sight of trash cans and the aroma of candles; she never had another nightmare about the bombings. She can talk about the events of that April day and feel none of the tingly, rising fear she once did. Her desire to party vanished; she stopped smoking pot instantly. "I felt immediately healed and freed from the anxiety and fear, which makes no sense," she said. "It was an on-the-spot miraculous healing and conversion, and I knew everything had changed."

A young man sits in a garden, mired in self-loathing. To the outsider, his hatred of himself appears outsize, as his indiscretions are downright quaint, at least by contemporary standards. In his youth he pursued silly mischief, like stealing to feel the thrill of transgression. He enjoyed the theater, but simultaneously found his delight in it repugnant, because his pleasure was derived from witnessing suffering, like a twenty-first-century person who relaxes to shows about emergency rooms. He lived for years with a young woman who wasn't his wife and reveled in their sexual relationship. As a young adult, he was enamored with a worldview that first appeared sound, but which over time he came to see as constructed on the words of a charismatic but foolish soothsayer. The man himself is extremely eloquent too—in his mouth, the general licentiousness of his hometown is transformed into "clouds of muddy carnal concupiscence"—but he greatly distrusts his articulation, counting himself among the vast class of knowledge merchants who do nothing but lead listeners astray with their empty, beautiful words. (In many ways, his biography is reminiscent of Tolstoy's.)

He desperately wants to be good, but it's hard to forgo baser pleasures. The turmoil has come to a head in this garden, where he is so tortured that he begins to almost physically spasm. A considerate friend hovers nearby, but the man wanders off to be alone ("Solitude seemed to me more appropriate for the business of weeping"). He throws himself at the foot of a tree and begs to be saved—not only from his propensity for "iniquities," but from his excruciating spiritual limbo.

The man, of course, is Augustine of Hippo, the early medieval theologian and philosopher, considered a saint in many Christian denominations, whose conversion is—apart from Saint Paul's—perhaps the most famous in history. Many, even those who've never read his proto-autobiography *Confessions*, know what happens next: from a nearby house, a voice emerges—A child? An angel?—and speaks to him. "Pick up and read," it chants. Augustine opens a nearby Bible, which lands on Romans 13: "Not in riots and drunken parties, not in eroticism and indecencies, not in strife and rivalry, but put on the Lord Jesus Christ and make no provision for the flesh in its lusts." This firm directive, he feels, speaks exactly to his predicament. His path forward is suddenly clear. Like Sara centuries later, he is instantly transformed: "I neither wished nor needed to read further. At once, with the last words of this sentence, it was as if a light of relief from all anxiety flooded into my heart. All of the shadows of doubt were dispelled."

That's a pretty neat and tidy summation of what actually happened though: while Augustine did resign from his teaching position and stayed celibate until his death (as far as we know, anyway), he does spend the second half of *Confessions* trying to answer some of the philosophical quandaries that continued to plague him, particularly locating God in the world, in time, and in human consciousness. One answer did not settle all of his questions; it exposed him to a host of new ones.

For centuries, Augustine's was the textbook redemption narrative, which goes something like this: The protagonist begins in an embryonic lost state (usually the opening vibe is chaotic neutral, at best), then descends downward into an emotional purgatory, reaches a nadir, and finally has—or is bequeathed, in Augustine's case—an epiphany. Everything before the instantaneous moment of salvation was assumed to be a result of the hero's sins, his state of being separated from God. But in 1901, the American biologist turned psychologist William James took the podium at the University of Edinburgh in Scotland to deliver the prestigious Gifford Lectures, in which he offered a slight twist on the usual arc: maybe an individual's spiritual transformation was not the result of divine intervention, but rather the *individual's* subconscious attempt to channel and heal his own pain.

Drawing on scant earlier scholarship on conversion, James roughly divides people into two camps: the "once-born" and the "twice-born" (the latter is a term borrowed from English philosopher Francis Newman). Of the once-born, who subscribe to what he calls "the religion of healthy-mindedness," he has less to say: a person whose "temperament

[is] organically weighted on the side of cheer" provides little fodder for analysis. As for the "twice-born" convert, James extols him as a religious "genius," but also recognizes that he often falls somewhere on the spectrum from neurasthenic to outright insane.*

James's lectures were later published in a book titled *The Varieties of Religious Experience*, in many ways a catalogue of redemption narratives, from a group of 652 early Methodists who attested to instantaneous awakenings to the health guru transformed by Buddhist teachings to the French secular Jew who had a chilling vision of God in a small Italian church and became a Catholic ("I came out as from a sepulchre, from an abyss of darkness; and I was living, perfectly living"). James is particularly enamored of figures like George Fox—whose spiritual mind was of "superior power," but who was also "a *detraque* of the deepest dye"—and Tolstoy, whose writings he quotes at great length.

At times, his subjects seem to have fashioned for themselves an early spiritual version of cognitive behavioral therapy, or CBT, which encourages people to focus on correcting maladaptive thoughts or habits as they arise, like psychic whack-a-mole, as opposed to the more introspection-focused therapies. For example, a woman who suffered from some undefined digestion issue describes achieving wellness by repeating mantras and conjuring images of vitality in a manner not dissimilar to what a CBT therapist might instruct a patient to do. "I succeeded in never losing sight after this of my real being, by constantly affirming this truth," the woman writes, "and by degrees . . . *I expressed health continuously throughout my whole body.*" As to whether there is actually a God who reached out to this woman and her fellow wretches, and whether His existence validates her experience, James is solidly neutral. Indeed, conversion, in James's view, is legitimate if the convert is

---

* I'm using "he" here because James's character studies are largely men.

made a better human (happier, more productive, kinder) as a result—what he calls the "fruits" of the transformation, paraphrasing the apostle Matthew.

The idea that the *purpose* of a religious experience is to heal a person would have been considered heretical from both the scientific and the religious perspective, a criticism James anticipated but ultimately denied. Though he wasn't a traditionally religious man, James comes across in the lectures as way more hostile to the scientific impulse to explain away mysticism than to spirituality itself. An early believer in nonoverlapping magisteria, James hated what he saw as science's mechanistic, condescending degradation of the spiritual. "Medical materialism," he said, suffered from the same hubristic stance as any "simple man": it just assumed it could wave away inexplicable human experiences by "vaguely associating them with nerves and liver, and connecting them with names connoting bodily affliction." He's sometimes positioned as the anti-Freud: his contemporary had a uniformly negative view of religion, seeing it as a collection of inherited, fear-based compulsions passed down from one's primitive ancestors, which would ultimately die out once the entirety of humanity became enlightened. (Jung, however, was an admirer.)

The Varieties of Religious Experience developed a rather eclectic following, from the prolific British writer Aldous Huxley to the analytic philosopher Ludwig Wittgenstein. But perhaps nowhere is its influence felt more strongly than in the history of Alcoholics Anonymous. Founded in 1935 by a cadre of repentant alcoholics, AA took many of its tenets directly from the Oxford Group, a Christian organization that stressed giving over one's life to God and regularly confessing one's sins and temptations to a fellow group member. The structure of *Alcoholics*

Anonymous: The Story of How Many Thousands of Men and Women Have Recovered from Alcoholism, also called the Big Book or sometimes AA's "Bible," is virtually the same as *Varieties of Religious Experience*, but shorn of any interspersed narrative commentary.

The writers of the personal stories in the Big Book, like "The Housewife Who Drank at Home," "Freedom from Bondage," and "Gutter Bravado," recount jail sentences, violent detoxes, family estrangements, and financial ruin. Each one describes relinquishing control to God—indeed, the introduction states spiritual experience is a nonnegotiable for recovery—often ambivalently, occasionally on the heels of some divine communion, like founder Bill Wilson's famous white-light moment. Many couch their recoveries in explicitly religious terms. "Henrietta," Bill Wilson said to the third member of AA's wife over lunch, in an episode recounted in one essay, "the Lord has been so wonderful to me, curing me of this terrible disease, that I just want to keep talking about it and telling people." (Decades later, the memoirist and Catholic convert Mary Karr would write similarly of her recovery from alcoholism: "I begin to feel like somebody snatched out of the fire, salvaged, saved.") Though there is a smidgen of medical language in the text—Dr. William Silkworth, the physician who treated Bill Wilson during his detoxes, contributes an essay—the biological view is clearly subservient to the spiritual one. "I earnestly advise every alcoholic to read this book through," Dr. Silkworth concludes his remarks, "and though perhaps he came to scoff, he may remain to pray."

Alcoholics Anonymous is a telling case, because it first presented as a successful blending of science and spirituality. Its prominence in the world of addiction only grew for its first seven-plus decades. But in the early 2000s, it began to fall out of favor. "Lacks scientific rigor" or "is not evidence based" came a chorus of critics, who rejected the idea of a spiritual disease but heartily embraced the idea of a physical one, to be treated with medications and secular therapies rather than mutual aid (never mind that AA had always insisted on a physical basis for alcoholism too). The American intellectual Philip Rieff noted that religion served as effective self-help because it offered "either a therapeutic control of everyday life or a therapeutic respite from that very control," but also posited that there was no room left for the kind of moralizing, authoritarian therapies of faith in an age of individualism. In the battle between human-as-soul and human-as-organism, the scientists had clearly won the day.

But instead of Rieff's theory that psychotherapy would free man from religious and cultural obligations, one could argue that psychotherapy and its medical enablers has just become a kind of replacement religion, one with its own oddities and obligations: both can involve confession to an intermediary, ideally on a regular, ritualized basis, offer psychic tools for human improvement, and sort humans and their experiences into categories (sin or symptom, Jew or schizophrenic). Both purport to help a person move from some negative state (damnable or anxious, despairing or depressive) to a "good" one (optimized, pure, mentally healthy, enlightened). Both are jargon heavy. Both have origin stories that look ridiculous prima facie (people love to say how crazy it is to believe the Joseph Smith discovered lost portions of the Bible on buried golden tablets, but isn't it also laughable to think that all women secretly want penises, just because some man sat in his little study and wrote that down?) Both deal heavily in narrative, encouraging adherents to locate a familiar, inevitable trajectory within the minutiae of their lives. That old Augustinian arc is still there in the analysand-cum-trauma-memoirist who is born into dysfunction, descends into despair, has an epiphany (meets a kindly therapist, receives a satisfying diagnosis, calibrates their meds), and ultimately achieves stasis.

——

Look closely, and one can see that the blurring and borrowing between psychology and spirituality exhibited in the interplay between Alcoholics Anonymous and Christianity continues apace in various contemporary therapeutic and wellness trends. Dialectical behavior therapy, a school of psychotherapy that focuses on distress tolerance and interpersonal relationships, is a gumbo of Zen and contemplative Christian practices; clinicians working in the trendy psychedelics space invoke both psychiatric argot and Indigenous spirituality in their dialogues with patients and their marketing materials. A friend married to a philosophy professor tells me that all the academics she knows are super into Jungian thought, obsessing over the Protestant magician's *The Red Book* and citing his vaguely religio-mythical archetypes.

Almost two years into the COVID-19 pandemic, I was reading *The New York Times* guest essay section when a headline caught my eye: "You've Done Self Care. You've Languished. Now Try This." Despite my innate suspicion of anyone whose job description contains some combination of the words "executive," "performance," and "mental health," as the author Brad Stulberg's did, I clicked. He opened by describing a client of his who was feeling blue despite her attempts to hold herself to generously low standards. Perhaps many of us were in similar situations, he suggested: we were resting, binge-watching TV, saying no to things, and ordering bath bombs by the dozen. "But at a certain point, rest creates inertia," he wrote. "Our minds and our bodies are as recovered as they're going to be. Yet we still feel off."

The solution, Stulberg posited, was "behavioral activation," which basically means doing all the things you know or suspect you *should* do, like exercising or volunteering, in the hopes that the action will energize you. Behavioral activation, Stulberg wrote, is not about forcing yourself to think optimistically. Rather, it is "based on the idea that action can *create* motivation, especially when you're in a rut."

Stulberg claimed that behavioral activation was first "developed" in the 1970s by a clinical psychologist named Peter Lewinsohn, by which I assume he meant that Lewinsohn coined the catchy corporate-therapeutic term. When I read the piece, the first thing I thought was that behavioral activation sounded exactly like the popular Alcoholics Anonymous aphorism "Fake it till you make it," and AA predates Lewinsohn's grand discovery by a good four decades. But then "fake it till you make it" was itself reminiscent of the work of Rabbi Nachman of Breslov, a somewhat eccentric eighteenth-century Hasidic rabbi whom many enjoy posthumously diagnosing with depression: "If you don't feel happy, pretend to be," he wrote to his followers. "Even if you are downright depressed, put on a smile. Genuine joy will follow." Following *that* trail all the way back leads one to a group of hungry, irritable, awestruck Jews, standing at the base of a mountain, telling a divine voice na'aseh v'nishma: "We will do and we will listen." Why would they agree to act before they'd even heard from God? Because, eons before Stulberg introduced behavioral activation to the *Times* readership as a nifty new life-enhancing concept, the Jews knew that, most of the time, behavior predates the feelings, and not the other way around.

I entered my junior year of college struggling with my third serious bout of anorexia in five years. Of all my episodes to date, this was by far the scariest, but not for health reasons. I had lost weight, but it wasn't plummeting, and none of the health problems of my previous relapse, like cardiac abnormalities, had resurfaced—at least as far as I knew, since I never really bothered going to the doctor. No, it was because I could feel the stability of logic, which I had always taken for granted, even in my darkest times prior, shifting, parting, creating crevices and chasms I could, at any moment, fall into.

What I mean by this is that during my earlier struggles, I had always recognized the obvious moral calculus I was flouting. Starving oneself to the point of physical harm was clearly wrong; pursuing mental and physical health was correct. But this time, I was starting to construct an argument in my head, as intricate and impressive to me as the great cathedrals of Europe, that, in fact, all moral presumptions about my behavior—and maybe moral presumptions altogether—were either man-made, meaningless, hypocritical, or all of the above.

My class schedule that semester was comprised of mostly English courses: Modern Drama, 19th-Century British Literature, Creative Writing. The material we were assigned was enthralling, but taken together, rather pessimistic, and I was all too eager to gather the depressing flotsam of postmodern thinkers for the systematic philosophy I was crafting to support my self-negating choices, like a little sparrow gathering withered sticks for the world's saddest nest. From *Women in Love*, I learned that every human is beholden to dark, vicious impulses, ones that society tries to repress, but we ignore at our own peril. From Foucault, I took that madness is labeled so because it is inconvenient to the mores of society, which is itself diseased; insanity, then, can serve as its own kind of righteous protest. Strindberg and Pirandello taught me that all life is essentially performance, that underneath this carapace we call a self is something else entirely (an unknowable mass, an emptiness, a stream of gibberish, a collage of stolen tics). The poor saps in *Waiting for Godot* were cautionary figures, warning against the pitiful danger of imagining that comfort for mere mortals would ever arrive.

It seemed as if every text we read had one underlying message: there is no inherent truth. That thing we call Truth is so endlessly malleable, so contextual, and usually so counter to whatever it is that mainstream society is offering us at any given time, that we can never rely on it, not really. Whatever truth we can find must be unearthed from within, chosen deliberately and consciously by each individual. Through the fog of starvation, I decided this was exciting, and exactly right.

Late one afternoon, I was milling about in the entryway of a campus building with a particularly crepuscular foyer, and I had what I took to be a flash of insight: even though I told everyone in my life I *wanted* to get better, this was actually a lie. After all, I had every incentive to recover. I could *choose* to do so—I believed in free will!—and yet I hadn't, and ultimately had no actual plan to. On this basis, I determined, I must *want* to remain sick. To borrow a term from economics, this was my "revealed preference": the thing that my behavior clearly showed I wanted, as opposed to what I *said* I wanted. In the meantime, based on a falsehood, I was wasting precious resources—the money of my parents, the time of my treatment care providers, the goodwill of my friends.

For years, I had deferred to these other figures in my life when it came to matters of health and self-esteem. Surely, as happier, more confident people, they must be right when they told me that starvation was terrible, that I should aspire to be well and functional. But what if, instead, the texts I was encountering—radical, nihilistic, thrillingly amoral—proved something else entirely: that anorexia was just another truth, no better or worse than any other guiding principle? That devoting my life to a thing I could argue (convincingly!) was spiritual, countercultural, and politically salient, was no different from devoting my life to any other cause (and in fact, might be materially better than living the unexamined life of a corporate automaton). And to those who would say that by choosing anorexia, I was choosing suicide, I could simply counter that a person has an unassailable right to nothing if not her own life, even if that meant hastening her own death.

Forget the fact that I could justify my anorexic behavior by quoting Sartre or Camus: regardless of whether or not it was the *right* choice, clearly it was the choice I was making, and asking me to go against it would be asking me to deny my own deepest desire, which was—in a weird, backward way—denying me my truth, and therefore wrong. The problem, therefore, lay not in the choice itself—in a postmoral world, who could say with any certainty that my choice was wrong, anyway?—but in my own hedging.

The right thing to do, then, the *noble* thing, would be to just come clean to everyone. Conveniently for me, I had a therapy appointment that very evening, so I concocted a plan: I would go to my therapist and explain to her that I had given my predicament a great deal of thought, and I had come to the conclusion that I needed to quit treatment and just accept the fact that I was going to be anorexic forever. I'd seen enough aged anorexics in institutions by that point to have glimpsed my likely future: not a dramatic premature death, like Millais's Ophelia, but a pathetic, uneventful life, with few friends, no lovers, no children, a studio apartment, a dead-end job—who could work wholeheartedly on so little fuel?—and a final demise at maybe . . . forty? forty-five? I realized this would be painful for my loved ones to accept. Indeed, it was deeply painful for me to think about—the me who once wanted a brood of children, to marry an artist and live in a loft, to travel the world—but it was honest, and that was the most important thing.

As I was having this conversation with myself, a little whisper inside me said: *no.* Something within—my conscience, my soul, whatever you want to call it—reacted quickly. *This is not right.* It felt like some soft, subtle kick from far away, something purely reactive, both inside and outside my mind. I tried, at first, to dismiss this as unnecessary guilt over harm done to others, the last gasp of my conventional self. But perhaps that impulse to self-preservation is what drove me to keep my therapy appointment that evening and lay out my whole diabolical plan to my doctor, like the idiot villain in a superhero movie.

I had seen many therapists over the course of my life, if you included the rotating cast of largely forgettable clinical characters one encounters in hospitals, but this particular therapist would have the greatest impact on me. She was a quirky, diminutive woman who sometimes asked me to bring her coffee (she took *six* sugar packets per cup) and shared with me an unusual amount about her life. For other patients, perhaps, this would have been annoying, but I have always been a nosy person so I relished it. For instance, I knew that she had been raised by Communists who decorated the top of their Christmas tree with a plastic head of Mao. She had originally gone to music school to study classical guitar, but had switched to pursuing psychology. (Her connection to music was so intense, she told me, that she could barely listen to it anymore, because it made her feel like she "had no skin.") A widow, she had converted to Christianity as an adult and had an intellectually disabled preteen son.

I sat on the familiar old couch in the darkening office that evening and launched right into my oral argument. When I was done, she paused to examine my face for a moment, then responded.

"See, what I think is that I should drive you up to Westchester tonight and have you admitted to the hospital there."

You can imagine what happened next: I immediately crumpled in tears, incensed—and also, sure, relieved—that my perfectly rational plan was being undermined. (Did I recognize my own part in its undoing? In the same volume as that little voice came the realization that, of course, I had *wanted* to be saved.) For an hour, we debated the merits of my view, me taking the side of the academy, her the side—I would later realize—of God. "We're not doing the moral relativism thing here, Kelsey," she shushed me, as I attempted to explain the implacability of individual truths. At the end of the session, bleary-eyed and exhausted, I had succeeded in doing nothing other than allowing myself one more week to increase my intake and gain (or at least not lose) weight. Did I feel I had been rescued from myself? Not really. Mostly, I felt like I had been thrust back into the tortured purgatory—*Will I get better, or won't I?*—that had consumed me for months or maybe years before, like Augustine in the garden, but with a quieter, less demanding voice instructing me from afar.

I sat still before her, unable to move. My hands lay open in my lap. "What am I going to do?" I asked.

She smiled sadly. "I'll pray for you."

Sara was still living in Los Angeles when I met her in person for the first time, six years after her conversion experience. A number of things in her life had changed. She'd gotten baptized again (she'd been baptized as a Catholic when she was a baby), in front of hundreds of observers, onstage at the Shrine Auditorium, an ornate, Moorish-style theater that's hosted the Oscars. While still working as a producer on the home improvement show, she began volunteering with a youth ministry organization, achieving the dual career path she'd always dreamed of. She and her roommate even decided to move into Koreatown to be closer to the low-income school where she spent her evenings playing games and reading scripture with students. One night, in spring of 2016, after meeting up with the ministry director, she got in her car to drive home, and she heard God speak to her aloud. "I am inviting you to leave your job and to work for this para-church youth organization full time," He said.

"I sat there in my car and I cried for a good while," she told me. "It was not anywhere in my plan or what I wanted to do." But having only recently had such a "radical" experience confirming God's power, she felt prepared to do anything for Him. *I will follow you anywhere and I will do whatever you want me to do because I know your way is better*, she responded. She was also attending seminary, in hopes of eventually working in some kind of church leadership position, perhaps even becoming a pastor (I got the sense she was sheepish about this ambition, and that this had something to do with being a woman). But Reality Church had remained a constant in her life since her first months in L.A., and on the Sunday morning I met her, she picked me up in her white Honda—an empty infant car seat sat in the backseat, in case she was called on to babysit a fellow churchgoer's daughter—and drove me all the way down Santa Monica Boulevard toward Helen Bernstein High School, which sits on land once owned by the Fox Television Center studios and has been home to Reality Los Angeles since 2009.

I felt pretty prepared for Reality's brand: the hip West Coast Evangelical aesthetic of Hillsong dialed down to 3, less movie-star bravado and more classic California chill (indeed, the network of churches Reality belongs to was founded by the heir to a surfboard fortune). Like Hillsong, Reality had been known to attract a celebrity or two—Joe Jonas and Demi Lovato have been spotted at services—but it cultivated a much more down-to-earth atmosphere than the Australian outfit. It's hard to tell how much of the signaling of humility, like the fact that they meet in a high school, or that they label the church "nondenominational" rather than "Evangelical," is a reflection of something solidly theological, and how much was in direct protest to the more aggressively cool Evangelical churches (though by the March day I sauntered onto the pavilion outside the school's entrance, Hillsong was in free fall from multiple scandals). Perhaps it was both.

Sara and I snagged cups of coffee from big jugs at a welcome station while a few friendly greeters waved at the steady stream of young, attractive Christians in vintage Hawaiian shirts and cropped jeans filtering in. We found seats about midway into the auditorium; I could make out the silhouettes of musical instruments in repose on the dark stage. The house band at Reality plays in front of a curtain a soothing cousin of Vermeer blue; the lighting is deliberately low enough to obscure the musicians' faces, so as to remind worshippers that it's Jesus they are seeking, not the shiny visage of a particularly talented singer. Still, I couldn't help but try to make out some features of the figures swaying on stage: the husky-voiced female vocalist appeared to have soft blond hair, and jutting out from the drummer's head was the unmistakable stiff brim of a trucker hat. Congregants were still arriving as the house lights lowered and the piano intro quickly rose to a crescendo. Sara began singing—the lyrics were projected onto a curtain, though I sensed everyone gathered there knew the words already. She had been sick the past two days, I knew, and as she reached her arms out in front of her toward the music, I could see the bare flesh of her arms was pale and goose bumpy.

> You are holy, holy
> The heavens shout
> You are worthy, worthy

I assumed the "you" in the lyrics was God, or Jesus, although it occurred to me also that, in classic crooner style, the listener would instinctively assume she is the one being sung to, dubbed worthy and holy by the dulcet voice, exalted above her lowly mortal station by Jesus's power. That people could be holy because Jesus was holy *and* a person, which is to say capable of feeling pain and of dying—the intimacy that creates, the sense of Jesus as being one's equal, of being capable of true empathy in a way that a noncorporeal God might be assumed not to be—was a theological draw that hadn't really ever occurred to me before I had met Sara.

A few months prior, when I asked in an email if her relationship to Christmas had changed since she'd converted, she told me about entering the Advent season reflecting on this very dichotomy: "The God of the Universe chose to come to us in one of the most vulnerable, miraculous ways—human birth. Mary was swollen, pregnant, and birth was messy, full of fluids. . . . And yet that is how the Creator chose to enter into this world—exactly how we all do. I think, as I reflect on Jesus's humanness, it makes me overwhelmed with gratitude and awe that the Divine came as God-with-Us to dwell and live with us, as one of us . . . yet was also fully God, and also fully human. Feels really relieving to know that God can FULLY relate and understand me, because he LIVED a very human life, as a human being."

Appropriately enough, that day's sermon was titled "Healing from Wounds," and it was delivered by Reality's head pastor, Jeremy Treat, a tall, handsome thirtysomething in a black Levi's jacket and expensive-looking but casual black high tops. Sara had told me one of her favorite things about Reality was that they were committed to scripture study, so it didn't surprise me when Treat opened by reading in its entirety a passage from Mark, about a miraculous healing performed for a woman with some kind of unspecified menstrual issue:

And there was a woman who had had a discharge of blood for twelve years and who had suffered much under many physicians, and had spent all that she had, and was no better, but rather grew worse. She had heard the reports about Jesus and came up behind him in the crowd and touched his garment. For she said, "If I touch even his garments, I will be made well." And immediately the flow of blood dried up, and she felt in her body that she was healed of her disease. And Jesus, perceiving in himself that power had gone out from him, immediately turned about in the crowd and said, "Who touched my garments?" And his disciples said to him, "You see the crowd pressing around you. And yet you say, 'Who touched me?'" And he looked around to see who had done it. But the woman, knowing what had happened to her, came in fear and trembling and fell down before him and told him the whole truth. And he said to her, "Daughter, your faith has made you well; go in peace and be healed of your disease."

After a brief prayer—"Would your spirit move in this time? Would you work in our hearts in a way that draws us to yourself that we might experience healing?"—Treat lightened the mood by relaying a brief humorous anecdote about a pantologist named Henry Gaylord Wilshire, for whom the famous boulevard is named. In the 1920s, Wilshire invented a "healing belt," which I envisioned as a kind of old-timey vibrating waist trainer. Wilshire claimed that the belt could cure everything from cancer to tuberculosis, and even though the medical community loudly labeled him a charlatan, thousands of people bought the belts. Why would people do this? "Because wounded people long for healing and will do just about anything to experience it."

"But Jesus isn't a gimmick or a moneymaking scheme," Treat continued. "He is the true source of healing. And not just for physical healing, but a healing that touches every aspect of our lives." There were different areas of life in which Treat said he believed Jesus could heal: socially/relationally, spiritually, emotionally/mentally, and physically, though the sermon focused mostly on the last three. He began by showing how scripture pointed to different ways in which Jesus himself experienced growth in these areas, before moving on to talk about the ways in which Christians could both expect healing from God and cultivate it in themselves. You could look to the Psalms ("a medicine cabinet for our souls") to see any human emotion poetically represented—I turned to the Psalms in my own life with great reward too—or you could see "every emotion [as] an opportunity to connect with God" (I assumed he meant in prayer, but it wasn't explicitly stated). But you had to do the work yourself, and that meant bringing in contemporary healing techniques. You couldn't be made well physically and then "eat Panda Express every meal," or experience emotional healing without learning to "identify our emotions and deal with our emotions rather than ignoring or stuffing them."

"God works through means," Treat said. "So you can pray for your physical health. But then you can also go see your trainer. And you can pray for your mental health. And then you can also see a therapist or a psychiatrist. We need a holistic approach to this that is centered on God."

During the sermon, Treat had announced that afterward, there would be stations for people who needed prayers for healing. "I really believe that the same way this woman experienced physical healing, we can experience that today," he said, one of the few times he came close to leaning on a stereotypical pastoral rhetoric. Later, though, he cautioned that people shouldn't expect immediate transformation: "A sermon or one church service isn't going to do that." I glanced over at Sara, who kept looking down at her arms self-consciously (she told me later it was rare for her to get that dressed up) and scribbling phrases in her notebook ("we get so used to our wounds," she wrote).

When the lights dimmed, a few people arranged themselves along the auditorium's walls; the music lifted again, and Sara made a beeline for one of the pastors she'd introduced me to earlier, who wore giant aviator glasses and had the tousled dirty-blond hair of a print model (he'd originally come to Los Angeles to be an actor).

I would never in a thousand lifetimes have risen from my chair and sought out one of the shadowy figures—indeed, it wasn't ideal for me, an Orthodox Jew, to be at a Christian worship service at all, no matter how much rabbinic guidance I've sought about how to navigate this aspect of my job, or how aggressively I kept my eyes open while those around me closed theirs in solemnity. But I sympathized with her, because I knew what it was like to crave a miraculous healing.

I had recently been devastated by the news that I had a condition that would make it difficult and potentially dangerous for me to bear a third child, the symptoms of which were weirdly similar to those of the woman Jesus encountered in this passage. Much of the time, my despair over this felt utterly impregnable. But sometimes, when I was alone holding my pain, I felt something widen inside, like existential doors were being pried open. The ache moved through me as if a storm roiling over the land's surface, kicking up all kinds of dust and dirt, moving rocks, damaging homes, but nourishing plants. At these times, my grief felt more honest than anything I'd ever said or done; the hurt became sentient and effective and purposeful, like it *meant* something— which, of course, is the only thing we can ask of pain, that it just not be absurd. God was not healing me, and yes, sometimes that seemed counterintuitive or unfair, so maybe it sounds like a lie to say that something useful was happening nonetheless, superimposing an idea of post-traumatic growth onto what really was senseless barrenness and despair. But it didn't *feel* like a lie. It felt like a great tapping into something universal and bottomless, an acknowledgment that despite the contemporary hubris that we can eradicate human pain, it would always be there, assaulting us, molding us, wearying us, carrying us.

I looked over to see if I could make out Sara's form, the handsome hipster pastor's hands resting gently on her head. Surely just as I knew that any person's touch would not cause my uterus to miraculously repair, she must have known that it was extremely unlikely that she would saunter onstage after this encounter and dramatically rip her insulin pump from her body, like the cripple who suddenly throws down his crutches at an old tent revival meeting. There seemed to be a categorical distinction between being healed of a psychic wound and a physical one, regardless of the occasional ways the two can intersect.

But I couldn't dismiss her impulse as ridiculous the way I assumed most would. I didn't think that she would be healed that day, that's true. But I didn't think praying for it, *believing* it was possible, was nonsensical either. I knew what it was like to go to whatever was cutting edge and not be cured, or even be harmed further. I knew how it felt to be told there was an explanation and a treatment, only to later learn it was a mirage, the promise of relief broken, the wound reopened. I'd come to the end of all that, with the pain still in my hands, and I'd think: *Well,* now *what do I do with this?*

Though Sara said her healing was spontaneous, in fact, it was a little more complicated than that. Shortly after switching careers, she realized while praying that she had an eating disorder—her official diagnosis ended up being binge eating disorder—and sought out the help of a counselor and a dietitian. The therapist she saw for her eating disorder was CBT oriented, and much of that process of replacing negative thoughts with uplifting ones was reminiscent of what she went through around her conversion, when she would write down passages from scripture reminding her of her inherent worth in God's eyes on her whiteboard and meditate on them when she felt overwhelmed by loneliness or sadness or a sense of personal inadequacy. Both journeys felt akin to taking care of a garden, rooting out the invasive plants and replacing them with flowers. "Each time God removed one of these weeds, it made space for Him to come in that area," she said. Self-negating thoughts were replaced by ones that said, *I am loved and chosen and holy and blameless.* The change in thinking wasn't always immediate, nor was the behavioral shift, as it had been with so many things after her miraculous healing: "It takes time to grow into maturity, grow into fruit, and to even *see* the fruit of all that work." But with repetition, just like Bill Wilson and his wretched drunks, she began to really *believe* these positive things about herself and to behave in kind.

Just as she was feeling she had a handle on her eating disorder, though, she decided to revisit EMDR to cope with a combination of new and old wounds: the sudden death of someone she knew through work; persistent anxiety around her diabetes; and a specific residual fear, related to the bombings, of being far from home and unprepared for imminent disaster. Her EMDR therapist was a Christian, which helped because Sara felt like she could be open about how much her faith meant to her. The therapist asked her to establish a "safe place" in her mind, so Sara envisioned a park bench overlooking the cliffs of Santa Cruz, Jesus sitting at her side. During most EMDR sessions, the patient is asked to replay the traumatizing event in their mind; Sara always began with a moment when she was walking down Newbury Street, just before she heard the first bomb go off. In her final session, she saw herself standing there on the street, and then noticed Jesus standing beside her. She felt a peace come over her. *Oh, he was there all along*, she thought.

All told, Sara was in therapy for about four years. She remains steadfastly grateful for the experience: she saw a lot of growth in it, and felt she was more self-aware than she'd be if she hadn't gone through it. She feels the positive ripple effects of it in her life constantly, in that it strengthens her relationships with everyone she interacts with, from the kids at the youth ministry program to the janitorial staff at the schools to the people she stands behind in line at the grocery store. "God doesn't waste anything," she told me. She considers herself to have fully recovered from PTSD.

But her feelings about her autoimmune conditions remain complicated. There are a few benefits, like when she meets a young diabetic and can make that person feel seen, but that feels like a paltry gift compared to what the condition takes away from her. *What is the why? What is the point of this?* she asks herself. Sometimes she avoids bringing it to God in prayer—she's afraid of how she'll feel when relief doesn't come—though, when I met her, she said she was in an intense season of praying to be healed. "I don't feel like I've seen yet the redemption side of it, and I might not in this lifetime. It might be in heaven only. But gosh, I pray for me to be able to see that in this lifetime too."

For Sara, it's not outside the realm of possibility: in addition to being cured of her PTSD, she's experienced other miraculous healings, she told me, like once when someone prayed over her shoulder injury and the soreness vanished. Even when we'd been to church, she told the pastor who prayed with her that she was getting over a cold, and when he touched her throat, she felt a warmth move down it. (As she recounted these incidents, I thought of Augustine's story of a postconversion toothache, which he claims was healed immediately after a prayer session.) God had rescued Sara before, just like He rescued Mary Karr and Bill Wilson and me, so too, she believed He could rescue her again. "I genuinely do trust God with my health. I know He is a good, redeeming God who only wants good things for me, who loves me endlessly and abundantly. I think that's really important, because I know who I'm turning to in the midst of my suffering."

My attitude is very close to Sara's when it comes to my physical suffering: of course I want to be healed, but I am also fearful of being let down, so only in times when I am really alone am I able to express my wish for it. I seek out allopathic medicine, though I steel myself for its possible failure, acutely aware as I am that it cannot address all the varied mysteries of human torment.

In terms of emotional suffering, though, my deconversion from the therapeutic model was relatively swift and ultimately comprehensive. My therapist's offer all those years earlier ended up confirming a suspicion I'd long held but never been confident enough to voice: that these clinicians whom I'd considered true cartographers of the human soul, whose affections I'd coveted more than my blood relatives' and whose pronouncements I held beyond reproach, actually had no special insight into suffering. Eventually, as the anorexic behavior started to correct, I was left to look at the nakedness of my personality underneath it, and it became clearer than it ever had that a major catalyst for my disease had been my lifelong existential leanings, ones that I'd felt without the vocabulary to articulate as a child, and that had left me feeling isolated and sad and desperately in need of some kind of outlet, ideally one that would communicate that pain to the outside world.

But these existential leanings weren't met with any greater under-standing in the doctor's office than they had been in tidy suburbia; instead, they were framed as part of yet another pathological state, one they sometimes called depression. I didn't mind carrying the label of anorexic—often, problematically, I enjoyed it—but I found this second diagnosis triggered a whole host of questions that I increasingly felt the science and psychological frameworks were unable to adequately ad-dress. A short, incomplete list: How happy is any given human *supposed* to be? Who decides where the line between acceptable suffering and unacceptable suffering is, and what kinds of suffering are worthwhile and what kinds are not? Is the pursuit of individual happiness the goal of earthly life? Are there virtues beyond mere self-satisfaction that are worthier of our efforts? Ultimately, is suffering a glitch in the system—a neurochemical mistake, perhaps, an evolutionary wrong turn—or, in the manner of the Buddha, was suffering the system *itself*?

I felt the complexity of my inner life reduced and flattened when experts attempted to explain me to myself using psychiatric or neuro-logical jargon, as if I were a broken car or a printer and they were the engineers. Though I once felt attached to my pain as something that made me special and unique, now I preferred to think of it as com-monplace, something that connected me to others stretching all the way back through history simply because it was so ordinary. This was freeing: of course, I'd like to have no pain at all, but there was a relief in submitting to a version of reality that said there was nothing to fix. (Who doesn't like to cross things off their to-do list?) Like James a cen-tury earlier, I felt that to address my big questions using medicine was, at best, an error in judgment, at worst, a major display of hubris. I be-gan to pull away from therapy just as I began to explore Judaism more seriously, although I've never been able to determine whether the for-mer directly caused the latter.

———

It's not like turning to God meant I never strove to change myself or things around me ever again, but ultimately, religion offered me three things that the therapy did not. The first is an off-ramp from introspection. "Psychological man takes on the attitude of a scientist," Rieff writes in *The Triumph of the Therapeutic*, "with himself alone as the ultimate object of his science." After more than a decade of plumbing my own depths, I was thoroughly bored, and I was growing increasingly skeptical that introspection could yield accruing results. I felt jolted when I first heard the lesson of na'aseh v'nishma: to hear that my emotions were actually not terribly relevant was a big relief, even though I recognize that it's deeply antithetical to the zeitgeist (perhaps that accounts for some of my attraction).

When I look at the ways religious texts provide emotional succor, I not infrequently find ideas that sound a lot like self-help concepts, but they rankle far less, because they're often balanced with the imperative to empty the self completely, rather than "center" it. These ideas differ from the academic explorations of the self I encountered in school, in that they offer a substitute—God, the ethical tenets of the faith, the community— while the former offers nothing, except occasionally art or sex. (Rieff thought that offering nothing was admirable and truthful; I think it *might* be truthful and it might not be, but it's clearly unsustainable.)

These days, I aspire to be something between dust and a kind of benevolent robot, one whose focus is on moving through the world performing right actions with an almost nonexistent inner monologue (this is not to say I come close to succeeding at this—my brain is *extremely* chatty by nature). "There is a state of mind, known to religious men, but to no others, in which the will to assert ourselves and hold our own has been displaced by a willingness to close our mouths and be as nothing in the floods and waterspouts of God," James wrote of such a state, which the Catholics might call contemplation, the Hasidim bitul hayesh, Muslims zuhd, and Anabaptists galassenheit: the idea of God's enormity whittling away at the self's centrality.* The secular, as far as I can tell, have no equivalent state.

Religion also gave me a healthy skepticism of the power of the intellect. "Some of us had already walked far over the Bridge of Reason toward the desired shore of faith," it says in the Big Book. "We were grateful that Reason had brought us so far. But somehow, we couldn't quite step ashore." Personally, I feel a little less grateful to my mind than this: sure, it helped me emerge from anorexia in some ways, but it also got me there in the first place. It was my reason, too, and reason alone, that had led me about as far down the dark tunnel of nihilism as I hope I'll ever go. I'm a far cry from Tolstoy, but his story resonates because he, too, looked first to the verifiable before finding a paucity of answers there. "For a long time I cowered before knowledge, and felt that the fact of my receiving no adequate answers to my question was a result of my naïveté and no fault of knowledge," he wrote. "I was finally forced to conclude that my questions were the only legitimate ones serving as the basis of all branches of knowledge, and that the fault did not lie with me and my questions, but with science if it had the pretension to answer these questions." Like him, I, too, came to faith quite unexpectedly, because I had found "nothing, absolute nothing" outside it "other than destruction."

One way in which I negate my own reason is by accepting and submitting to the larger demands of my belief system. Do I think there is

---

* Galassenheit has many meanings and implications; the scholar Donald Kraybill describes it as "self-surrender, resignation to God's will, yielding to God and others, [and] self-denial," although it has other more cultural meanings as well, such as simplicity of lifestyle and "thrift."

really some ethical value in not wearing clothing made of linen and wool, as I'm prohibited from doing? Not particularly, but I do it, because there's meaning in putting your own will aside at times. (In Judaism, a mitzvah like shatnez, which is a rule without any reason or obvious purpose, is called chok.) I spent many years trying to methodically determine whether it would be braver to kill myself than to live feebly, as I felt myself to be doing. When I became religious, the internal argument abruptly ended, because I considered myself to have signed a metaphorical contract that forbade me from suicide. It was really just that simple.

Even beyond that, there is much in Judaism to suggest that a person is commanded to be *joyful*. "[B]eing happy is so important you should even force yourself to be happy, if that's what it takes," Reb Nachman wrote. This is, again, an idea that would be met with much suspicion in the twenty-first century, where the prevailing sentiment is that forcing inauthentic emotions is wrong, even tantamount to violence. But how different is this, really, from being told in CBT to replace one's negative thoughts with positive ones? What is the difference between labeling difficult thoughts "demons," as early monks did, and personifying them as "Ed," as people with anorexia often do, or "the depression," when all of these amount to envisioning bad feelings as nefarious external forces one is in constant combat with? How is precluding suicide by invoking God all that far removed from what all us sad young anorexics recognized in the hospital: that it became paradoxically easier to eat in an institutionalized setting, simply because we felt the option had been taken away from us?

Finally, religion gave me a model of redemption and resilience far beyond what the biomedical view did. When I was sick, there was an idea very much in the ether—it might still be out there now, but I haven't checked lately—that if you had an eating disorder, you would always be grappling with it. I totally rejected this from the outset, and to be fair, I never had a treatment provider who affirmed it. But when the focus shifted from the anorexia to the depression that my clinicians believed lay underneath it, the future they offered me was very much one of management rather than transformation. And I just couldn't live with that. To submit to the idea of me-as-synapses over me-as-soul was far more depressing than, well, depression itself. I needed to believe I could grow and heal; if I couldn't do that, then what was the point of anything?

When I started to open myself to the idea of God, I found a new, unending source of power and joy. If it is possible, as James suggested, that "one who lived more habitually on one side of the pain threshold might need a different sort of religion from one who lived on the other"—in other words, if different personality types require different religions—then Judaism revealed itself as the perfect medicine for my particular soul. Equal parts reverent and skeptical of the cerebral and the atavistic, the ecstatic and the disciplined, respectful of human pain but insistent on its subservience to happiness—on which the therapeutic had little if nothing to say—Judaism is, as Rieff suggested, both a private refuge from a zeitgeist I find lacking and a set of tools to navigate it more adeptly. Through Judaism, God took my wannabe monkish self and forced her to recognize the inherent worth in earthly things like rising in the morning, enjoying a meal, savoring moments of human connection, and living in community, to say nothing of having attached oneself to a group that could be the poster children for survival. "The whole world is a narrow bridge," goes one of Rabbi Nachman's most famous dictums. "The most important thing is not to be afraid." And thanks largely to my coreligionists, I no longer am.

In the first years I observed Yom Kippur—one of the holiest Jewish holidays, a day of repentance and atonement that is marked by fasting—I wondered halfheartedly if the experience would "trigger" me, in the anorexic sense. Even then, though, I recognized that this was a remnant of an old, backwardly self-aggrandizing idea: that because I had *suffered* so greatly while sick, I should be excused from any hardship, no matter how small, for the rest of my life. Even a suggestion of self-evaluation, let alone self-criticism, felt tantamount to victim blaming. My entire life, from the moment I could be declared "recovering," should be focused on making sure I was treated (by myself, by those around me, by the universe) with as much tender care as possible.

But that first year I fasted, at the Reform temple in New Jersey where my then-boyfriend's (now-husband's) family worshipped, I stole away to the bathroom and rested my head, throbbing from caffeine withdrawal, on the cool metal top of the toilet paper dispenser, and I realized many things: that my anorexia had been as much about avoiding pain—all that gum and diet soda, to stave off the *true* hunger!—as it had been about courting it; that the universe owed me nothing; that I was no better than any other person on the planet; that my pain was no more important than theirs; that no one was exempt from the obligation to take stock of their lives; that I was, as we all are, "more a worm than a human being," to borrow a phrase from Tefilla Zaka, a prayer said in the early hours of the holiday.

That didn't mean I should spend my entire life repenting though. The psychic genius of Judaism is to say, yes, repent, yes, examine yourself, yes, remind yourself of your insignificance—but in a controlled, contextual, time-limited way. Some of the philosophical underpinnings of my anorexia, like the desire to be fully spirit, were not wrong in essence, but rather improperly directed and magnified beyond all rationality. Judaism showed me how to channel those impulses, and then let them go, knowing, as I did full well, that I would fall short and then be given yet another chance, the next Yom Kippur.

On Yom Kippur in 2021, exactly a decade after my first agonizing fast, my tired eyes were scanning the pages of the machzor, a prayer book, when something caught my attention. Though I had read these prayers so many times before, somehow I had never stopped to really contemplate the text found at the end of the famous Unetaneh Tokef prayer, which depicts a vision of divine justice in dramatic terms. The best-known portion is the rather graphic catalogue of ways to die—"Who by water and who by fire; / who by sword and who by beast"—but the part that captured me that day was at the end:

> Man is founded in dust / and ends in dust.
>
> He lays down his soul to bring home bread. / He is like a
> broken shard,
>
> like grass dried up, like a faded flower,
>
> like a fleeting shadow, like a passing cloud,
>
> like a breath of wind, like whirling dust, like a dream that
> slips away.

Like a broken shard. Nothing I had ever read had so concisely and accurately captured the experience of being human. My heart ironically swelled at this phrase, and indeed this whole paragraph, for here was the truth of human life, which, depressing though it may be, is without a doubt more honest than any of the equivocations or outright falsehoods that are daily sold to us: that we are small, that we are ephemeral, that our lives are suffering, and that nothing, absolutely nothing, is going to change that. We *can* be happier; we *can* wrest whatever joy there is available out of what is ultimately a brief and befuddling tenure on earth. God can and does help us to do that. "He is a God of redemption and restoration and taking broken things, broken people, broken stories and making something new," Sara had told me. This is true, but it is also true that because we are human, we cannot make ourselves wholly secure or wholly satisfied, and for this reason we will always tremble.

And yet here I was, surrounded by people who, though they had perched at the precipice of their demise time and time again, though they knew better than many peoples on earth that life could be a nightmare and the world a hell, chose to pursue it and cherish it. Though the world outside the synagogue that day often dismissed our rituals as archaic, would understand our idea of standing before an Almighty King that day as simply an extended metaphor, we could tap into something they couldn't: at the end of the day, we're all just broken shards, begging for mercy, doomed to fall and rise and fall and rise again.

3.

KATE, TO THE OVERPOWERING REVELATION OF MORMONISM

For verily the voice of the Lord is unto all men,
and there is none to escape; and there is no eye
that shall not see, neither ear that shall not
hear, neither heart that shall not be penetrated.

—REVELATIONS OF JOSEPH SMITH COMPILED
AS DOCTRINES AND COVENANTS, 1:2

K ate first met the Mormon missionaries at a diner near her college campus in the northern New Jersey suburbs.* The decor
was a bit more Cracker Barrel–folksy than classic rest-stop

---

* A note on the term "Mormon": Despite its prevalence in their holy texts and Church
promotional materials, Russell M. Nelson, the president of the Church, announced in
2018 that he had a revelation that the Church should completely abandon Mormon in
favor of the more official Church of Jesus Christ of Latter-day Saints. He alluded to the
fact that Mormon had a pejorative edge to it—"A nickname may offend either the one
named or the parents who gave the name," he said in explaining the shift—while others
suspected it might also be an effort to rebrand the faith so as to seem more closely
aligned with mainstream Christianity. Many Mormons and non-Mormons alike continue to cite it as the term they most commonly associate with the LDS Church (the
longer name is also significantly harder to use in writing). In the last few years, Mor-

joint—no checkerboard tile floors or miniature jukeboxes at each individual booth—but it did have the endless menu and reasonably priced all-day breakfast staples beloved by so many Americans. The coffee managed to be simultaneously watery and bitter, but of course, no one would be drinking coffee that day.

That January meeting had been a long time coming: though she'd only recently reached out to a Latter-day Saint friend named Amanda from back home and asked to be connected with some local missionaries, she'd become an "investigator"—the term used to describe a person learning about the Church of Jesus Christ of Latter-day Saints while considering a conversion—about seven months prior. That past June, her boyfriend, Andrew, a kind, clean-cut basketball player and lifelong member of the Church, had broken up with her. He was leaving to serve a two-year mission in San Francisco, after which he would go to Brigham Young University in the Mormon stronghold of Provo, Utah, where Andrew's five older siblings and his parents and *their* parents had gone before him.

Though he never said outright that the reason for the breakup was because Kate wasn't LDS—What was she anyway, though? Lapsed Catholic, like her mom? Some kind of undefined atheist-agnostic type, like her father?—the difference in their religion was clearly causing the path they had been walking down together to fork, at least temporarily. To Kate, his farewell seemed more like a soft breakup than a real schism, because he couched his goodbye in caveats: he didn't really *want* to break up with her, he said, but his sister had told him he shouldn't have a girlfriend while on a mission, so they had to press pause.

"I want to get married in the Temple," he told her, a rite available

mon has come to imply the "culture" of the faith, while the longer title is more often used to refer to the actual theology or the Church itself. Throughout the text, I toggle between the two, using Mormon when there is a cultural element at play, when I'm quoting someone who used it, or when style or brevity requires it.

only to those of good standing in the Church. "And I don't want you to change for my sake." She had thought she heard a "wishfulness" in his voice when he said this, like perhaps he hoped she *would* change.

None of this came as a shock to Kate. The pair had only been formally dating for a few months, though they had been friends since their junior year. They'd played cello together in the school orchestra and been in the same calculus class. When she told me about their relationship later, she made it sound as if she had known that the romance would be short-lived: they were just high school sweethearts, figuring out how to love in the first place, of *course* it wasn't meant to last. Besides, she knew that he would only be allowed minimal contact with people from back home during his mission; he'd also be prohibited from actively dating, especially if the object of affection was not a Latter-day Saint herself. For him, graduating high school marked the beginning of his journey into Mormon adulthood, a life that was full of obligations and social pressures but was intimately familiar to him: a mission, BYU, marriage in the Temple, a gaggle of kids. A different person might have chafed against such expectations, but for him they were clearly defined and, therefore, comforting.

For the first time in Kate's eighteen years on earth, though, she felt totally out of control. She had always imagined herself just drifting through life, in an easygoing, pleasant way, like a leaf that had fallen into a stream and was bobbing along with the gentle current. Now, everything was changing, and she had nothing to reach out and grab hold of. She was leaving the city she'd lived in for most of her life to attend a small university not far from Newark, New Jersey, and she'd only been to the East Coast once before. Her close-knit friend group was about to scatter across the country, and her first romance was coming to an end. In a "spiritual autobiography" she wrote in college years later, she used words like "crisis" and "collapsing" to describe how unstable her life felt at that time.

Two weeks after Kate and Andrew ended their relationship, Kate downloaded the Book of Mormon from iBooks. She did not consider revisiting the Catholicism she had a passing familiarity with; she didn't reach out to her uncle, who'd become a committed Evangelical Christian in his adulthood. Indeed, she hadn't considered looking into any other faiths aside from Mormonism, which she admits is a little odd. She was drawn to the Book of Mormon, she told me, because it had provided "peace" to so many of her friends. She told Andrew, with whom she remained friendly, that she was planning to read it, and he suggested they do it together, because he was trying to get through the entire thing before he left for California in July. She thought he seemed "a little too excited" about this plan—although whether it was the first sign of the missionary's compulsory zeal for conversions or his way of revealing he wanted to keep the door open for a future reunion, she wasn't sure.

They didn't accomplish their ambitious goal of tackling ten chapters a day, but Kate kept going after Andrew departed and they could no longer text each other their progress reports. Without the benefit of a teacher or study buddy, she'd made it through the dense sermonizing sections, the infamously endless parable of the wild olive trees in the Book of Jacob; she'd bristled at the famously punishing rhetoric of 2 Nephi 6:15 and even skipped over the chunks of Nephi in which he wholesale quotes the biblical prophet Isaiah, who beseeched God, poetically but rather cruelly, never to show sinners any mercy, no matter how much they repent. She'd later compare the experience of reading what she'd eventually come to see as the divine word to "trudging through mud." But trudge on she did.

The missionaries Kate met that January day struck her as pretty typical teenagers, not particularly incisive theological minds or spiritually exalted souls. Even then, she recognized that the whole thing was a little ridiculous. "I don't trust nineteen-year-old boys most of the time," she told me later.

"Why am I trusting them to *teach* me?" She wondered how she ever would have been able to take them seriously if she were in her forties or fifties.

Kate finds it easy to go with the flow, though, so she didn't spend much time worrying about this. And anyway, the missionaries had a lot less to do in her case than they did when they were knocking on strangers' doors to preach—that involved a lot of harsh rejection and occasional ridicule. By far the biggest part of a missionary's job is convincing reluctant people to read the Book of Mormon, a task Kate had already accomplished, so there was some confusion as the party of three tried to figure out exactly what it was they were supposed to do between now and whenever Kate decided she was ready to get baptized, even though she told them right off the bat that she had no intentions of doing that soon, or maybe ever.

This is one of many examples of Kate professing, either in the moment or in retrospect, low expectations or lack of commitment: she said she was never interested in the faith of a large number of her friends when she was young, never expected to find anything emotionally moving or nourishing when she began reading their sacred text, that she was reading it just to "humor myself," that on the day she sat across from the missionaries she was, at best, ambivalent about becoming a full-fledged member of the Church of Jesus Christ of Latter-day Saints. But from the outside, it looks very much like Kate moved deliberately and without hesitation directly into the warm heart of belief.

When she was growing up in an upper-middle-class enclave on the outskirts of Tucson, Arizona, God was not discussed in Kate's house. Her grandparents were religious—on her mom's side, Catholic, and on her dad's, Lutheran—but her parents had stopped believing at some point, and Kate and her younger sister were not expected to participate in religious life really at all, though the family still attended Mass when Kate's grandmother was visiting from San Francisco or if they were visiting her there. To young Kate, Mass was beyond boring: it seemed to drag on forever, and with all the standing and sitting and vocal repetition involved, she often felt like a performer who hadn't been given the play's script in advance. Kate got the sense that her father didn't believe in God because he would occasionally make disparaging comments about religion, wondering aloud, for example, why anyone would ever be so gullible as to believe the Red Sea parted for the Jews when they fled Egypt. But when Kate asked her mother if her dad was an atheist, her mother said, "I think he just doesn't know."

It wasn't that Kate would have been disturbed to learn definitively that he was not a believer: Kate didn't believe in God either. Intellectually, she just couldn't comprehend feeling connected to a figure you couldn't see or whose existence you could never actually validate. *You can prove gravity*, she would think to herself. *You can't prove God.* Still, there were times when she did have wistful thoughts about faith, like that it would be nice to believe in *something*. When she read *Harry Potter and the Deathly Hallows* at eleven, she was so frightened by its themes of death and resurrection that she found herself wishing she had some vision of the afterlife to cling to. "I think it would be nice if I believed in something, but I don't," she summed up the existential stance of her youth, "and I don't think that's going to change." Besides, even the occasional longing for God was usually fleeting. It didn't cause her any real distress, so she just let the thoughts float through her mind without interrogating them.

In middle school, Kate quickly fell in with a group of about eight friends, three of whom were Latter-day Saints. In a sense, it was surprising that she hadn't made any Mormon friends before then: Arizona has a significant Mormon population, having been home to some of its earliest colonies. Kate knew virtually nothing about Mormons, but lots of other kids at her school did. Classmates of hers relayed that their parents would often express exasperation at yet another visit from local missionaries, saying it was "awkward" when they came around, no matter how friendly they were. Though she no longer remembers when, at some point Kate learned about the less savory aspects of Mormon history, like the polygamy widely practiced in the early days and the fact that Black men were denied the priesthood, the highest religious authority granted, until 1978, but she figured every religion had a blemished past. Ultimately, she didn't think of her Mormon peers as any different than her other religious classmates—she had a friend whose mom was Jewish and who celebrated both Hanukkah and Christmas, and another from a Mexican American family who would go on to attend a Catholic high school— and besides, it wasn't something that came up very often.

When Kate switched schools for high school, she fell in with a new crowd that included Andrew—her future boyfriend—and his buddy Tommy, a wry, red-haired kid, both lifelong members of the LDS Church. The three became inseparable; for Halloween senior year, they dressed up as Ron, Harry, and Hermione from *Harry Potter* ("We were *them*," she said, rolling her eyes). Nearly all the other students who ate lunch at their table were kids the two boys had known since early childhood through the Church. Kate did sometimes feel like an outsider in the group, but she chalked that up to the fact that most of these people had known each other for years. The exception was the one time a sophomore girl announced that she wished all members of the Church could go somewhere and live under the Prophet, separate from everyone else. Andrew nudged Kate surreptitiously under the table. "And the nice people, too, right?" he said to the girl who had made the comment.

"The *nice* people?" Kate replied.

Kate wasn't upset, exactly, though she recognized another person in her shoes might have been offended to hear something that sounded a lot like an assumption of Latter-day Saint superiority. It's not like she'd never entertained the possibility that there was something more significant separating her from her new friends beyond the fact that she was a recent addition. She wasn't jealous, either, that her friends would have immediate entrée into this hypothetical utopia, whereas she'd be relegated to some bleak spiritual wasteland, whatever that looked like. But she was curious, and for the first time, perhaps a little put off, about what the incident revealed about her friends and their religion. *Is this how they are when it's just them?* she wondered. *Is this what they* really *believe?*

The summer before her senior year of high school, Kate's friend Amanda suggested she go visit the newly constructed Mormon Temple in Tucson, which would be open to the public before being consecrated, after which it would be closed to non-Mormons. After watching a brief introductory video in the waning heat of the summer evening, the tour group was instructed to put mesh booties over their shoes, the kind exterminators might wear in clients' homes while looking for rodents, so as not to sully the pristine new floors.

Walking down the slick, shining hallways of God's house, Kate didn't feel any sense of wonder or transcendence. She appreciated the fact that no detail of the design went ignored: the thirty-eight-thousand-square-foot building featured stained-glass windows etched with images of ocotillo plants and prickly pears, both native to the region, a dome covered in blue tile imported from Germany, multiple diamond chandeliers, and a baptismal font that stood atop the backs of twelve cast-metal oxen statues, black as obsidian, meant to represent the twelve tribes of Israel, all surrounded by seven acres of desert, landscaped so as to coax whatever cacti and spindly trees would come forth. She'd never been to New York City, but she assumed the way she enjoyed the Temple was similar to the way she might like strolling through the Metropolitan Museum, even though the ostentatiousness made her a little uneasy. She wondered if it wouldn't be just as nice if they used less expensive materials and then done something charitable with the leftover funds. But aside from that fleeting connection between faith and financial ethics, she left unaltered.

If the aesthetics of the faith failed to hook her, what initially did was the Mormon family unit, in all its archetypal American glory. It wasn't that Kate's family was wildly dysfunctional, to contrast; they were just definitively *not close*. "Impersonal," is the word she came up with, after a long pause to mull it over. "It's not like my parents don't love each other, but I can't *see* it," she said, trying to be diplomatic. It was like she and her parents and sister were individual atoms in a petri dish, confined to the same space, circling each other, but never truly meeting. When she spent lots of time at her Mormon friends' houses, she couldn't help but compare the natural intimacy they seemed to enjoy with her own family's relative repression. The kids all chipped in when it was time to prepare food, they talked about their siblings fondly even when they were irritated with them, they hugged and kissed each other regularly. In middle school, she had gone to gatherings at Amanda's house and seen her parents openly flirt with one another, which she found just wild. She couldn't remember ever seeing her parents behave that way; if they were watching TV and her dad rested his head in her mom's lap, Kate would instinctively recoil, just because it seemed so abnormal.

When Kate and Andrew began dating—which mainly consisted of chaste activities like going to see Marvel movies together—neither worried about his family accepting her, even though she wasn't a member of the Church. To the contrary, Andrew would often tell Kate that his mom "loved" her, yet another example of the open communication policy among her Mormon friends' families she found both deeply enticing and seriously bizarre. She was pretty sure her dad would not be as enthusiastic about Andrew. He saved the lion's share of his anti-religion sentiment for the LDS Church, which he called a "cult." "We're just Gentiles to them," he'd scoff. Kate asked her mom to pass along the news of her relationship to her dad, but her mom procrastinated for so long—either because she thought he'd be angry or because she, like Kate, had some strange resistance to or laziness around sharing even the most innocuous information with her family, Kate still isn't really sure—that by the time her dad *did* learn about the relationship, it was basically over.

The summer she began reading the Book of Mormon, Kate began praying every evening, because her friends in the Church had encouraged her to try it. They didn't give her many specific instructions, so she simply told God about her day, emphasizing the things she was grateful for, perhaps asking for some guidance. The only formulaic part was the concluding script her friends had offered: "I say these things in the name of Jesus Christ, amen." The whole thing was nice enough, but mostly because it meant she "was able to reflect on my day a bit before I went to sleep," as one does in a guided meditation or a gratitude journal. She would sit on her bed in the dark, "legs crossed and arms folded" like a kindergartener, and talked to this entity she neither understood nor technically believed existed. She often felt a little ridiculous speaking into the void, night after night, getting no response—until, one August night, she did.

※

Though I often forget in the fog of my adult mordancy, the natural world I inhabited as a child bewitched me. I'd often stand very still when I spotted a rabbit in the ivy-covered land abutting the stream next to my yard and stare laser-like into its eyes, hoping to transmit some kind of message that would incite it to hop right up to me and snuggle into my lap. That stream was an endless wonder for me and my best friend, Anna, who lived next door: we would put on our jellies in the summer and slosh through it until we reached the bridge beneath the street, watching as amebic white dots wriggled beneath the surface of the water, trying in vain to catch frogs, and digging up onion grass, even, on occasion, eating the thickest of the bulbs we unearthed, satisfied at our harvesting prowess. We would roam the woods beside our neighbors' yards, daring ourselves to go a bit farther than we had the last time. Once, we saw a completely white deer race off behind the trees, frightened by the cracking of twigs beneath our feet, and were convinced it was the rarest and most special of creatures. (We later figured out it probably had albinism, but that didn't seem to dampen our awe.) When my family drove in our car at night, I'd look up at the friendly white moon and wonder how it was that it always seemed to be following me, no matter where I went; even though I knew intellectually there was such a thing called gravity that kept my feet planted to the earth, I still couldn't quite believe that I never *once* felt even the slightest spin or jerk.

When the cicadas—invisible though clearly populous, considering their volume—sang their evening chorus, when I was walking through the path to Anna's house and looked up at the giant tree that stood alone at the back end of my yard and saw its leaves swaying against the bright azure sky above, it seemed completely logical to assume that this was God, always playing His favorite instrument with His giant, invisible fingers. It was the effortless animism of a child's mind, and it was equal parts lovely and terrifying. For if some great spirit could be so omnipotent as to manipulate the smallest leaf on a tree, and all the other small leaves on all the other trees across the globe—not to mention the tides of the oceans and the volcanos and the tectonic plates shifting beneath us and the feverish molten core down at the center of it all—then clearly that spirit was capable of doing terrible things as well.

My unthinking assumption about God wasn't that He was only present in the natural world; no, He was also deeply attentive to *me*, a little girl with a pretty uneventful life in Connecticut. I could speak to Him within the confines of my own skull—He heard all of my inner monologue, in fact—and He, in turn, could send me messages through my dreams. Like many kids, I was interested in what happens after someone dies, but I was equally invested in painting some kind of picture of the heavenly space humans lived in *before* we were born. So when I had a recurring dream that a playmate of mine from school rode to my window in the middle of the night on the back of a puppet-like dragon (it looked like one of the giant, plush characters from the psychedelic children's show *H.R. Pufnstuf*), beckoning me to come out and ride off to the land where babies live before they arrive on earth, a cloudy plane where she and I were princesses together, I thought, *Well, of course, I had this special, spiritual job.*

This innate spirituality, so tied to the natural world, was quietly at odds with my cultural environment. I was born in the mid-1980s and raised in a hyperprosperous environment, among people who seemed wholly unperturbed by the inherent *peculiarity* of human existence. (Of course, as I've aged, I've wondered if perhaps some, if not most, of these people were just better at hiding their spiritual confusion than I was.) Life seemed pretty clear-cut for most of my fellow suburbanites: If you wanted something, you bought it; if you were sick, you went to the doctor; if you wanted to succeed, you worked harder.

The milieu was not an overly religious one. In town, we had a handful of Christian churches, including the Presbyterian one, where I attended nursery school, and the Catholic one, where Anna and her family, and also my childhood nanny, went. (The town was, and still is, a very homogenous place, with a miniscule population of religious or ethnic minorities.) My nanny would take me to Mass when I was a little girl, and the priest would bless my stuffed animals and dolls, and I was heartened to know that my precious Baby—the doll I'd had since I was born, whose hair stood straight on its ends like a Troll figurine and whose plastic limbs were marred by errant crayon markings—had been touched by God, because, of course, my stuffed animals had souls, just as the plants and the rabbit and I did. I know my nanny talked to me about God, although I was too young to remember the actual content of these conversations, because my parents later recalled being annoyed by my habit of praying on my knees constantly. On the rare occasions when God and Jesus came up outside this context, such as during the handful of times my parents took us to church on Christmas, I listened to the stories raptly, deep as I was in what philosopher Paul Ricoeur called the "first naïveté," when the absurd, supernatural events of the Bible are taken at face value. While I didn't feel a strong emotional connection to Jesus in particular, I did not doubt that what I was hearing was, in a very literal way, true.

Until, eventually, I did. Starting early in the third grade, I began to have questions. How could three people—or entities, or whatever—also be One Thing, as was suggested by the Trinity? How is it that people could do miraculous things in the Bible, like walk on water or raise the dead, but no one seemed to be able to do those things now? (I myself had tried to walk on water, but I was pretty sure the two steps I completed were just a result of the fact that I sprinted off the dock.) How is it that Jesus came to save the world, but we were all still here, living our puny little lives, rather than basking in some glorious post-messianic bliss? The image of God I felt most equipped to conjure, of the creator of the universe as an old man with a white beard on a throne, was one common enough to children. This irritated me: could the creator of the entire universe really be so cartoonish? I started to wonder, intermittently, if God didn't fall into the category where I placed things like school and Santa: a ruse presented as nonnegotiable to children by adults, constructed in order to keep us behaving in an optimal fashion. It was a kind of precocious Marxism, with the children as the proletariat and the adults as the bourgeoisie, that, despite what followed, feels amusing to contemplate now.

One day, when I was eight, I was walking the regular path over to Anna's house, and I looked up at that giant tree, this time backdropped by a sad gray sky, and I finally made my decision: You cannot see God, you cannot hear Him; therefore, He must not exist. To believe in Him was a fantasy, and I was not going to be the kind of person who indulged in fantasies. It was time to put away childish things and face the reality of the world's emptiness. What followed was thirteen years of silence like the kind experienced by characters in Bergman films and Shūsaku Endō novels. Silence inside, and silence beyond. Silence that felt dense and depressing, but also angry and bitter and tense, like spiritual tinnitus. Sensory-deprivation-chamber silence, rather than its opposite: that of the countryside, of the bottom of a canyon, of the night sky.

Sure, over the ensuing years there were some moments when I attempted to inject a little magic into my universe, like my fourth-grade Wiccan phase, inspired by a family trip to Salem, Massachusetts, that saw me conducting crude séances and hypnotism sessions with friends during sleepovers. I dabbled in Tarot, romanticized meditation, but never really committed to anything. These felt like silly romps into the metaphysical, endeavors I knew were performative even at the outset, like willing my starved imagination to bear exotic fruit. It would be over a decade before I started to see my renunciation of God as a failure of vision rather than a triumph of the intellect, a willful narrowing of life rather than the liberation I assumed it would be. I used to taunt my friends on the playground over the fact that they'd been baptized as infants: now they were stuck with a farce! I all but laughed and pointed, though I realized later that I did this because I was afraid—afraid that I'd trapped myself alone with nothingness.

The Torah, the first canonical text for the Abrahamic faiths, begins with Hashem—the Jewish term for God—inciting acts of creation through mere speech: yi-hi or, He says. *Let there be light.* And so too with the sky, the oceans, the earth, the vegetation: Hashem's voice is so powerful, it causes objects to spring forth from the void. Throughout the Torah, and on through the canonical texts and traditions of Christianity and Islam, some of the most impactful moments are when God speaks out of the nothingness and directly to the individual. When Moses saw the burning bush in the hot, dusty wilderness, he peered closer to marvel at it, and Hashem called him by name from within the flames. When Jesus ascended a mountain with Peter, James, and John, the disciples heard a bellow from on high, affirming Jesus's identity as God's son and commanding the disciples to listen to him. Allah never speaks *to* Muhammad in the Quran—the angel Jibrīl (Gabriel in English) acts as an intermediary—but in the hadith, Muhammad ascends to paradise, and has a tête-à-tête with the divine about, among other things, the number of times Muslims should be required to pray daily (Muhammad bargains down from fifty to five). In the mid-nineteenth century, a secretary of Joseph Smith's described what it was like to watch his prophet receive God's messages: "[T]he Spirit of God descended upon him, and a measure of it upon me, insomuch that I could fully realize that God, or the Holy Ghost, was talking through him. . . . I felt so small and humble I could have freely kissed his feet." Often, God's voice appears in conjunction with a natural phenomenon: a clap of thunder, the form of a dove, a bright cloud, a "pillar of light." Other times, it's less dramatic: when Hashem calls Elijah out from the mountain, He sends an earth-shattering (literally) wind, but only speaks in the quiet afterward, in a still, small voice.

Today, people are not inclined to hear God: If they do so literally, it's more likely to get them institutionalized than venerated, but even if they admit to experiencing such low-grade divine interventions as promptings, nudges, or inexplicable intuitions, they'll be written off by many as hopeless kooks. How did we get from a time when God's presence was so easily accepted as to be nearly unremarkable, to today, when to acknowledge it is to risk potential cultural exile?

In his oft cited magisterial book *A Secular Age*, the philosopher Charles Taylor charts Western history from a time of experiential religion—when everyone saw God in everything—to our current era, in which a growing number of people feel, or believe, or have *chosen* to believe, that He is absent. Taylor's theory is dense and winding, but the skeletal version goes something like this: The average person living in fifteenth-century Europe saw everything—from the king who ruled over him, to the bugs creeping at his feet, to the *mysterium tremendum* of the cosmos swirling above him—as reflecting God's presence. The dominant Church was infused with residual sprinklings of Pagan alchemy, whereby objects like the tibia bone of a saint could contain within them a pulse of sacral potency.

To ask whether the medieval leper "believed" that "the sweat-cloth Saint Veronica had used to wipe [Christ's] face" would heal him is misguided, because we'd be assuming the leper had a choice to endow the relic with meaning, rather than that the meaning simply, for him, existed in the relic independent of his thoughts. (That this fact is very difficult to grasp should give you a sense of how wide the chasm is between then and now.) The leper's world was an "enchanted" one—a play on "disenchantment," a term made famous by sociologist Max Weber, which describes how modern secularism leached mystery and wonder from everyday life—where "demons, spirits, and moral forces" lurked everywhere. The human being was a "porous" creature, just as capable of being enacted upon by these and other forces outside itself as it was capable of imposing its own will on the world. The universe had a Swiss watch quality to it: every king and man and beast had its place in the order, and all objects in the world related to some perfect version of it in the godly sphere, in a kind of Christianized riff on Plato's Forms.

The subsequent story of secularization is not one of pure "subtraction," Taylor says. But it's clear that he sees the Protestant Reformation as a major, if not *the* major, turning point. It remains a debate whether the Abrahamic faiths acted as disenchanting forces or enchanting ones, and further, if they were historically disenchanting, whether they are now, in fact, enchanting. Taylor, who is Catholic, clearly sees Catholicism as a means of enchantment, but posits that the Protestant Reformation opened the door to our era, in which the individual is increasingly prone to view the world via an interior, subjective understanding—indeed, sometimes has no *choice* but to do that—rather than a holistic, mystical one. Though all the Abrahamic religions purported to be antimagic—"let no one be found among you who consigns a son or daughter to the fire, or who is an augur, a soothsayer, a diviner, a sorcerer, one who casts spells, or one who consults ghosts or familiar spirits, or one who inquires of the dead," it says in Deuteronomy—they had up until that point retained what the esteemed Rabbi Lord Jonathan Sacks called a "folk penumbra," a kind of social fringe in which usually peasants or those of lower classes dabbled in magical practices in a way that was largely tolerated. Take, for example, the aforementioned sweat cloth, or the amulets engraved with curses or blessings to help shepherd Jewish women in the ancient world safely through childbirth. But Luther and his Protestant followers deemed even the "good" religious hocus-pocus heretical and therefore sought to eradicate it. Instead of salvation arriving through public rites, organized by the interlocutor figure of the priest, people were taught to turn inward and to locate it solely within themselves.

This sparked a slow and occasionally subtle shift, from God being around and above us, to Him being *within* us, and it laid the groundwork for all sorts of other smaller societal changes that further alienated us from the divine voice. We no longer saw God as participating in the world; instead, He became a kind of remote "architect" who drives away from the house once it's been erected, leaving its new residents to play happily within, as Hugo Grotius and John Locke argued. The natural stuffs of the earth—boulders, rabbits, blades of grass— were no longer spiritually laden, but tools for our usage; the intricate, harmonious, evolutionary workings of an ecosystem a matter of "a silent but beneficent machine" on autopilot; the miraculous advancements of modern medicine the result of the effort of human intellect rather than divine gift (science and religion weren't always at odds— the discoveries of the Scientific Revolution were originally regarded as evidence of or service to God's glory, after all). Civilization and nature alike were beholden only to human reason, increasingly the most exalted force of all, which eventually meant that meaning became the exclusive right of people to bestow upon things outside themselves. The human being was no longer porous; it was "incarcerated," to use Stanford psychological anthropologist T. M. Luhrmann's word, in the "citadel" of the mind, which "is central to one's own identity but fundamentally disconnected from one's world."

This notion persists in the present, an era in which even many self-identified religious people who profess verbally that God controls the world—myself included—feel a tension between our expressed beliefs and our *experience* of the world, which is mostly secular in nature. At best, many of us have inherited a kind of presumed Deism: even if we *believe* in God's existence, we usually hold that He no longer interferes directly in earthly matters. When it comes to the practical workings of our lives, we default to other ideologies, like biology or geopolitics or psychotherapy; we seek to make spirituality somehow compatible with reason and flourishing, to keep it relevant and fresh, to ensure it remains a desirable consumer good. The "immanent frame"—what Taylor calls this brave new worldview—is how it's possible to have Buddhist meditation classes shorn of any reference to the cycle of death and rebirth; or "therapeutic churches," to borrow a phrase from theology professor Brad East, where the pastor feels more comfortable speaking of wellness than sins or hell; or a synagogue that declares itself "God optional" (because the synagogue's job is to serve a congregant, who of course has many other options for frameworks of meaning, rather than to provide a space in which the congregant can adapt themselves to serve God).

Case in point: one afternoon, I was telling a friend of mine on the phone about accompanying Kate to a service in New Jersey. During a Sunday school lesson taught by a parishioner, a man who seemed to be a long-time Latter-day Saint asked a question about Joseph Smith's revelation concerning Adam-ondi-Ahman, a place in northwestern Missouri Smith said was the original site of the Garden of Eden. "So how did this *work* exactly?" the man asked. "Because we know the Jews came from Adam, and the Jews were all the way over in Israel, and Missouri's *really* far away from Israel, so how did they get from one place to the other?"

I told my friend that this was somewhat odd for me to listen to, as a Jew, but that ultimately I understood that faith requires a kind of letting go, a willingness to treat scripture as both factually true *and* symbolically true (for many believers, anyway), and that submitting to incomprehensibility in an era besotted with certainty is part of the intellectual and emotional challenge of belief. But my friend seemed to think I was making a case for the inherent stupidity of Latter-day Saint doctrine. "I mean, has she tried *science*?" she scoffed. Which I thought was strange, considering this friend is a practicing Catholic, who regularly consumes a cracker that she is told is quite literally the body of a man who died centuries ago. Such is the deal many of us "modern" religious people make with society: the spiritual and supernatural remain within our halls of worship, but outside those contexts, such things often seem incoherent.

Though humans have reaped the benefits of Taylor's version of secularity in many ways, in the process of divesting our universe of God's presence, we've lost an awful lot too. We inhabit a world with, in Weber's words, "no mysterious incalculable forces intervening in our lives," but where "all things, in theory, can be *mastered* through *calculation*," which *sounds* like a good thing—unequivocally so, if you're a rationalist—but often renders the universe cold and mechanistic and vast. Nihilism is always crouching at our doors, scratching, asking to be let in. We experience a kind of mass longing for an enchantment most of us have never actually experienced.

This is what underpinned my desire, as a young atheist, to see a ghost, the prospect as terrifying as it was alluring; it's what drives young women in hipster Brooklyn to buy crystals and recite love spells, whether wholly genuinely or in some kind of half-ironic counterpose; or what leads travelers into the depths of the rainforests or to the maw of the Grand Canyon (because the wonder of creation is *out there*, in the dwindling sublime ur-wilderness and its primitive residents, and not in our own dull little lives). It's why moviegoers flock to watch demons sink their teeth into regular-Joe protagonists on giant screens: they crave even a simulacrum of a danger that our predecessors would have experienced as part of everyday life. Would that a bush burst into flames in front of us, I'm guessing many of us would actually be pretty excited.

Today, we are standing in our finery, stabbing the sharp stake of our flag into the ground, grinning in self-satisfaction at all we've managed to do, but the wild world—what's left of it, anyway, ecologically *and* spiritually—still encircles us, infinitely more powerful than we are, only now, by virtue of our own solipsism, we've made it so we can't hear God's voice there. Which is a shame, because maybe He has something important to tell us: that the universe, and our relationship to it, is not only comprised of verifiable facts but awesome secrets, not only explications but poetry.

✳

That August night, Kate prayed, as always, in the dark. Right after she thanked God for the chance to perform with her orchestra that day—they were playing the soundtrack to a documentary on a local historic village—something unexpected happened: a warm blast of heat seemed to burst from her chest, flooding her with joy. Every time she is tasked with describing it, she paints roughly the same image: it was "a light in my heart," "an explosion of goodness," "a bloom of happiness," "like the most vibrant sunrise you've ever seen, so bright you can't look directly at it." What made the experience so enthralling was that it was entirely unprecedented. "It was so unlike anything else I had felt that I was like, *Well, this has to be something more.* The only way I could explain that was it was God." In that fraction of a second, Kate's perception of herself shifted from a nonbeliever—an "atheist-atheist," she called herself—to a person of faith. "I knew my prayers were being heard," she wrote later, "and there was a force out there I was just beginning to know."

She lay awake most of the night, adrenaline coursing through her body, unable to quell her excitement at having "found something." Still, she wasn't convinced this experience was a validation of Mormonism in particular, even if it did come in the context of Latter-day Saint prayer. Instead, she saw it as a general confirmation of God's existence. "I know there's something out there that cares about me that I can have a relationship with," she said, a knowledge that gave her such an intensely positive, rapturous sensation she was anxious to experience it again.

Years later, my friend Matthew Wickman, a professor of English and head of the Humanities Center at Brigham Young University, told me that many LDS Church members describe the presence of the Spirit exactly as Kate did, as a feeling of warmth in and around one's heart. The phrasing is lifted from a short passage in Doctrine and Covenants, a book of LDS scripture that catalogues Joseph Smith's revelations. "But, behold, I say unto you, that you must study it out in your mind; then you must ask me if it be right, and if it is right I will be cause that your bosom shall burn within you."

I met Kate in late summer of 2019, a year after her revelation of God. In a flurry of emails, often written while she DJed the graveyard shift at her college radio station (they played mostly metal), Kate told me her story. She'd come East for college that previous fall and finished reading the Book of Mormon in October. She was proud that she had fulfilled the dictate set out by the angel Moroni near the book's close, which she had found moving: "And when ye shall receive these things, I would exhort you that ye would ask God, the Eternal Father, in the name of Christ, if these things are not true; and if ye shall ask with a sincere heart, with real intent, having faith in Christ, he will manifest the truth of it unto you, by the power of the Holy Ghost."

She met a girl in her year at school who was a member of the Church, which she described as one of many "small miracles" that had started happening since she began praying and reading scripture. Another of these was that a Latter-day Saint church was a mere five minutes away from campus—and all this, she told me, in a state with the lowest percentage of Latter-day Saints of any state in the country! ("I'm really into population statistics.") It was clear, even then, that a new filter had been applied, as if slightly changing the prescription on one's glasses, so that the kinds of occurrences that many people would have chalked up to chance or deemed only mildly interesting—there are LDS Temples in Paris and Tokyo, after all, so how strange is it really to find one in the New York tristate area?—had a touch of the mystical about them.

That October, Kate and I met in real life for the first time, at a brightly colored, popular Cuban café on a corner in SoHo that I'd walked by many times in my hedonistic early twenties. My first impressions of her personality turned out to be long-lasting ones: a curious combination of taciturn and forthcoming, her frame was so lanky she seemed to almost hover over her plate of food, and her brown hair hung limply just below her shoulders. She and Andrew had all but stopped talking by this point, but she didn't really need his mentorship, because she'd begun meeting formally with the local missionaries. At first, they urged her to read the Book of Mormon again—"It's the keystone of the faith!" they insisted—but, having so recently read the whole thing, she wasn't interested. Then they mostly offered lessons from the standard teaching manual.

In January, she had asked her friend Rebecca, the first Latter-day Saint she'd met at school, if she could accompany her to church. Back home, if a friend of Kate's had been leaving on a mission or returning from one, she'd go to church to hear them give a little speech, so this wasn't her first time at a service. But her missionary friends seemed a little nervous that Kate had chosen this particular Sunday to attend, because it wasn't the usual sacrament meeting. Instead, it was a "fast and testimony meeting": about once a month, congregants abstain from food for some amount of time before church, then spend the meeting delivering personal accounts of the way faith impacts their lives. The church Kate ended up visiting, near her school (Latter-day Saints go to church within their geographical area, which is called a "ward"), was unique in that the attendants were largely immigrants from Haiti and continental Africa, and almost all were converts who displayed an exuberant spirituality; during fast and testimony meeting, sometimes people would break out in song, which Kate later realized was very much not the norm in other locales.

Though she had little in common with the other attendees, she felt immediately relaxed there, so much so that within two months, she decided to text her family and let them know that she had been going to church. She sent the message in the frigid March air, then turned off her phone and tucked it into her purse, determined to enjoy the service regardless of her parents' reactions. When she turned it on again, she was greeted by three texts: her dad had written "ok," while her mom had texted her to the side, telling her that her dad had "freaked out," and said that if Kate joined this cult, he would cut her off. She advised

Kate that if she didn't want to completely rip the family apart, she should simply stop bringing it up with her father. So Kate did, and the family resumed its usual complacent silence.

Even though Kate felt warmly cradled by her new faith community, it was also an arena in which she found herself taking initiative to an unprecedented degree. She had seen the pitfalls of making a commitment like this without understanding how demanding it would be—converts in her ward who didn't attend church for more than a month after being baptized, investigators flabbergasted when they learned the church's well-documented history of polygamy—so she decided that if she was planning for a future as a Latter-day Saint, she would do her own research, to ensure she was going in eyes achingly wide open.

Technically, people who aren't Church members in good standing aren't supposed to know the details of what goes on inside Temples, but online Kate found a script of the Endowment Ceremony, an elaborate pageantesque ritual in which attendees clad in white reenact the human cycle, beginning with creation, through the expulsion of Adam and Eve from Eden, up through humanity's reunion with God. "I was like, *I'm not joining unless I know what's happening there. I need to know!*" It's easy enough to find footage taken inside with clandestine cameras on YouTube, including a two-hour-long video of the entire Endowment Ceremony, but Kate didn't feel right watching that, even if she did understand the voyeuristic impulse of others. "It's weird," she said of the ritual, laughing. "Even the people I've talked to who are lifelong members say, 'It's weird.'" The whole Temple hoopla scared her, to the point where she wrote another high school friend serving a mission to confess that she was having second thoughts. But in the end, her trepidation wasn't strong enough for her to swear off that feeling of "sunshine inside" she was now certain arose directly from praying and reading scripture. Over and over again, I asked Kate to describe this sensation, but she'd usually smile in confusion before landing on something simple like, "I just feel *good*." Whatever the sensation was, it was something that was sublingual and subcutaneous, some kind of euphonious movement within her heart that she didn't feel capable of living without.

In the summertime and during school breaks, when Kate was home in Tucson, she would sometimes test the waters by making a reference to something LDS-related in the news, but her family didn't seem to pick up on this. They didn't call her out for not drinking iced tea anymore, formerly her favorite summertime beverage. Bereft of the spiritual sustenance that church provided, she spent evenings in her room streaming BYU speeches or reading scripture, which always kept bad feelings at bay. But a weight hung over her, because she knew she was hiding the most important thing in her life from those she was, in theory, supposed to be closest to.

Maybe prebelief Kate would have been fine with compartmentalizing, but new, assertive Kate was unsettled by this subterfuge. ("I mean, I *am* lying," she insisted once, when I characterized what she was doing as "sort of lying.") At the rate things were going, she assumed she'd have to wait until after she'd graduated and achieved some financial independence from her parents to be baptized. That was disappointing, but delaying baptism specifically didn't feel like that big a deal. She was ambitious about ramping up her observance in the future—"I can see myself continually adding on," she told me—but she was content with her level of involvement for the moment, and even though missionaries often encourage people to get baptized quickly, the ones she was meeting with at this time were chill, so it didn't seem like there was any reason to make a bad situation worse.

In January 2020, though, a few months after we'd met and a year after she'd started attending church, something significant but ineffable shifted. In the course of praying the way she always had, she unexpectedly felt an "urge" to get baptized, and soon. *You should do it now*, something inside her insisted, despite the fact that she says she hadn't really been thinking about it all. She told me later that the decision to get baptized came "out of nowhere," one that felt like it was made in a "singular moment," even though she can't really remember that moment itself, only that she started to make plans as if it were already a fait accompli.

I guess I should tell my mom now, Kate thought, before drafting an email to her, in which she stressed that she had done her own lengthy research, knew all the criticisms people lobbed at the Church, and assured her mom that she did not view the Church as the only true religious expression, despite this being a bulwark of Latter-day Saint belief. "My personal experience means more to me than anything I could read on the internet or what someone else could tell me," she closed, "and in my personal experience I have felt more peace at church then I have anywhere else." She then sat through an agonizingly long school lecture with the email sitting like a digital hand grenade in her drafts folder, obsessing for the entire two and a half hours over how her mom would react. As everyone rose from their seats and gathered their belongings, another realization arrived, fully formed: *You might as well send the email, otherwise this stress will have been for nothing.*

Kate's mom texted her back. She had seen this coming, she said, though she wasn't exactly enthusiastic about it, particularly because she'd heard rumors of the LDS Church's authoritarian behavior. "They keep track!" her mom said. "They take attendance!" Kate rolled her eyes at this. "This is something that I truly love and that brings me happiness," she told her mother. "No one is forcing me to do this." Her mom asked her to go to Mass regularly for a month before she took the plunge—better the weirdness you know than the weirdness you don't, was my read on this request—which Kate agreed to, because she had actually grown to love the intensity of Catholic ritual and imagery. Sometimes, when she was having a bad day, she'd pray at the campus chapel, a Gothic Revival–style church with a mural of the Virgin Mary surrounded by golden-haloed apostles above the apse. The irony, unbeknownst to Kate's mother, was that Kate felt closer to Catholicism now that she was a near Latter-day Saint than she ever had in her apathetic youth, when those golden glowing figures so lovingly adorned on the church walls were strangers to her.

In late February 2020, Kate emailed me to let me know that the date for her baptism had been set for Saturday, March 28. Some friends back home, including Amanda and Andrew's parents, were already booking flights so they could attend. News about the coronavirus was starting to trickle in—New York City had its very first recorded case on March 1, and big chunks of suburban Westchester were declared a "containment zone" less than two weeks later—but in those early, surreal days of the pandemic, we all thought things would blow over just as quickly as they'd blown up. Kate didn't even panic when, on March 12, the Church announced it would ban all large gatherings under its auspices worldwide. "Bummer for me because I love going to church— but baptism is still on!" Kate said.

But things moved rapidly in the New York City area in the early days of COVID-19. On Thursday, March 19, Kate's university informed all its students they had forty-eight hours to evacuate the campus, much to the chagrin of the students. The missionaries scrambled to reschedule Kate's baptism so she could have it before she left to go home, which gave the whole thing the frantic air of a wartime operation. "Isn't it crazy that Satan caused a worldwide pandemic to stop you from getting baptized?" Amanda's mom joked with her a few days before the big event.

Kate was a little disappointed to have fewer guests than she'd originally anticipated, but she mostly felt relieved it was actually happening. It was a warm evening for March when she walked through the doors of the brick building that had become her home over the last year. The sister missionaries in her area baked brownies; the last two missionaries to teach her—she'd cycled through a number by this time, and mostly just hung out with the most recent appointees, two hilarious young men from Haiti and Thailand—sang a hymn that was unmistakably off-key. A woman named Frances, who regularly gave Kate rides to sacrament meeting and who had herself converted as a young woman, came with her two young kids. When Frances's six-year-old daughter spontaneously gave Kate a big hug, Frances whispered awkwardly, "*Ruthie,* we're not supposed to be hugging people right now." There were a few opening remarks and a prayer before Kate, clad in a white jumpsuit to signify purity just as those attending those "weird" Temple rites did, descended into water. She expected it to be cold, but it actually felt like a bathtub. One of the missionaries walked down into the font with her, clasped her wrist, and intoned the standard blessing.

"Having been commissioned of Jesus Christ, I baptize you in the name of the Father, and of the Son, and of the Holy Ghost." From behind the glass partition, the handful of attendees responded "Amen." And she was plunged backward into the warm water, emerging seconds later, dripping and new, but feeling less than changed. *Am I a Mormon now?* she wondered.

Before they left that evening—Frances and her children back to their home; the elders and sisters to their impersonal, furnished apartments; Kate to a friend's to spend one last night before boarding a flight to Tucson the next day, as the world around all of them was grinding to a screeching halt—Kate spoke briefly to those assembled. It was a very short speech, in which she acknowledged the struggles she'd faced on her journey to the font that evening. But she was comforted beyond all measure by the certainty that she had found her place in the Church, and she closed on a note of optimism: "I know I have felt God's love and hand in my life, and I know this is just the next step to continue to grow closer to Him."

The flaming sensation Kate felt in her chest the night of her spiritual awakening is what's called "personal revelation," the LDS term for the way in which God interacts with people in their everyday lives. In theory, Augustine's voice in the garden, Bill Wilson's white light, Sara's vision of being freed from chains, many instances in George Fox's life, and the jolt that deterred me from pursuing a premature death could all qualify as personal revelation. Many faith traditions have a version of God speaking directly to the person (you might argue that almost the entirety of Quakerism is about facilitating that exchange); for Latter-day Saints, that dialogue is a cornerstone of belief.

In Latter-day Saint theology, God sends messages to humans via the Holy Ghost, a figure of pure pneuma who is able to move between heavenly and earthly realms, not unlike the fleet-footed Hermes in Greek mythology. These messages can be instantaneous and straightforward, or drawn out and hard to parse; they can be a clear directive—

go on this mission, take this church posting, move to this city—or an invitation to greater inquiry or reflection. Often people describe the message they receive as at least a little counterintuitive, as Matthew Wickman told me he did: "It will have something familiar to it, and pop open something you had not considered." The messages can be soothing feelings of peace or comfort. They can arrive directly to the individual or come through a particularly resonant passage in scripture, in the cold light of day or as one sleeps at night, unearthed from the hallucinogenic remainders of "day's residues," as Freud called dreams.

For Latter-day Saints, though, knowing how to recognize personal revelation is, above all, a skill that is honed at church, where one's attention, drawn away as it is during "regular" life by grocery lists, work deadlines, childcare, or whatever else, is refocused again and again on God. To an outsider, a house of worship appears to be a place where people go to get their already-entrenched beliefs validated. In her book *How God Becomes Real*, T. M. Luhrmann argues this is actually backward: very few people, she writes—even the deeply religious—effortlessly sense God as real and present in the same way that they understand other things in the world to be real and present. Even the devout behave as if He (and His emissaries, like angels or spirits) is of a fundamentally different category than all other entities, even invisible ones, like atoms or wind. Rather than go to church to commune with a God whose existence they take for granted, then, Luhrmann says that people attend services to actively *create* the sense of God's presence.

"Of course, one might say, they believe, and so they build cathedrals," she writes. "I am asking what we might learn if we shift our focus: if rather than presuming that people worship because they believe, we ask instead whether people believe because they worship." Or, as Kate recalled someone saying once at church, "Having a relationship with God is like having a relationship with any other person. You have to maintain it."

How exactly is this accomplished? Through ritual, prayer, the plumbing of religious narratives, services, even, in the case of tightly communal faiths like Latter-day Saints, nonreligious activities done with other church members. (Kate's told me about the panoply of events put on by her local ward: bingo, speed dating, basketball, choir. Maybe being in a bowling league doesn't seem like it would qualify as a spiritually strengthening activity, but it does if you're with others who'll attribute your strike to the hand of God.) Some faiths are very smart about using smells and tastes—the incense wafting through the air at a Catholic Mass, the crunch of the matzah eaten during Pesach seder—to burrow into your brain, creating links between the emotional element of holiness and sensory stimuli. This all amounts to a process Luhrmann calls "kindling": like a fire, she says—or a lover, Kate's church acquaintance might argue—God's presence needs to be continually nurtured.

There are a few main goals to all this kindling. One is that it trains people to tap into God's presence more regularly, in just the same way that it becomes easier to ski with practice, or to feel sad or cynical when those neural pathways are more deeply carved out by repeated pessimism. (Some people need less training than others: Luhrmann says they have "talent," whereas William James called them "'geniuses' in the religious line.") Prayer facilitates a feeling of intense absorption, and it allows people to be transported to a "paracosm," a metaphorical separate world, serious but simultaneously fantastic. When religious people enter their own paracosms, they find themselves in a sphere where the wild stories in scripture are applicable to their own, not very fantastic lives. They enter a space where miracles are real, where magic still exists, where utterly ordinary people can actually *meet* God and speak to Him.

Does it matter whether the God we encounter isn't real in the way that cats and trees and fathers are? Maybe it's the same as for the leper stroking Saint Veronica's cloth: that even asking reveals our fundamental flaw, which is our insistence that we are the only ones with the power to apportion meaning. Or maybe proving in some mathematical way God's existence isn't the point at all. Maybe it is as Luhrmann says and James said before her: that the power of religious behavior isn't in its obvious successes—the prayers answered, the belief inured to doubt—but in its capacity to change the people engaged in it.

When I first started trying to wrap my head around the concept of personal revelation, I found the idea maddeningly slippery: How would a person know, for example, that it was God speaking to them, and not their own inner voice? How do you not assume you are making sublime connections out of mere coincidence, or seeing God's presence even when He wasn't there, like Scrooge's insistence that his apparitions were just a bit of indigestion? (Perhaps a bad analogy: those ghosts were *real*.) Despite the insistence on a counterintuitive quality, wasn't there a significant risk that you would just use the concept to reaffirm what you already wanted or believed?

There are answers to each of these questions, but they're not particularly relevant here, because after some time furrowing my brow in confusion at this concept, I realized what I was actually after was a way to understand what it *felt* like, as an individual, to have God speak to you. The desire to capture and codify the concept arose from not a small amount of envy: it took me years to come to terms with the fact that I am more academic than mystic, and even though Judaism is uniquely suited to those who meet God more in their cerebrum than their chest, ultimately I think I'd rather be a person who doesn't need to be *taught* to see God. Sometimes I worry that I am "unmusical" in religious matters, as Max Weber once called himself: I appreciate the melodies for what they are, but I can't create them because I'm tone-deaf, can't get completely carried away by them (or anything, really) because I'm too busy *analyzing*.

There is a famous Hasidic mini-story—which also serves as one of the epigraphs to this book—about the grandson of a spiritual master who was playing hide-and-seek with his friends. After a long time crouched in his concealed spot, the boy realized his friends weren't looking for him at all, and he ran to his grandfather in tears. "What's wrong?" the rebbe asked. "I am hiding, but no one has come to find me!" the boy said. "This is what God says too," the rebbe sighed. "I am hiding, but no one wants to seek me!" When I read this story, which I used to do every year at Rosh Hashanah, I see myself as both the boy and the grandfather, lamenting that God appears to have forgotten me *and* that I have neglected to look more doggedly for Him.

Latter-day Saints would say that my envy is for naught, because while I am able to have some contact with the Holy Spirit—we all are, as humans made in the divine image—only those who have been baptized into the LDS Church are guaranteed that relationship. And Judaism doesn't seem to engender quite the same intimacy with God as other faiths do, at least not in the modern academically oriented community I affiliate with. We believe He's there, of course, in the way of the popular children's song my kids learned at Jewish daycare, with its cloying pop melody that gets you in its clutches and never releases you: "Up, up, down, down / Right, left, and all around / Here, there, and everywhere / That's where He can be found!" But because His inconceivability is an idea very central and sacred to Judaism, and because He is decidedly *not* anything that we have here on earth—though they are intimately connected, an artist is not their own painting, nor a parent their own child—there is a sense that trying too hard to see Him in the world might bring us uncomfortably close to idolatry.

For any semblance of direct contact, you'd have to go to the mystics, like Rabbi Kalonymus Kalman Shapira, the so-called rebbe of the Warsaw Ghetto. "If you haven't yet tasted prayer that is completely cleaned from asking your needs, if you haven't yet cried as you describe the greatness of the Holy One," Rabbi Shapira wrote, "this is what you have to do: go out, for one or two hours, abandon the world and its tumult, and all its requests and clever manipulations that are in you, and be alone, by yourself, and if possible, go walking in the woods, and see yourself as a simple and honest creation among God's creations. Become one with the sun and the moon, the birds and all the trees, and sing before the Holy One."

Can a person dismantle their mind's citadel and run out into the open pastures? Can one change one's orientation from a closed sensibility to an open one, to borrow more of Taylor's wording? In a sense, I started to do that when I considered the possibility of God again in my early twenties, and I'm still working at it, right now, chipping away at that foundation of the fortress, despite my natural inclination to let my head drown out my heart. At the risk of taking a metaphor too far, many musicians say you actually *can* learn to sing if you're tone-deaf, and indeed, most people who believe themselves to be tone-deaf are actually just suffering from lack of confidence. Some would argue that seeing God is itself a choice, just another way of superimposing your mind onto the tableau in front of you. We can't go back to the enchanted days, that's true; we will never again be naïve. The marketplace of belief systems isn't going to get shut down in the modern era, so any concept of a transcendent reality will remain one of many on offer, and only the few born mystics among us will find it requires no work to maintain. It isn't like once you start to entertain the idea of God's presence that every single other framework of meaning is foreclosed to you, as so many secular people assume. Perhaps some are, but the ideological explanations that remain are enriched by the possibility of numinous intention behind them. In this way, it really does feel like a literal opening, because there become *more* explanations for earthly action, rather than fewer. The moon is following me because of relative distance; the moon is following me because it loves me.

Above all, though, it's beautiful and enlivening. When you think it's possible that God is communicating to you in the "texture of everyday life," as Matthew Wickman put it, you tend to pay closer attention. You peer at the things around you to perceive the intrinsic meaning shining out from within them (blades of grass, rocks, rabbits, other people). One recent winter day, a light snow fell early in the morning, but only a few hours later, it looked like the snow had ended, until I strained to see across the street to my neighbor's house and, in changing my perspective, saw the flakes again, so tiny they were floating *upward* with the breeze. "Is that You?" I asked. No one answered, but I felt a subtle warmth. It's a wonderful challenge, trying to see God everywhere. You should try it sometime.

On a bright, unseasonably warm Sunday morning one February, I made the drive from Park City, Utah, where my husband's family lives, to the outskirts of Salt Lake City. The trip from the mountains down to the valley around the city never fails to terrify me: a winding highway, often crammed with semitrucks going seventy miles an hour, perched on the side of the mountains, that makes me feel as if the car will tip over and fall into some unseen precipice. But it's undoubtedly beautiful—the dusty, craggy rock outcroppings, the spiky pines clinging to the sides of the canyon—and it isn't hard to see why early Mormon pioneers, exhausted, starved, diminished in numbers by the illnesses that ravaged their cohort en route from Illinois, would arrive at this land and decide to make a home here.

Of course, upon each descent into the valley of the Great Salt Lake, the land fills up with low-lying buildings and the air turns gray with smoke. "[A]nd the heavens were veiled; and all the creations of God mourned; and the earth groaned," it says in Latter-day Saint scripture. A wave of sadness lapped at my spiritual shores, to see such evidence of man's domination of his natural environment, and I wished I could momentarily wipe the landscape clean in my mind, purge it of the billboards and the Costcos and the car dealerships, suck the smog from atop its peaks, and see it renewed, clean and abundant and sacred.

The funny thing is, Kate had insisted to me many times that she would never move to Utah. Once, the summer before her senior year in college, she went out to visit her friends from high school at BYU in Provo. She came back enamored of Utah's environmental splendor—"the pine trees! it just smelled so good!"—and she loved that it was possible to casually strike up conversations about faith. But she maintained it would never be her home. "I think I would find the culture *overwhelming*," she told me, which I took to mean it would be just a little *too* Mormon for her, that there would be a holy one-upmanship that she wouldn't be able to stomach. But after graduation, Kate snagged a job managing social media at a news outlet run by the LDS Church, and relocated to Salt Lake City, the closest equivalent Latter-day Saints have to Mecca. (This was not terribly surprising to me, as someone who also felt, early on in my religious life, that it would be preferable to have a little geographical space from my religious brethren, only to pretty quickly realize how isolating such an approach can be, especially in intensely communal faiths.)

When I met her outside her townhouse, Kate looked better than I'd ever seen her: she was wearing a hot-pink, retro-style sweater, gold-rimmed eyeglasses, a denim pencil skirt that fell just below her knees, hoop earrings, and pristine Doc Marten boots. Even her skin and hair looked healthier. She also seemed way more upbeat and energetic, chatting happily about how much she liked her new environs, how she'd gotten a new "calling" that day (to be "mingle cochair," which involves organizing postservice snacks), how she spent one of her days off touring the LDS historical sites downtown. I knew that real stressors remained in her life—she was still working up the courage to tell her dad she'd been baptized—but she wore them very lightly.

On the drive over to her church—she attended a Young Single Adults ward, which was geared specifically to members ages eighteen to thirty—she flipped on BYU Radio, which played the soothing tones of the Mormon Tabernacle Choir, interrupted every so often by a soft-spoken radio announcer giving a lesson on a passage in Genesis, or a recorded testimony by a random Latter-day Saint whose name I couldn't quite discern over the whooshing sounds of the wind beating at the sides of the Jeep. It occurred to me, not for the first time that day, that this person who once told me she faltered at joining the Church because of its many requirements, now lived a life that was, for lack of a better way to put it, so very *Mormon*.

Today she would be attending a fast and testimony meeting, just like the first service she'd ever gone to back in New Jersey. "It's kind of like if improv was church," Kate whispered to me as we took our seats, but it reminded me more of an AA meeting. The hundred or so congregants looked to me like near embryos: their skin was smooth, their hair naturally lustrous, that famous Mormon friendliness often palpable even in the smallest of interactions (asking to borrow a pen from the woman next to me evoked such a panicked reaction of disappointment on her part that she didn't have one to offer that I felt very sorry I had asked). I could single out the odd, giggly romantic pairings in the way a young woman picked lint off a young man's suit jacket or squeezed the knee of the boy sitting next to her. It was almost impossible for me not to project a universal innocence onto them, to assume that their lives remained, for them, ones of spiritual certainty, of easy, unbidden confidence.

But one by one, these young people stood up at the wooden lectern in front of the congregation, in their flowery dresses and their Hawaiian-style ties and their ironic lumberjackesque beards, and they spoke of struggle: of parents diagnosed with brain tumors; of being abandoned by their betrothed; of friends and loved ones passing away; of feeling like the biblical Jonah, called to an extraordinary task but ill-equipped to fulfill it. Many said they had great difficulty seeing God in their lives, but they "worked" at it and they "trusted" in Him, and when they felt bereft of proof that He was really there, they read their scripture and prayed and thought of the times He had shown Himself before, and when that failed, they did it again. A few wept.

After the confessions came a kind of salvation in progress, an exhortation directed both to the speaker and the listeners to seek divine presence everywhere. "So for me, I just need to get up here and say that I trust Him. I have faith that He's right. I don't have any evidence of it right now other than whisperings of the Spirit, but it will work out. And it will be okay. And I *know* that God is saying the same thing to you," one young girl said. "God wants us to know who He is and find the truth," a soft-spoken man replied. "Know that you *do* have someone who understands and knows what you're feeling." Some reported that when they were at their lowest, God revealed Himself: they bumped into an LDS apostle during a Temple visit, they thought of someone they could minister to, or they *felt* Him nearby. I admit that I hadn't been very moved the previous time I went to church with Kate—it felt subdued, lacking in the ancient patina of my own Orthodox worship, or the evocative "smells and bells" of Catholic Mass—but listening to these young people speak of a palpable God in their lives, I could see how a heart might be filled this way. This was kindling, in real time.

I didn't hear God that day, at Kate's ward. At times, I do feel a warm glow akin to the one Kate felt in her room that evening: when I am davening in a group and we lift up our voices in song or lament, for example, or when I light the Shabbos candles and peek through my fingers and see my children gazing up at me, love written all over their little faces. And I talk to God, too, all the time. What I get back, of course, is silence. I frequently feel like Job, dust covering my downturned head, looking in vain in every direction for Him, or like Blaise Pascal, though without the mathematical prowess: *The eternal silence of these infinite spaces terrifies me.* But this silence, unlike my earlier one, is contemplative. I wager, as Pascal did, on God's presence. Do I hope that I'm right? Of course. Does it really matter if I'm wrong? It does not, for the ramifications of the seeking alone ripple throughout my life in ways that both ground me to the earth and expand me to the above. Whichever narrative I choose would be just that—a choice, made in the absence of any meaningful data proving or disproving some transcendent force—so I might as well pick the open one, the hopeful one, the magical one.

4

HANA, TO THE COLLECTIVE EMBRACE OF ISLAM

Anas ibn Malik reported: The Messenger of
Allah, peace and blessings be upon him, said,
"The believer is the mirror of another believer."

—AL-MU'JAM AL-AWSAṬ LIL-ṬABARĀNĪ 2114

In a way, I met Hana Nemec twice: the second time the traditional way, and the first time by watching her on a short-lived Oxygen Network docuseries called *Living Different*, which aired in early 2015. Each episode of the show tackled a particular lifestyle deemed "different" by producers: one featured a bisexual, "androgynous" model; another a psychic medium; another a female MMA fighter. Hana's episode was titled "#MyExtremeDevotion" (hashtag included) and revolved around her attempt to become a successful realtor in Los Angeles despite being a devout Muslim. The camera crew captured Hana, then in her early twenties, as she knelt down on a sajjāda to pray on Los Angeles sidewalks, handed out literature on Islam to passersby on the Santa Monica promenade, and talked about her decision to start wearing an abaya (a hijab plus an all-black sheath that covers her entire body to her wrists and ankles) with her theatrical boss over lunch. ("Once you get past the initial shock, I'm a totally normal person," Hana says. "No, you're not normal," her boss counters, shaking her head and raising her eyebrows. "You're nowhere close to normal.")

Even more than most reality shows of the time, the episode features an array of obviously manufactured scenarios: it seemed too serendipitous that on the evening Hana was proselytizing on the boardwalk, a liberal professor of Islamic Studies would materialize with his super chic, bespectacled wife to start an argument on the religious necessity of wearing a hijab, or that Hana's boss would out of the blue give her the allegedly enormous responsibility of running a seminar on buying a house—or indeed, that such an event would be considered high stakes at all, considering this occurred when people would surely be able to access whatever information they needed on escrow via the internet.

In one of the scenes in *Living Different*, Hana goes out to a hookah bar with her friend Rana, a young Saudi Arabian woman Hana describes as "one of [her] first Muslim friends in L.A."

"So, how was Saudi?" Hana asks, pronouncing it with a slight Arabic accent, "sow-di," and using the familiarized shortened version of the country's name.

Rana seems somewhat bemused by Hana's newfound sartorial zeal. "Now that you started wearing your abaya you're actually one step closer to Saudi," Rana says, laughing dryly. "I never thought that you would actually wear it." Rana is wearing a deep blue hijab and red cardigan over a bright patterned dress, her mouth a slight moue. "I don't think that I would wear abaya."

"You wouldn't wear abaya?" An inch or so of brown hair peeks out from beneath Hana's black headscarf; a tiny amount of fabric creeps up over her chin, in accordance with conservative Muslim style.

"Here? No, I don't think so. As long as I am covered, I feel like it's okay, like I don't need to wear abaya."

"You wear it in Saudi."

"Yeah, that's the point! I want to change. I don't want to wear it—like, I'm wearing it the whole time over there, I like to have my options."

"All of my friends are interested in being Americanized, because it's cool and it's popular and it's where they live now," Hana says, back alone with the camera. "As opposed to me, I'm more interested in following their culture and their traditions, because I can't imagine my life without them."

Hana wasn't only compelled by Islam itself, then: she was drawn specifically to the religion as it was practiced by Saudi Arabians, which is different from the way it's practiced by Egyptians, Iranians, Indonesians, diaspora Muslims, and so on. Of course, no religion exists in a theological vacuum, no matter how much some might claim to transcend culture or ethnicity or other earthly influences, which means when a person converts, they often find themselves gravitating toward a particular cultural *expression* of that religion. Sometimes the chasm between two expressions of faith are huge, as it is between African Quakerism and its European and American cousins, and sometimes the devil is in the details: many Amish women in Lancaster wear heart-shaped gauze bonnets, while those in the Midwest are pleated and stiffer; Sephardi Jews will eat beans during Passover, while those of Eastern European descent abstain.

Frequently, a person cannot explain to you why it is that they chose one iteration or another; it's some kind of ineffable chemistry they feel with the aura of a people, the lilt of their dialects, the spice of their food, the look of their art and their clothing. Often, there's some element of geographical convenience involved. I once met a Dominican Muslim convert whose mentor was Pakistani, so she wore traditional Pakistani dress on special occasions. In London, I was briefly acquainted with a young woman who had a fling with a Sephardi man and was pursuing a conversion through the Sephardic religious court, though she likely had less in common culturally with people of Iberian or North African origin than with the larger Ashkenazi community, comprised of Jews of Eastern European descent. When I later talked to Hana about this, she told me that she first became enamored with Saudi culture when she'd moved to Los Angeles after college and fallen in with a group of Saudi friends, who always told her she was "so Saudi." When I asked her what that meant, she said it was just an indescribable way of being: the way she walks, the way she carries her purse, the way she touches her face, her mannerisms, the way she teases those she loves. "I never felt like I fit in until I hung out with Saudi people. With them, I never felt like I was putting on a front and trying to be something I wasn't."

Sometimes, the invitation to join a new culture quite literally shows up and knocks on your door. Years ago, when I was living in England, I binge-watched *The District*, a web-based reality miniseries produced by the Church of Latter-day Saints that followed missionaries evangelizing in San Antonio and San Diego. Some of the relationships between the missionaries and the investigators seemed pretty straightforward, like when they taught a young woman whose serious boyfriend was a Latter-day Saint. But other interactions were discomfiting. I couldn't help but cringe while watching a pair of missionaries minister to an isolated Chinese university exchange student with a poor grasp of English and an even poorer grasp of Latter-day Saint theology ("I don't really understand and then he's just confusing me," the student admitted during a private interview). In some ways it was even worse when the Mormon family of a diminutive, soft-spoken Mexican man asked a pair of missionaries to come and convince the patriarch to abandon his Catholicism (although then again, I wondered if maybe that Catholicism was itself really "his," imposed upon his ancestors as it likely was by conquistadors). "Right now, I have my religion, and I believe in it," he tells the young men. "In other words, I'm not lost."

One can imagine why a member of a minority would want to take on something that brings them closer, at least in theory, to the majority wherever it is they live. But what about when someone takes on the identity—the beliefs, the characteristics, the vernacular, the dress—of a minority, as Hana and I did? And what if that minority culture is one that has been historically persecuted, but you can't claim that distinction with your birth identity? At a time when people are sensitive—occasionally hypersensitive—to the idea of adopting a new cultural persona, what are we to make of religious converts, who inevitably do just that?

✳

When Hana was a little girl, her family told her that her father was dead. She saw his family, who were part of a well-off real estate clan, on occasion—"maybe once a year, on a holiday"—but they were never close; later on, when she learned that her father was not in fact dead, but rather just had no interest in a relationship with her, she figured his family must have been comfortable going along with the ruse. Hana was attached to her mother, a sassy blonde of Czech descent named Cherie. Cherie, in turn, was devoted to Hana, her only child: she worked two jobs so she could live in what Hana described a "hoity-toity suburb of Cleveland" where "everyone is a doctor or a lawyer."

Cherie herself was unpretentious and uninterested in the trappings of fancy society. Once, when Hana was in elementary school, Cherie got a big tip from a customer at the restaurant where she worked as a waitress, and she took Hana to the mall to buy some new school clothes. At the mall's entrance, a man who appeared homeless sat asking for money, but Cherie didn't have change, only the single hundred, which she handed over without hesitation. Hana was deflated—her dreams of a new shirt from Limited Too had vanished before her very eyes!—but she never forgot her mother's selflessness that day. In nearly every photo of the two from Hana's early life, they are clutching each other adoringly, Cherie's voluminous, frosted early nineties blond do framing a face that is positively beaming with joy.

One ordinary early March morning while driving thirteen-year-old Hana to school, Cherie announced nonchalantly that she had cancer. She assured her daughter that there was nothing to worry about, that she was getting treatment and would be perfectly fine. The next morning, when Hana was getting ready for school, she could hear her mother screaming in pain from her bedroom. *I don't want to bother her, so I'll just slip out quietly*, Hana thought to herself. A week later, on March 19, 2004, Cherie Nemec was dead.

When Cherie died, Hana remembers thinking, "How could anybody let this happen to me? I'm a little kid, and this is like a movie; it can't be real." She entered into something of an uneasy truce with God. She had prayed to Him the night before her mother died, begging him for a cure. "If you love me, don't take her from me," she asked, zooming right past denial and anger and straight into the bargaining phase. But the tragedy hadn't dampened her natural faith. After all, she didn't see how else she could have summoned the strength to endure her grief, if not from some higher power.

The problem was that Hana didn't feel that she saw God reflected in any of the religions she was familiar with. Her mother's family were unaffiliated Christians, who encouraged Hana to have a relationship with the divine but were not overly dogmatic. Hana attended Sunday school on occasion, and had been made to go through some parish Religious Education classes at a local Catholic Church in order to get access to the financial trust controlled by her father's family, who wanted her to take Communion (her mother told her to just be quiet and get it over with; in the end, she never got access to the money).

But overall, Christianity didn't sit well with Hana. She was too much of a natural contrarian to take the religious lessons at face value. She once argued with a teacher at catechism class who told her she couldn't pray to win an upcoming basketball game because the other team would surely be praying for the same thing and thus Hana's prayer would be in conflict, which struck Hana as ridiculous: shouldn't she be able to pray for whatever she wanted? Wasn't that the whole point? ("I was annoying, but I was a thinker," she told me.) Plus, the concept of the Trinity evaded her entirely. Why, in the Bible, would Jesus pray to God if he himself *was* God? "I LOVED the big guy," she would later write on her blog, "but had some questions about the other two."

Cherie had been married to Hana's stepdad, whom Hana called "a lovely person," for only a year at the time of her death, and he didn't feel equipped to be a single father to a preteen girl. As her grandparents were already in their seventies, everyone thought maybe it was time for Hana's father to step up to the plate. He took a cheap apartment in a location that allowed her to remain in the same school district—she was a stellar student, and no one wanted to jeopardize any scholarship opportunities she might earn—but then "he just never came," she said. For months, he'd disappear somewhere (she presumed Florida, where his mother owned property) only to show up at random for a few days at a time and make erratic, unreasonable demands, like that Hana go grocery shopping in the middle of the night or keep the doors to the apartment—which was adjacent to a highway and any stranded driver's first port of call—unlocked.

"I remember that one time, he took my door off my bedroom, because in the time that he was away, I moved the computer into my bedroom because it was just more convenient. And he was like, *Oh no, you're trying to do stinky stuff.* So he took off my bedroom door. He took off the bathroom door." Hana's friends' parents would sometimes park outside in the lot and just sit in their cars, trying to make sure she was okay, but when she mentioned her situation to her mother's family, they assumed she was exaggerating, at least a little bit. Only when Hana got her license and her friends were also able to drive did things get easier, because she could run errands on her own terms, but the sting of being abandoned remained.

"I won a scholarship to go to college and they call your parents to tell them," she remembered. "And so they called my dad. They made contact with him. I showed up on the day of the event and I looked in the audience and I didn't see my dad. So I figured, Oh, I'm not winning. Somebody else must be winning. And then I *did* win and I won the biggest one, and I was the only kid that walked up onstage by themselves. And they kept calling for my parents because the lady that was announcing didn't know," she said. "He didn't care enough to be there."

When Hana matriculated at the University of Toledo in 2008, her life became more structured than it had been in years, which was an enormous relief. "I have a job, I can work, I have a place to live. It was great," she told me. Still, something seemed to be missing. She looked for succor in the wisdom of religious traditions—in her honors class, they read a number of religious texts, including portions of the Bible and Tao Te Ching—but nothing gave her the "warm fuzzies" she was seeking. She was curious as to why Islam never came up in her class, given that it was a major religion, and thought she might "close the loop" by looking into it herself, although all she really did at first was chat casually about the faith with a Facebook acquaintance. Her roommate at the time was Palestinian, though not a particularly devout Muslim: she said "Bismillah," a blessing that means "in the name of Allah," before she ate, but she also partied and drank alcohol and wore her hair uncovered. One day, for some reason Hana no longer remembers, this roommate sent Hana an email with a short chapter from the Quran known as the Surah ad Duha in it. Hana opened the message in her college library's computer lab:

> Thy Guardian-Lord hath not forsaken thee, nor is He displeased.
>
> And verily the Hereafter will be better for thee than the present.
>
> And soon will thy Guardian-Lord give thee (that wherewith) thou shalt be well-pleased.
>
> Did He not find thee an orphan and give thee shelter (and care)?
>
> And He found thee wandering, and He gave thee guidance.
>
> And He found thee in need, and made thee independent.

Hana was vaguely familiar with the early lines of this surah, which is well known, because her Facebook acquaintance had it as his profile picture for a while, but she had never read it in its entirety. She felt immediately that the text eerily encapsulated her entire life. For was not

Hana still that lonely, orphaned girl who had managed to mysteriously summon the fortitude to weather the years of living on her own far earlier than any child should have to? Didn't she, against all the odds, rise unbroken and surefooted from that hardship, into the pillar of self-reliance she now was? In that tiny computer console, Hana stifled sobs. Her eye makeup dripped down her cheeks; her throat closed in on itself.

After wiping her eyes, Hana closed up her computer, got into her car, and drove straight to Barnes & Noble to buy a copy of the Quran. It disturbed her that she felt such a profound connection to the verse. She knew from watching CNN and reading the news that Muslims were violent, backward people whose sacred book sanctioned blood-shed and polygamy, and she wanted to show her roommate that her fealty to the text was misguided. "I'm reading it with a negative, criti-cal eye," Hana recounted on a podcast called *Salam Girl!* years later. "I thought the worst possible things."

But Hana devoured the Quran in less than two weeks, spending hours reading after school and work, staying up until four in the morn-ing poring over the text and crying, and she found nothing to incite her ire. She also started scouring the internet for information and watching YouTube videos, especially a talk show–style series called Convertfessions. Everything she'd thought previously awful about Is-lam, like the idea that men could marry up to four wives, made sense in historical context; she also noticed far more similarities between Is-lam and Christianity than she expected. The short prayer that opens the Quran, often called the Exordium, was reminiscent of the Lord's Prayer: *Praise be to God, Lord of the Universe, The compassionate, the Merciful*, it began. *You alone we worship, and to You alone we turn for help.* What was so objectionable about that? *This feels right*, she thought to herself. *This feels good.*

But Hana had no idea what to do with these feelings. There had been maybe two Muslim families in her entire hometown, neither of which she'd known well, and even though her roommate had opened the door for her, she couldn't offer much guidance because she was not practicing herself. Hana had no idea where to find a mosque or how to go about deepening her knowledge. There was a girl she saw sometimes on campus who always wore a hijab, so the next time Hana was at the library, she decided on a canny strategy: when you printed something on the public printer, the person's name popped up on its screen, so Hana immediately printed something right after "hijabi girl," as she dubbed her, so she could catch sight of her name. She was too nervous to approach her directly, but she thought she could find the courage to write her on Facebook.

"This is so weird and so random," Hana remembers the note reading, "but I see you on campus, I know you wear hijab so I know you're Muslim. I'm interested in becoming Muslim but I don't know what to do." As it turned out, this young woman's father was involved with the board at the local mosque, and there was a little old lady on staff there who assisted the people interested in conversion. She offered to put Hana in touch with her. "You can learn all about it," the campus hijabi girl, whose name turned out to be Afaf, said. Hana was happy to be offered support, but also a little defensive, because she felt like she'd already learned a lot in the seven months since she began investigating; she felt like she was ready *now*. Hers was not the normal path: most people would make their way to the mosque or a trusted Muslim friend at the first stirrings of a spiritual awakening—unlike in Judaism or Catholicism, no formal test of knowledge or period of study is required to convert to Islam, only a verbal confirmation of faith—but like Kate, Hana had felt compelled to "gather all the information" on her own before she reached out to anyone. There was only one thing she hadn't learned in all that study, and that was how to actually convert.

Afaf took her to study sessions at the masjid and to a local woman's house for lessons on the Quran. Eventually, Hana met with the little old lady, whose name was Fadia, at a local Wendy's. Over Frosties, Fadia soft-quizzed her and was surprised at the depth of Hana's knowledge. Hana knew the five pillars of Islam in both English and Arabic; she knew the difference between Shia and Sunni Muslims. When Fadia asked Hana why she wanted to convert, Hana told her about her lifelong attraction to religion and inability to find one that fully spoke to her until now; she also told her about her mother's death, how it had accelerated her seeking. Both women cried into their ice cream. "I'm obsessed with this," Hana told Fadia. "It's all I ever think about."

By the end of the meeting, the date for Hana's conversion had been set for later that week. The ceremony took place on May 27, 2011, at their local mosque in Toledo, where Afaf and her family and Fadia worshipped. The community welcomed her warmly, to a degree that Hana sensed might have been unusual, perhaps because a young, single American woman converting was seen as a major boon (most often, in Hana's estimation, converts come as part of a romantic pair). The men stayed in the room, which she wasn't sure was allowed, and the mosque had hired a videographer for the occasion. "All of the women came; they all brought me gifts," she recalled. "They wanted some pomp and circumstance around it." Afterward, she went home and took a shower, as was required. "It's supposed to be the most cleansing shower of your life," Hana said. Despite seeing herself as "very cynical," she "really did feel that."

But life as a Muslim in the Midwest post-9/11 was hard. It probably doesn't help that a tall, pale-skinned woman in a hijab at a Walmart in Ohio is bound to attract some attention. On occasion, people would yell at Hana to "go back where I came from" ("I'm from Cleveland," she'd retort) or feel compelled to let her know that Jesus loved her (she'd always say she too loved Jesus, who is considered a prophet, albeit not divine, in Islam). Hana got the distinct sense that people would steer clear of her in stores or restaurants; she overheard adults whisper to children that the reason her hair was covered was because she probably had cancer. Once, in a checkout line at a clothing store, a woman began speaking loudly about how she felt bad for Hana, because she must be oppressed to dress the way she did. Hana surveyed the middle-aged woman's tube top and miniskirt. "Honey," she said, "I feel even worse for you."

Six months after she graduated from college, in January 2013, Hana relocated to Los Angeles, where she'd gotten a job in real estate. She found refuge in the sprawling, diverse city (there were far fewer incidents of people spitting on her, for one). Through an online acquaintance, she met Rana, who would appear alongside her in *Living Different* and is still her closest friend. Saudi by birth, Rana lived in an apartment complex with a handful of other Saudi and khaleeji girls, most of whom were studying in the United States under a scholarship program organized by then-King Abdullah and former President George Bush to encourage crosscultural exchange. (When Abdullah died in 2015, Hana openly wept at a café frequented by Saudis: "If it wasn't for this man, I wouldn't know about this culture," she told them. "I wouldn't know about so many people in my life that I consider family now.") Though Hana never officially lived in the same building as Rana, she became a de facto resident, spending lazy evenings after work with her friends there and watching *Friends* until two in the morning before falling asleep on their couches. "We would go out and sit by the pool and people were smoking hookah outside," she told me. "People were playing old Arabic music through the windows. It was such a cool vibe."

It wasn't long before an absurd idea began to wriggle its way into

Hana's mind: she loved her Saudi friends, she loved their culture, and once they all moved back home, she'd have little tying her to America. What if *she* could find a way to live in Saudi too? It was a daunting task: "I didn't really think that it was possible because it *wasn't* really possible." In 2014, even getting a tourist's visa was a significant challenge; paths to actual residency were nearly nil. Though, as a noncitizen, she'd be exempt from some of the more draconian national rules for women, like being subject to male guardianship, Hana still would be prohibited from driving; she'd be encouraged to cover her entire body at all times, and she would have to learn to navigate a highly gender-segregated society. (Full coverings for women weren't technically a legal requirement at the time, but were widespread, especially in Riyadh, where Hana wanted to live.)

To her, though, this all sounded ideal: Saudi Arabia was the birthplace of her beloved faith, and if she relocated there, she'd go from being one of few to one of many—in America, less than 1 percent of the population is Muslim, whereas over 90 percent is in Saudi Arabia. (She'd turn into a minority in another distinct way, though: so few Saudi Arabian residents are white that they don't even register statistically.) She sent out hundreds of blind messages on LinkedIn to Saudi Arabians holding middle-management roles in the kingdom, hoping someone would be intrigued enough by her story to want to give her a chance. Finally, someone bit: a medical research center was hiring secretaries and would be willing to interview her. The second a job offer came through, she began to prep. "I literally packed everything by November and I didn't move until April," she said. In April 2015, she landed in Riyadh, the capital and largest city of Saudi Arabia, which over its history had morphed from a backwater along a trading route to the bustling, sleek—albeit reputationally conservative—seat of Wahhabi

Islam. "The first time I stepped off the plane in Riyadh," she wrote later on her blog, "my soul felt like it was home."

＊

When I was a little girl, my mother used to take my brothers and me back to visit her extended family, who lived in the suburbs of Columbus, Ohio, every August. When I was old enough, I developed a ritual: every visit, I would spend at least one day visiting the condo of my Aunt Margnie, a lifelong bachelorette and the keeper of the family history books. We'd sit in her clean little parlor with ham sandwiches, and she would flip through the pages, pointing to each sepia-toned, frilly-necked little creature, tracing her fingers down the delicately written pedigree chart. I was into drama and intrigue, so I remember only the ancestors whose stories were rife with both, like the man who sailed off to Brazil, or another who, my aunt whispered, hanged himself, *but we don't talk about those things.* Most of these long-dead relatives, though, I naïvely dubbed boring: Midwestern farmers, truck company owners, white and middle class to a one.

Which is why, perhaps, I clung to the mention of the lone Irish relative who married in. Irish blood! *I* had Irish blood! I had always known there was something troubled and garrulous about my very nature, something that justified my longing for that wet little downtrodden island. My nanny since infancy was also Irish, and had raised me on a steady diet of Irish nationalism—peculiar, given that her childhood was full of the kinds of horrors early-twentieth-century Irish childhoods were known for (orphanages, alcoholism, malnutrition). Once, she walked me over to a nearby convent to knock on the door just so we could say hi to the nuns, which I thought was odd given that she always made the nuns who taught school in Ireland sound like monsters. She also told me that leprechauns were real and that her friend had once captured one and kept it as a pet, something I believed until I was entirely too old.

Together, my nanny and I sang Irish folk songs; she taught me bits of Gaelic. The exotic language, the shared references, the ancient history, and above all, the rich and varied hardships, the exquisite suffering, the clearly defined Other: stir for centuries, and you have yourself a real *heritage*. And I felt so strongly about it all, wanted it so very much, that I thought surely there must be something in my very marrow that made it so. And here, with this one ancestor, was proof there was.

This dovetailed neatly with something I'd noticed in myself from an early age: a desire for immersive anthropological experimentation, a kind of extreme cosplay. In kindergarten, when everyone in my class was assigned a role as a colonial child in order to learn about Pilgrims, I encouraged my friends to make up elaborate and cohesive biographies for themselves and stay in character all day, a challenge virtually none of them took up. (My enthusiasm waned when I was given the rather unfashionable name of Prudence, who was meant to be a tanner's daughter, which I learned from a book meant I'd be lower class and smell of animal hides.) Later in elementary school, I was disappointed to learn upon a family trip to Colonial Williamsburg that the reenactors there did not actually live full-time colonial lifestyles by choice, like the Amish. In high school, I even conducted some tours of our local historical society in costume, explaining to visitors how we would have made soap in 1775 while carrying around a chamberstick with an unlit candle stuck in it, a role I had basically asked the society if I could originate. The fact that these anecdotes are all about the American colonial era says more about the culture into which I was born than it does about any actual fascination of mine with that particular time period, except perhaps an interest in what it meant to live without modern conveniences. (I clearly had no idea what it *actually* meant to live without modern conveniences: I just thought bonnets were cute and churning butter seemed wholesome.)

I lost my fascination with all things Irish around age ten or so, though I still retain a fondness for Irish people and culture. But nearly a decade later, I would find myself enthralled with another small group, a people with their own tragic history, ancient roots, and inscrutable foreign tongues.

"Other people have a nationality," the Irish writer Brendan Behan once wrote. "The Irish and Jews have a psychosis."

※

Deep into the twenty-first century, we all know what cultural appropriation looks like: on the relatively harmless and inane end of the spectrum, it's Gwen Stefani in a Harajuku get-up; on the odious and destructive, it's academics posing as Indigenous people, acting as mouthpieces for communities they don't belong to and coopting causes that aren't theirs. But is there such a thing as religious appropriation?

According to the scholar Liz Bucar, author of the book *Stealing My Religion: Not Just Any Cultural Appropriation*, the answer is yes. Bucar defines religious appropriation as "when individuals adopt religious practices without committing to religious doctrines, ethical values, systems of authority, or institutions, in ways that exacerbate existing systems of structural injustice." (On the structural injustice front, this might mean that appropriating the aesthetics or practices of Evangelical Christianity in America wouldn't inflict the same harm as appropriating the aesthetics or practices of Islam or Judaism.) The examples she uses include wearing a hijab temporarily as a sign of political, but not spiritual, solidarity, trekking the Camino de Santiago as a tourist rather than a Catholic pilgrim, which Bucar did for many years with her college students as a professor over a summer-school session, or—in an accusation she knows will hurt many Americans, including herself—developing a yoga practice without any interest in or connection to its Vedantic origins.

To this list, I might add (somewhat provocatively) celebrating Christmas as an atheist, decorating one's fireplace mantel with Buddha statues despite not being a Buddhist, and the occasional bizarre stories that pop up of Evangelical Christians living secretly as Haredi (ultra-Orthodox) Jews, sometimes for years, in the hopes of covertly ministering to the original holdouts. (Considering how hard it is to assimilate even to a more moderate Orthodox life, when I hear these stories, I'm sometimes tempted to quote Ron Burgundy from *Anchorman*, upon discovering his dog has eaten an entire wheel of cheese: "How'd you do that? Actually, I'm not even mad. That's amazing.")

My own most shameful story of religious appropriation is from 2012, when I went to Paris, on vacation, alone. While there, I stayed in a famous English-language bookshop that looked directly out at Notre Dame, and after staring at the cathedral for a great many days, I decided on a whim that it might be fun to attend a Mass there one day—not because I was particularly interested in Catholicism, but because it seemed like an *experience* in fitting with my grand solo European adventure. So the next evening, I found myself a seat in one of the sparsely populated pews and tried to follow along with the service—which, being neither Catholic nor French-speaking, I obviously failed at doing. A very tiny and primly dressed old lady, who looked like she'd been to services at Notre Dame every day of her life and who was seated one row in front of me, kept turning around to glare at me in a way that made it clear she knew I was an interloper. I couldn't decide what made me feel worse: that or the fact that, the entire time, a horde of loud, gawking tourists swarmed up and down the aisles, snapping photos—with flash—of the iconography, the altar, and even the parishioners. At that moment, I decided to never visit a religious site as a tourist again while a service was under way.

But religious appropriation is a far stickier wicket than cultural, for multiple reasons. For one thing, most religions have always maintained some path to assimilation, whether arduous (like in Judaism or Conservative Anabaptism) or relatively simple (like Evangelical Christianity, Islam, or Mormonism); unlike race, there's at least some historical precedent for accepting new members. Indeed, many faiths actively recruit new members and are delighted when converts shape themselves to fit the dominant cultural mold. Even those with more ambivalent or outright hostile views toward outsiders can welcome the usurpation of their ideas. Once, while attending a religious studies class in Israel, the very sharp, very religiously conservative rebbetzin instructing us brought up the subject of non-Jews claiming ownership over Jewish ideas or performing Jewish rituals. I assumed she was referring to things like the fact that, if you go on YouTube and look up "blowing a shofar," the lion's share of results will be of Evangelicals on windy hilltops, or the fact that people online like to dabble in Shabbat observance as a means of detoxing from tech, both of which irked me. But the rebbetzin was unbothered, even enthusiastic. "People are always getting upset about people taking our traditions," she said. "'They're stealing our stuff!' they say. But that's a *good* thing. Here—take our morality! Take *more* of it!"*

---

* Jewish theology is very clear that non-Jews are not required to keep the mitzvot; there are seven rules non-Jews have to abide by, most of which are the standard "don't

Still, all religions have an ethnic component to them, in that all faiths originate in a specific geographical place, often among a specific ethnic group. The Mormons were a band of white Americans; the Amish, Swiss and lowland European dissenters; and the Jews, a tribe of Semites from a tiny patch of land on the Mediterranean. "Islam is in its origins an Arab religion," V. S. Naipaul wrote in *Beyond Belief: Islamic Excursions Among the Converted Peoples*, about his travels in Indonesia, Pakistan, and Malaysia, among other places. "Islam is not simply a matter of conscience or private belief. It makes imperial demands. A convert's worldview alters. His holy places are in Arab lands; his sacred language is Arabic. His idea of history alters. He rejects his own; he becomes, whether he likes it or not, part of the Arab story." The individual convert has little choice in the matter: sooner or later, she'll *have* to start culturally assimilating.

In certain faiths where the ethnic plays a larger role—like Islam, Judaism, and Anabaptism—the person who comes to convert claiming a genetic link, however tenuous, might be seen as more legitimate. In his book, *Am I a Jew?*, the writer Theodore Ross visits with the conversos of the Southwestern United States, people who believe they are descended from Jews forced to convert to Christianity during the Spanish Inquisition. Sometimes, they confirm this suspicion by pointing to odd family traditions—like that their grandmother lit candles on Friday nights—and sometimes not; sometimes they pursue a formal conversion (which would be required if they couldn't prove direct, unbroken matrilineal descent) and sometimes not. It seemed to Ross that, regardless of plausibility, the idea of conversos seemed to catch on like wildfire in the

---

kill" and "don't steal" stuff. What this rebbetzin meant was that a greater affinity for Jews and Jewish ideas might bring these interested parties closer to an appropriate moral life.

brush: "Thus, in New Mexico, people 'came out' as Jewish; they spoke of reclaiming their 'compromised identities'; they read significance into the fact that they 'looked Jewish' (translation: had big noses) or had an unusual number of Jewish friends." Once, Kate texted me a funny anecdote: a Mormon guy she'd messaged with on a Latter-day Saint dating app had in his profile that he was "the most Jewish person you'd ever meet." (Turns out 23andMe had told him he had a small percentage of Sephardic ancestry.)

Like with cultural appropriation, there seems to be a spectrum of social acceptability. Converting because of ethnic heritage: neutral, good if it leads to genuine spiritual change. Converting for the jokes, a la Tim Whatley on *Seinfeld*: bad. Converting out of genuine spiritual conviction, like Hana: good. But what constitutes "genuine spiritual conviction" and who gets to decide? What if the main instigator is not a beloved vision of a religious future, but a desire to abandon a loathed past? What if there's some political agenda entwined with the new-found religious affinity?

In August 2022, *The New York Times* published a guest essay by Julia Yost, an editor at the Catholic magazine *First Things*, in which she described a "mass" conversion to Catholicism among a mildly famous, insouciant downtown New York City crowd affiliated with a Lower East Side neighborhood that had come to be known as Dimes Square. (The word "mass" is in quotes because the entire body of converts constituted only a handful of people, but a noticeable proportion of the Dimes Square crowd.) Yost wondered if Catholicism's retrograde reputation might in fact be the main draw for these types: "Traditional morality acquired a transgressive glamour. Disaffection with the progressive moral majority—combined with Catholicism's historic ability to accommodate cultural subversion—has produced an in-your-face style of traditionalism." But readers largely dismissed these people as poseurs. "Madonna did it all in the 80s and nobody thought she was an intellectual," one commenter wrote. The writer Ann Manov, in a piece for the online publication *UnHerd*, accused them of feigning an interest in Catholicism "in pursuit of attention and in the exercise of branding."

If it was indeed a branding exercise, at least in part, it would have to be in service of a brand that is contrarian and reactionary. What's unique about the Dimes Square Catholics is that while most urban trendsetters in the past—punk musicians, abstract artists—have sought to undermine the historical status quo, this one seeks to *restore* it, by championing supposedly antiquated values. Why would it benefit their "branding" to be associated with an institution that is viewed as problematically backward, even, to some, evil? In sociologist Erving Goffman's 1963 book *Stigma*, he describes the experience of "the individual who is disqualified from full social acceptance," which could mean, according to my copy's rather archaic summary, "the dwarf, the disfigured person, the blind man, the homosexual, the ex-mental patient and the member of a racial or religious minority [who] are often considered socially 'abnormal,' and therefore in danger of being considered less than human." The book isn't only about the hardships stigmatized persons face; Goffman also deals, less often but deftly, with the contextuality of stigma—the way the same trait can, under two different circumstances, be a blemish or a boon—and also, on occasion, its *attractiveness* (recall, if you will, that an early linguistic reference point is the Christian stigmata, the wounds caused by Jesus's Crucifixion, which lent the bearer an unmistakable and unique quality of holiness).

And why would a stigma be *attractive*? To personify this phenomenon, Goffman uses the term "the wise." Who are the wise? They are those whose "special situation has made them intimately privy to the secret life of the stigmatized individual and sympathetic with it, and who find themselves accorded a measure of acceptance, a measure of courtesy membership in the clan." This "special situation" could be a familial or social link, like the child of an ex-con; or proximity, like a white person who lives in a predominantly Black neighborhood; or profession, like a nurse working with the infirm. Goffman doesn't provide a full accounting of what the wise person's motivation might be, but aside from the practical ones like those already listed, one can imagine another option: the wise feel themselves *invisibly* stigmatized—like because they were orphaned at a young age, or experienced trauma, or were once ill and carry the marks of that experience with them—and are drawn to other stigmatized individuals, even those whose aberrance is obvious and unavoidable. Goffman alternately refers to the wise as "marginal men," the "sympathetic normal," those who bear a "courtesy stigma," or a "stigmaphile."

The latter term recalls, for me, the way the writer Amy Levy's Jewish characters mock a potential convert in their midst for thinking they must all be paragons of piety, or various quotes from firebrand British journalist Julie Burchill's book *Unchosen: The Memoirs of a Philo-Semite*: "The Jew had become a symbol to me . . . of outsiderness not just embraced but made magnificent." Though often welcomed by the stigmatized, the stigmaphile can also create discomfort, both for the inherently stigmatized and for themselves. The sympathetic normal may usurp attention by "always being ready to carry a burden that is not 'really' theirs." For the bearer of the courtesy stigma, they might find that they have to deal with the same issues navigating society as those with the "real" or authentic stigma, without knowing for sure that they share in the benefits of the group identity.

In my late twenties, when I was spending more time in Jewish environs, I remember asking friends what they were doing for Pesach, eminently pleased with myself for my accent. A few years later, I was given a book to review, written by an acquaintance who'd left religious observance. I read the gentle ridicule of the newly religious in their community, those who started by attending services regularly before decamping for a seminary in Israel, returning to Pittsburgh with "shining eyes, throats hairy with the guttural *ch* sound they had mastered and yielded proudly in their triumphant blessings." Alone, reading, I grimaced in recognition of myself. "To our ears, the ancient words seemed to fall from their tongues like bricks off the back of a truck." Hana "stalked" the hijabi girl on her college campus (her word, not mine, and obviously hyperbole) and then joined a group of Saudi friends who joked with her that she was even *more* essentially Saudi than they were. We were both, in our way, becoming *the wise*.

※

I met Hana in real life in the winters of 2021 and 2022, when she visited her family in Atlanta, where her maternal uncle and grandmother had relocated (after a brief and disastrous attempt to reconnect with her father, the two were estranged again). On both occasions, she was intimidatingly elegant and composed: a flowing scarf perched perilously atop her head, cascading down alongside her long hair like a waterfall, her eyes heavily lined in black, her cheeks chiseled by Kardashian-level contour, her brows and hair thicker and much darker than they were when I saw her on television ("I have grays now," she told me, when I asked her if she dyed it). On her feet she wore pointy, studded designer shoes.

If we had met just two years earlier, I never would have seen anything other than Hana's eyes, visible through the narrow angular peephole cut into her niqab, the veil worn by some Muslim women that covers the entirety of the face. She'd decided to start wearing it in January 2015, shortly after the show aired. On the *Salam Girl!* podcast, she told the host that she was uncomfortable being recognized after her TV appearance. She'd originally done the show because she'd wanted to provide a positive portrayal of Islam, and though she'd had some qualms about the production along the way—how they kept encouraging her to engage with people who conveniently showed up to antagonize her, or the fact that they paid her to bring her own acquaintances to her staged professional event—she'd been optimistic. "I just felt like they never showed normal Muslims, especially in 2015," she told me.

But even though the response was largely positive, she ended up feeling the show was very sensationalized, and she didn't like being associated with it. By the time it aired, the wheels of her plan to move to Saudi Arabia were already in motion, and because she'd planned to wear the veil there, she wanted to practice to see if she could hack it. Her Instagram selfies from her five niqabi years show a black column of a person, her eyes increasingly accentuated with liner and the occasional splashes of pink shadow. These shots are interspersed with pictures of her travels—home to Cleveland to visit family, or to more exotic environs, like Paris and Toronto—and uplifting graph-irmations of both the Islamic and the girlboss variety ("Well behaved women don't make history," one read).

Though I of all people am disinclined to make assumptions about a person's feminist credentials based on their outfits, I'll admit even I found it a little difficult to square Hana the up-and-coming, worldly entrepreneur with Hana the hidden. And eventually, so did Hana herself: on January 1, 2020, Hana debuted her new niqab-less look in an

Instagram post featuring a trio of photos of her bare face, a slight smile on her lips, and a white scarf so far back on her scalp it seemed to be almost draped over her shoulders. "I love niqab. It makes me feel safe and secure . . ." she wrote in the caption. "[But] the world doesn't love the idea of not seeing someone's face—tying it to the person's identity instead of realizing that her identity is not in how she looks but in who she is inside. [I]t's a shame, but it's real. I made this decision—despite feeling uncomfortable uncovered—after I missed out on many opportunities that could have benefitted other people."

When we met, Hana confirmed that, overall, she had loved wearing the niqab. Being unseen meant that she was judged solely by her merits, whereas as soon as she removed it, she felt the usual lookism creeping in, like when people refused to believe she graduated among the top students in her college or assumed she was a flight attendant, because what other attractive, single American would be living in Saudi? "I miss that aspect of it," she said, the way it was "really about my personality, my work and all of that." When I asked if she'd found it difficult to travel outside Saudi while wearing a niqab, she said the uplifting interactions she had with people far outweighed the bad ones. "I think I had a lot more positive experiences than negative in that I really was able to show the normal side of it. I could joke with people, I knew rap songs they didn't expect me to know . . ."

Though Hana didn't necessarily sign up to be an "ambassador" for Islam, she relished opportunities to alter people's perceptions of Muslims. But a few things happened that gnawed at her and eventually resulted in her decision to uncover herself. First, in 2017, she'd gotten an offer to work for the philanthropy office of a very wealthy, high-profile person in Saudi Arabia. Because the organization did a lot of business internationally, they wanted to present a unified, modernized image, which meant Hana would have to remove her niqab. Offended, she turned the job down. Afterward, a woman who worked there called and told her she'd made a mistake. "You can do whatever you want," the woman said, "but you could have made a huge impact. Is it worth the cloth on your face?" On a more Freudian note, she began to dream of herself wearing a niqab, which freaked her out. It was one thing to feel protected from the prying eyes of others, she felt, but it was entirely another to not even see *yourself.* The symbolism of it felt ominous. "I thought, *that is not healthy.* I can completely understand how disassociated I am from who I am as a person."

The Saudi Arabia of 2020 was a very different place from the Saudi Arabia of 2015, the year Hana relocated. Because of an ambitious plan put into place by Crown Prince Mohammed bin Salman called Vision 2030, Saudi Arabia was rapidly modernizing, and in few arenas was this more obvious than that of women's rights: the number of women in the workforce nearly doubled over the course of five years; more and more public spaces became mixed gender; and in 2018, women were granted the right to drive. When the niqab was the uniform regardless of marital status or socioeconomic class, it was something of an equalizing force among women; by 2020, it was a clear signal of religious conservatism, which was no longer an unequivocal good, especially if, like Hana, one was professionally ambitious. "It's gotten to the point in Saudi where they think that if you wear niqab, you're probably under your husband or your father's control, you're probably not going to come to work because you probably will get pregnant and have twenty kids, because you're *real* conservative," she said. "Everything's changed." Hana's friends liked to joke with her that "oh, Hana opened because Saudi opened"—I made the same comment to her, the first time we met—which she both understands and finds a little simplistic. "People put a lot of emphasis on the outside, but I don't feel like I've changed that much on the inside."

When Hana talks about her adoptive home, she sometimes sounds like a one-woman PR campaign for the Kingdom (this makes sense given that, when we met, she worked as a marketing consultant for, among other outfits, the American Chamber of Commerce in Saudi Arabia, a nonprofit that encourages American businesses to "connect, grow, and prosper" there). Her enthusiasm seems to have remained steady over time, regardless of the changes. In 2016, she was commissioned to write an article about living as an expat in Saudi for an American magazine (they didn't end up publishing it), in which she said she was fine with, even happy about, the fact that she was legally prohibited from driving there. "From the bottom of my heart, I thank God every day that I do not drive here," she wrote. "Driving is INCREDIBLY dangerous. I fear my imminent death every time I'm in a vehicle of any sort. Accidents are the number one cause of death—I'm okay in the back seat, thanks." Just a few years later, in a blog post celebrating Saudi National Day, she listed among her favorite things the country's "modernism." "Women's rights including driving. Forward-thinking technology. Mixed events. New media sources and outlets." Recent Instagram photos show her cruising through lunar-like desert landscapes, mouthing the words to hip-hop songs alongside various friends.

For Hana, the country's constant transformation itself has turned out to be part of the draw. "It's the only place on earth where there's so much change going on. And you can be physically part of the change. I make a decision and tomorrow that decision is implemented and has a ripple effect and an impact." With this, we traded our knowledge of dizzying futuristic projects. She mentioned a floating industrial city— I look it up later and find it's real, called Oxagon, set to jut out into the Red Sea not far from the Suez Canal—and I counter with what I vaguely remember is a city made entirely of mirrors the prince is planning to build. (The Line, a "tall and narrow stripe of a city more than

105 miles long, teeming with 9 million residents and running entirely on renewable energy," according to NPR, which will cost "hundreds of billions of dollars to build"; in the years since our discussion, reporting on the Line has revealed the project has been beset with financial and logistical problems and may end up being much smaller in scale than originally projected.) When we met in 2021, Hana seemed hesitant for me to visit her; by our second meeting in 2022, she was touting the ease of the visa process—I, too, had noticed sponcon tastefully hidden between articles on *Condé Nast Traveler*'s website, urging Americans to "apply for an e-visa with a quick online application" and promising it will be ready "within minutes upon completion"—and telling me all the things she'd show me if I was able to swing it. It was as if any hint of fear over my status—as American, or Jewish, or a female solo traveler—had evaporated.

No one can like absolutely everything about where they live, though, and Hana does cop to one major challenge: dating. Hana is a self-described workaholic, and I didn't get the impression that she is truly desperate to marry, but she is a traditionalist at heart, and she ultimately wants to start a family. The problem, in her estimation, isn't that she doesn't measure up as a convert or an American, but rather because Saudi is still a highly "tribal" nation, where parents often have the final say over their child's choice of spouse. She recounted story after story to me of meeting a guy she liked, only to have his parents reject the match, or, alternatively, of being set up with a man by a mother or sister, only to find he was flaky or ill-suited for her in the end. (It's normal for a mother to see a young woman at a women's-only event—say, before a wedding—where the female attendees remove their niqabs and hijabs, and then get the number of a pretty guest for her son.)

When I asked her if there was ever a scenario where a couple was rebellious and defied the parents' wishes, she said yes, but it was difficult.

It just so happened she was most often attracted to men from a particular region of Saudi that was rather conservative, which meant she frequently found herself in situations with rigid parents. As the child of a small and broken family herself, she didn't want to be responsible for breaking up those bonds and cutting off her future progeny from a relationship with their grandparents. "Because I don't have parents, I don't want to put my kids through a situation where they're not going to have any family like I did. I don't want my kids to feel that if—God forbid—something happened to me and my husband, they would have nobody to care for them." There were dating apps in the Kingdom, like MuzMeet, but she was too "picky" to find them useful.

The second time Hana and I were together, in December 2022, I sensed a new weariness—or perhaps she had only just then decided to let me in on it—with being typecast as the perfect convert, the quintessential Saudi expat. She bemoaned the fact that whenever anyone she knew had an American friend visiting the kingdom, she'd be called on to give a makeshift tour; when her company had a TED speaker come in to run a small, select group session and she was chosen to participate, she knew with absolute certainty why and resented it. "What they see in me is just that I'm going to regurgitate a story that I've told a hundred times about me moving to Saudi and loving it," she said, exasperated. "And I believe it. Deeply in my soul, I believe it. But the more times I tell it, the less authentic it is, because I'm just rushing through it, because for me, it's not that interesting." Once upon a time, she'd maintained a blog called *Convert Confessions*, and she had of course agreed to be on reality TV as a representative of her faith, but now, watching convert influencers on Instagram post pictures of themselves on sponsored trips to Dubai, she felt an instinctive aversion to branding herself that way.

In Muslim theology, everyone is born internally Muslim before out-

side influences corrupt their natural faith, so converts are actually referred to as "reverts." But Hana was uneasy with this framework. "I
don't think my parents messed me up or that in my preconversion time
I was a bad person," she said. When others focused excessively on her
change, it tended to obscure some essential things she valued about
herself: how thoughtful a friend she was (I can attest to this, as Hana
never failed to bring me a gift when we'd meet, like a container of
Saudi dates sprinkled with pistachios arranged like jewels inside a little
box); how extraordinarily hard she worked at her job; how generous
and accommodating she could be. And there were the silly things too:
she liked hip-hop; she adored her pet cats; she loved traveling; she used
the word "gucci" to describe something cool, which was something
I'd only ever heard teenagers do in the movies. Underneath her incon-
veniently extraordinary conversion story, despite her former boss's pro-
testations, she really *was* normal. "People expect it to then also be the
entirety of your identity," she said, speaking both of her faith and her
cultural transition. "But I'm not *just* that. I'm a million other things.
Islam happens to be the most important to me; that happens to be the
one that guides me and gives solace and is a reflection of me. But it's
not the whole picture of who I am."

There is no actual concept of conversion to Judaism in the Old Testament. In the biblical era, belief and worship practices had more to do
with tribal allegiance than spiritual leanings. What there is, instead, is
a concept of the stranger, alternately called the ger or sometimes ger
v'toshav (meaning, respectively, "sojourner" and "resident alien," the latter implying more permanence). Of the multiple terms used to denote

foreigner in the Tanakh, ger is the one that implies the most familiarity and fondness, and numerous times throughout the Torah, particularly in the books of Deuteronomy and Leviticus, God exhorts the Jewish people to treat the ger—whose vulnerable status is akin to that of the orphan or the widow—with special consideration. The ger's status in the biblical Jewish world is an uneasy one: a resident of Israelite society and yet not a full Israelite, he is beholden to certain laws and not others, the recipient of a number of privileges but not the full spectrum of those on offer to Jews, invited to participate in some rituals but not all of them. In many cases, a crime that would incur a severe punishment for a Jew incurs a lesser one for a ger. He is an outsider, with all the stigma and advantages such a position usually entails.

Though the rabbis of the Talmud retroactively propose conversion stories for a number of righteous non-Jews in the Bible—among them Batya, the daughter of the Pharaoh who rescues baby Moses from the river (and my Hebrew namesake)—the only figure whose trajectory actually looks conversionesque in situ is Ruth, the Moabite woman who remains with her mother-in-law, Naomi, after both are widowed. "Do not urge me to leave you, to turn back and not follow you," Ruth implores Naomi, in what has to be one of the loveliest expressions of fealty in the Tanakh, or anywhere else, for that matter. "For wherever you go, I will go; wherever you lodge, I will lodge; your people shall be my people, and your God my God."

Despite the mention of God here, not much about Ruth's pledge of allegiance looks anything like what we expect a religious conversion to look like today: she expresses no knowledge of Jewish practice and confesses to no great spiritual awakening. Some scholars take this to mean that religious affinity actually isn't an important element in conversion. "There is no provision for accepting a convert who searches for religion," writes Rabbi Moshe Miller in *Rising Moon: Unraveling the*

Book of Ruth. "There is no law that states that it is even permitted to accept an applicant who claims a philosophical belief in Judaism. The only basis for accepting applicants is if they claim that their life will be complete only if they join Yisrael." And though Ruth is held in the highest esteem in Judaism—wisdom holds that the Messiah will descend from her line—there is some textual evidence that even after she'd begun the process of assimilation, she continued to view herself and be viewed by others with some suspicion. When she first encounters Boaz, who will become her husband, she asks, "Why are you so kind as to single me out, when I am a foreigner?" but for "foreigner," she uses the word "nachriyah," the term that connotes the greatest degree of difference: a very *foreign* foreigner, one who possibly poses a threat.

By the Talmudic era, the meaning of ger had shifted so that it came to almost exclusively mean "convert" instead of stranger. Today, an Orthodox conversion candidate usually takes at least a year to complete the process, which can require taking classes, learning the rudiments of a new language, embedding oneself in a community, and in some cases, relocating entirely, but in the Talmudic era, the rabbis outlined something swifter and less challenging. Back then, once a candidate was accepted, he was informed of "some of the lenient mitzvot and some of the stringent mitzvot"—obviously not a comprehensive overview, given that there are 613 of them—and a few of the punishments involved in breaking these new rules. "They do not overwhelm him with threats, and they are not exacting with him about the details of the mitzvot," the text continues. "If he accepts upon himself all of these ramifications, then they circumcise him immediately."

Although this seems quick by contemporary standards, much of the other content about the ger in the Talmud is written with obvious skepticism. Can we really trust these people, whose backgrounds are surely rife with orgies, murder, gluttony, and generally immoral behavior?

If we remind them of their origins, will they inevitably backslide? What would possibly motivate them to want to do something like this? Any exploration of a convert's motivation in the halakhic literature is done almost exclusively from an outside view, usually with an aim toward ruling out what doesn't qualify as acceptable: doing so to marry a Jew, during a period of relative Jewish success (converts, it is said, were not accepted during Solomon's kingship and won't be accepted after the Messiah comes), because they feel threatened by Jewish military might or otherwise coerced, because the idea came to them in a dream. In a passage in his legal work *Mishneh Torah*, Maimonides—who elsewhere displays an undeniable bookish elitism—even implies that "intellectual conviction" isn't a worthy reason for a change of faith among Gentiles, in a passage that makes me, as a person who often thinks about faith, feel chastised. In all these delineations of improper intentions, we're often left wondering what a proper and pure one might be, especially as the Talmud offers numerous examples of converts who became righteous even after the most inauspicious beginnings—Hillel converted a man simply because the latter coveted the high priest's ritual garments, while one prostitute felt compelled to convert after a Jew rejected her despite her beauty (and even more shockingly, it is implied she was allowed to marry this man later).

It's only really in the more mystical texts that we start to see a picture emerge of who the convert is *inside*. In the Kabbalistic view, there are a few explicable, albeit esoteric and therefore somewhat incomprehensible, reasons a person converts. One says that a convert is a "spiritual child" of Avraham and Sara, the product of one of their many failed attempts to conceive a child. Another goes as follows: at the beginning of time, God, who once occupied everything, retracted Himself so as to make room for the universe. In the vacuum created by His withdrawal, He put ten "spiritual vessels," into which He shined a light. But the light was so intense that the vessels shattered, and the resulting sparks were dispersed across the earth. The entirety of human history since has been in service of gathering these sparks through the performance of mitzvot; once they're all retrieved, the Messiah will arrive. A ger is a person whose soul contains one of these fallen sparks, and his conversion is part of this redressing.

As to how a person in our current age could contain a spark of something that originates at the beginning of creation, the answer is actually reincarnation, which, though more commonly associated with Buddhism, is a rather central part of Hasidic (though not mainstream, nonmystical Orthodox) Jewish belief. Throughout mystical texts, the tone toward the ger is at once reverent, awestruck—"There is a precious quality found in a ger that is not found within someone who was born Jewish," the Izhbitzer Rebbe wrote, citing the ger's independently honed reverence and dedication to God—but also wary, even bigoted. "In order to truly understand who a ger is, you must know that . . . God did not give gerim the merit to be born into the Jewish people," the nineteenth-century Hasidic rabbi Shlomo Hakohen Rabinowicz wrote. "They were forced to wander among the nations in order to achieve the rectification of their souls." This is a dichotomy one sees reflected across the Orthodox spectrum, albeit in different ways: although it's stated in many places that, legally speaking, converts are full Jews, they are often viewed simultaneously as both a true embodiment of spirituality and simultaneously flawed or less than. This suspicion persists even in environs where Jews are relatively cosseted: born Jews in my own modern Orthodox community often profess to being impressed at my having changed my life, but are also usually open about the fact that they find it profoundly weird I would have ever wanted to be *one of them.*

Today, it is extremely common for Jewish converts to speak of having been "born with a Jewish soul." "I've always *felt* Jewish," I've heard quite a number say; the common phrase for this is the Yiddish pintele Yid, meaning literally point of Jewishness, but more commonly referring to some tiny inner bit of Jewishness that cannot be eradicated—though, often, these people grew up knowing few or no Jews and without any concept of Jewish practice or belief. This appears to arise from the Kabbalah—hence a common loose translation, "spark" of Jewishness—where the idea of a mismatch between body and soul is fleshed out and emphasized, and also the legend that when God offered the Torah to the nations of the world, they refused, although certain individuals within those nations were in favor but outvoted. Over time, these ideas were flattened and simplified via an elaborate, long game of cultural telephone until they became sweet bromides about authenticity and innate selfhood divorced from their sources and cited by the least mystical of Jews.

Before I converted, I thought the idea of a core Jewish self was pretty appealing: if you ever had doubts about whether or not it was what you were "meant" to do, or if you were in it for the wrong reasons, you can just nicely plaster over that with some vaguely romantic and wholly unfalsifiable language about how *it was meant to be* and *you've always known it.* But unlike most converts I know, I was also always slightly wary of it, and as time has gone on, I've grown to become downright resistant toward it, perhaps to a heretical degree. When I hear my husband tell my sons that "mama's neshama was always Jewish," I bristle a little, although I don't openly object to him framing it that way (my own explanation would be too complicated for children, and I recognize that the one he's giving them is likely the one they'll hear repeated most often).

Frankly, it reminds me a little too much of anorexia: when you feel like a messy, inchoate, aimless person, in swoops this airtight explanation to make everything coherent. You can look back over the entire course of your life and superimpose this new narrative over every past slight and grievance and misstep. "Well, of course I didn't fit in with my family of origin. Of course I didn't feel comfortable in my childhood environment. Of course I struggled to figure out who I am and what I should be doing in life. *I was different all along.*" (Not that I felt I had actually *been* anorexic prior to the illness developing, but more like the seeds of my discontent, which grew into my eating disorder, were planted in my personality long before I was ever conscious of them.) The Talmud says that when a person completes their conversion, they are like an infant, stripped of any relationship to their family of origin, but I held all those painful memories of feeling like if I could just lose a little more weight, if only I stuck to my punishing plans, I would be transformed into a New Person, one who carried none of the shameful flaws of Past Me—only to be proven wrong, of course. I would not make the mistake of believing I could overhaul myself entirely ever again.

Here's the other thing: what does it mean to *feel* Jewish? It seems most often that when people invoke this idea, they aren't talking about emotional range—that idea always struck me as nonsensical and somewhat patronizing, as surely Jews feel the entire spectrum of human emotions just as anyone else does?—but rather some kind of Weltanschauung, one that encompasses feelings but goes beyond it, toward some kind of indefinable ontology. An orientation, a *way of being in the world*, one recognized by both the individual and their observers. Sometimes, this "feeling" has to do with embodying the stereotypical Jew as neurotic, prone to excessive doubt, with a dry wit, verbose; alternatively, as Theodore Ross puts it, "a culture, a sensibility, a form of humor, an array of tastes, a canon of literature, a philosophy of work and education."

But these summations don't, in my opinion, conform so easily to the Israeli Jew, the French Jew, or even American Orthodox Jews. When I lived in England, I often felt a subtle chaffing of personalities between me and many British Jews, but I *also* noticed that same subtle disconnect between me and British Gentiles: could this be chalked up to my not having that same kind of Jewish *feeling* as the Jews-by-birth, or was I reacting to the foreign Britishness in my new neighbors? Instead, it seems to be a descriptor that largely applies to secular or at least less observant American—specifically northeastern or even more specifically New York–area—Ashkenazi Jews. If I had a nickel for every time someone told me that someone they knew was "the most Jewish person ever" because they liked smoked fish and shunned religious practice and behaved like Larry David, before I reminded the speaker that I spent a significant amount of time with Hasidim, I'd be richer than any anti-Semite could fantasize. Besides, "dispossessed, persecuted, misunderstood, outsider": that buffet of negativity that people once associated most commonly with Jews is now claimed by greater and greater swaths of humanity, as academic Devorah Baum argues in her book *Feeling Jewish (A Book for Just About Anyone)*. All this to say: Is my expression of being in the world a product of some secret but very real immutable inner self, one that I liberated upon my conversion, or is that expression constructed, over time, with fragments of the culture in which I was raised and socialized, my life experiences, and my personal quirks? (Or—maddeningly—some combination thereof?)

The Jew of *feeling* takes on sociopolitical connotations too. It is a Jew who is less a figure who lives a particular kind of lifestyle—one of "ultimate concern," which is Paul Tillich's definition of religion, actualized via ritual and communal life—than it is a symbol, very often that of victimhood. This is the Jew in Sylvia Plath's "Daddy," in which she wrote "A Jew to Dachau, Auschwitz, Belsen. / I began to talk like a Jew. / I think I may well be a Jew," equating her exiled status as fatherless, hysterical female to the experience of being Jewish in the Third Reich Germany, a device some found brilliant and some found wildly offensive (personally, I think it's both!). It's the one Plath's contemporary Anne Sexton longingly writes of in her poem "My Friend, My Friend": "Who will forgive me for the things I do? / To have your reasonable hurt to belong to / Might ease my trouble like liquor or aspirin. / I think it would be better to be a Jew." It's what Misha Defonseca, a woman who fabricated an outlandish story about surviving the Nazis by hiding in the woods and befriending a pack of wolves, meant when she offered up this explanation for why she lied about being Jewish: "I felt different. It's true that, since forever, I felt Jewish and later in life could come to terms with myself by being welcomed by part of this community." Paula Winkler, the wife of philosopher Martin Buber, might have had this Jew in mind when she penned her essay "Reflections of a Philo-Zionist," first published in Theodor Herzl's *Die Welt*, in which she recounts feeling roused by her future husband's speech to the 1899 Zionist Congress: "How I love you, people of pain! . . . you should not perish in the maze of foreign peoples. All of your beauty, all happiness and all earthly joy lies in difference."

It's not that I don't understand the impulse to identify this way, the stigmaphilic way; many times in my life I have felt dispossessed, persecuted, misunderstood, outside of, though arguably so have many— maybe even most—people living, for reasons both inscrutable and obvious, reasonable and illegitimate. As repulsive as Defonseca's falsehoods were, both her parents *did* actually die in a concentration camp, but for the Belgian resistance (her father was later accused of giving the names of fellow resistance members to the Nazis). How else could she make that pain legible to the wider world? (The writer and critic Daniel Mendelsohn could muster no sympathy for her explanation: "'Felt Jewish' is repellent: real Jewish children were being murdered however they may have felt.") Sylvia Plath and Anne Sexton were female poets at a time when the world still favored the voices of men, and they looked for the most effective metaphors they could find. Should anything be totally off limits to the artist?

If forced, I'd cast my vote for "no." Of all my examples, it's perhaps most unfair to include Paula Winkler, who ended up actually converting not once but twice, the first under a Reform rabbi in Germany, and the second under the auspices of the Orthodox rabbinate there during the rise of the Nazis, before the family had to flee to Israel. No one could dare cast aspersions on such a courageous act, even if it was not motivated solely by religious belief (her granddaughter recalled that in her later years, Winkler referred to herself as a "pagan").

People of pain. The line makes me bristle every time I read it, despite my admiration for Winkler. I didn't want to convert because I wanted to find a new way to understand my individual pain, a new concept onto which to project it, a new story to superimpose on top of it. Though obviously self-negating, anorexia also involves a serious amount of ego: I'm better, or different, or more special than others, because I have this secret power. Thinking of myself as singled out for an exceptional life, one that involves being both especially exalted and especially persecuted, brought back the logic of that dark past again. The writer David Foster Wallace, when pressed once to admit he knew he was unique, pushed back by saying he couldn't indulge such thinking. "The parts of me that used to think I was different or smarter or whatever, almost made me die," he told the reporter David Lipsky. To see in my conversion echoes of my anorexia, though they were unavoidably there in some ways, was equal parts gross and scary. I wanted to think of myself as a simple religious person, and I saw as much optimism, if not more, in Judaism as pessimism, despite its reputation. The Talmudic sages might have disagreed with me here: when discussing how to handle a potential convert, the sages instructed the court to ask, "Don't you know that the Jewish people at the present time are anguished, suppressed, despised, and harassed, and hardships are frequently visited upon them?" (The rabbis ask these same questions of converts at the mivkah today.) What is the appropriate response, according to them? "I know, and although I am unworthy of joining the Jewish people and sharing in their sorrow, I nevertheless desire to do so."

So perhaps some amount of self-flagellation is indeed in order. But the idea that the conversion would be somehow about my *feelings* sounded frankly, well, rather un-Jewish to me. I was much more drawn, again, to the notion of na'aseh v'nishma. To imagine that your religion is determined based on a mysterious welling up of affinities and emotions seems much more akin to Christianity than it does to law-based Judaism, or to Islam for that matter. Just as my friend Angela was concerned about relying too much on moments of big feelings, I didn't want to go to Judaism expecting spiritual ecstasy and identity cohesion for the rest of my life. I figured that, despite its opportunities for spiritual transcendence, Jewish life, just like secular life, is sometimes a slog. I didn't want my relationship to faith to be ultimately contingent upon what it gave *me*; I wanted to serve *it*.

Finally, I worry that this idea of needing to "feel Jewish" supports a system in which converts need to deny or suppress their former selves in order to fit in, which seems fundamentally unhealthy. There is plenty to suggest that the convert is obligated in all the same ways a Jew is, but little to say that one must be culturally identical to the Jew (which also raises the question of *which* Jew: The Yemenite? The Hasidic? The Upper West Sider?). I was never at real risk for full self-sublimation, if I'm being honest: I'm not the bravest of nonconformists, but I have strong tastes, am quirky, and can be opinionated, so I've never felt enormous pressure to fit in under most circumstances. And I was already one half of a couple when I came to Judaism, which meant that I didn't need to worry about presenting myself in the right way to find a spouse, which can be difficult depending on the community ("As a principle I wouldn't want [my child to marry a convert]," a Haredi man tells the YouTube personality Corey Gil-Shuster in one of his videos. "At the end of the day there is a small imperfection [in them]"). All things considered, I would ultimately have preferred to have been raised Jewish, but only because I would like to have had that time to garner adequate skills to live the life I've chosen.

I've always felt like I'm simultaneously living and observing, existing and performing—a trait that, for whatever it's worth, is one quite common among writers—which has made me inordinately preoccupied with the impossibility of total authenticity. Given this, it makes sense that nearly a decade after a conversion, with children in Orthodox school, a giant water boiler that enables me to drink coffee on Shabbat morning, and counters that would never be debased by a bread crumb days before Pesach, I would still balk at the idea that I'm a "real" Jew. I'd prefer to make the rather Talmudic argument above than tell you of the more sentimental aspects of my religious life, like that I cry every year on Yom Kippur, so moved am I at being given a second chance to live a good and upright life, or that I chose the Hebrew name Batya because it means "daughter of God," and I wanted to feel I was walking with Him all the time (not that I always do feel that way; it's aspirational). Certainly most of the converts I've met don't purport to have these same hang-ups; most seem to much prefer the idea of total assimilation to perpetual relegation to the fringes. A close friend, the wife of a rabbi, told me of a young convert in her midst who was having trouble finding her place in her new community: "I'm inordinately grateful when I'm recognized as a member of the tribe without question," she texted my rebbetzin friend once. Another friend, who teaches at a rabbinical school, told me that when a member of the staff mentioned he had forgotten one student was a convert, the convert student responded, "Thank you."

But me: I don't know. It's basically irrelevant to ask whether I would want total assimilation, because I just don't feel that it's possible in my case. I will never be as proficient in Hebrew or as learned in halakha as someone born to this; I could never give up theater and literature in service of only consuming Jewish content (Does one *have* to do that? It depends on who you ask; certainly, if I wanted to free up my time for the sake of learning halakha or Hebrew, I could reallocate it from TV). These days, I tend not to think of myself as a Jew because of how I feel, but rather because I've made a commitment to live a particular (and demanding) way, and because I try really, really hard to do that. Maybe my resignation to never fitting in, not to mention my propensity to obsess over details, is actually one of the most Jewish things about me in the end. A powerful midrash—ancient books of biblical exegesis and occasionally wild stories—I love says that the ger is special because many of our prophets felt like, were, or referred to themselves as strangers, implying that there is something spiritually productive about the experience of being a little separate, a little distinct, a little vulnerable, like I'm the Jew of Jewish society, in a way. I have given up citizenship in my native land; I hold a passport to my new country, but I can barely speak the language, and I fumble through the customs. The local styles look awkward on me, the food on my plate triggers no nostalgia for my youth. Judaism—as many religious traditions do—often extols its original act of rebellion, its status as macrocosmic outsider, but flinches at signs of noncompliance internally; maybe my presence reminds people of the occasional value of breaking the mold.

Perhaps my favorite text of all time on conversion is another midrash. In this one, a king—understood to be God—has a flock of working animals. One day, a gazelle randomly wanders into the pen with the cattle at night. In the morning, the gazelle goes out to graze with the herd, and at night, the gazelle went back into the pen, and so on and so forth.

The shepherd mentioned this strange development to the king. "Be careful with this gazelle, that he is not struck by any person," the king commands him. The king showed his family members the gazelle and instructed them to give it food and water. "And he loved the gazelle the most."

The shepherd watches the king dote on the gazelle in this way. Finally, feeling confused, he asks the king why he's so fixated. "My master the king, how many male goats and how many female goats and how many sheep and how many kids do you have? And you have never told me to be careful with them! But for the gazelle, every day you command me about him!"

"The cattle, this is the usual way to shepherd," the king responds. "But the gazelles, they dwell in the wilderness, and it is not their usual way to enter to dwell with people. But this gazelle entered and dwelled with us! We will not hold him back from going to the great open wilderness, in the place where gazelles and deer graze," the king said. "[But] we need to support him well. So too, the Holy One, blessed be He, said it is a great need that I need to support the convert, because he put aside his family and the house of his father and came to me."

A contemporary interpretation of this passage might see the reader miffed on numerous points. What about the poor other animals, who work tirelessly, give their milk and their wool and their literal flesh for the king? Why does the comparatively useless, interloping gazelle get such royal affection? The gazelle is being fetishized! It is loved for its sleek good looks, its aberrance, its mysterious ways! The gazelle is like Hana, towering over her fellow Saudis, inviting stares as she wanders through a souk; or it is me, at a new synagogue, being peered at warily by a fellow congregant. ("Where are you from? You look kind of *Irish* to me.")

But I find it rather moving, and true, because it admits some things that most other texts on conversion do not: it recognizes that the gazelle has given something up to be part of this flock; it also acknowledges it won't ever fully fit in. It doesn't pretend to know the gazelle's motivations, and it lets the king's remain enigmatic. It lets it come down to befuddling, agonizing, mystifying love, and love alone.

5.

CHRISTINA, TO THE PASTORAL RESTRAINT OF THE AMISH

Nevertheless, these and similar evil examples are constantly presented to our eyes, and they are the more pernicious and dangerous for the reason that some worldly-minded people pronounce them to be non-essential, unimportant for either good or evil, and therefore, allowable; while it is the same with them as with the fruit from the tree of knowledge, which stood in the midst of Paradise, and was pleasant to the eyes, but deadly in the use.

—THE BLOODY THEATRE, OR MARTYRS MIRROR
OF THE DEFENSELESS CHRISTIANS

Though I have been to Lancaster County, Pennsylvania, many times, the prospect of a trip there still excites me. It's a little over two hours from my house, and I always look forward to the drive, forgetting that about 80 percent of it is down long, exceedingly dull stretches of highway in New Jersey and into Pennsylvania. Then at the very end, Route 340 narrows into a single lane, which cuts straight through the middle of Intercourse, Pennsylvania, the beating heart of

Pennsylvania's Amish country, or at least the town that's best capitalized on its distinctive denizens. Turn onto one of the many country roads off the main drag and you'll be met with gorgeous expanses so green the grass seems to be emitting its own light. Clothes drying on lines sway languidly in the breeze; cows crowd under trees for shade, occasionally swatting at one of many flies that swarm around their warm, muddy bodies. Off in the distance, you might see a man in a straw hat behind a line of mules plowing a field. The air everywhere, even in the parking lot of the CVS in town, smells, not unpleasantly, of excrement.

I enjoy spending time in Amish country, but I am always suspicious of my own enjoyment. I've read enough tourism theory to know that being in proximity to the Amish makes me feel like I'm absorbing elements I worry are lacking in modern life: slowness, simplicity, wholesomeness, a relationship with the land, a sense of practical know-how and self-sufficiency (the Amish, after all, can fix or build nearly anything; I have six years of higher education and can barely put together a piece of Ikea furniture). Sometimes I feel like my credentials as a journalistic chronicler of the Amish and other groups of Conservative Anabaptists gives me at least an entry visa, which allows me some extra claim to affection and expertise beyond that of the average tourist; other times, I feel like a basic parasite. I avoid shopping centers like Kitchen Kettle Village, a faux mini-hamlet of stores selling everything from locally made ceramics to yarn to music boxes, as if it's a particularly seedy downtown. When I do purchase something, like a small wooden airplane for my son during a research trip or an intricate cream-white quilt during a family vacation, I cringe a little when I hand over the money. My terror at participating in a commercial activity there is because I once read that the average tourist to Amish environs doesn't really want to learn about "Plain" history or culture at all: they just want to shop *near* the Amish. "The tourist purchases much more than a piece of lawn furniture; the tourist is also purchasing an element of Amish culture," the sociologist Thomas J. Meyers wrote in his paper "Amish Tourism: 'Visiting Shipshewana Is Better Than Going to the Mall.'" "The transaction that includes the sale of a chair or a table also includes cultural commodification."

Thankfully, I don't really have to deal with these neuroses in Oakland, Maryland, because the Amish community there is so small that there's no real tourism around it to speak of, save for one couple who offers sleigh and carriage rides for paying customers (including, if you're in need, a horse-drawn funeral hearse). Nestled into a verdant Appalachian enclave deservedly called Pleasant Valley near the border of West Virginia, the tiny town of Oakland is known for its historic B&O Railroad station; its proximity to one of Maryland's most popular ski resorts; and being home to the oldest Amish community in the state, founded around 1850. No restaurant shaped like a windmill or oversize buggy stuffed with iPhone-wielding tourists signal your arrival. In the early hours of the first Sunday morning I drove into town, there was nothing to greet me except the sleepily rotating wind turbines perched atop the nearby hills, and a smattering of jet-black buggies moseying down the road toward the Gortner Amish Church, a short distance yet a world away from the Denny's and the Taco Bell, the Chrysler dealership and the public golf course, a few miles away in town.

Nearby, a white farmhouse sits far back from the main road down a long, rocky driveway. To the right of the driveway is a barn that used to house dairy cows before it burned down in 2014—now it just contains debris and some ash-enriched soil, which has been turned into a strawberry patch—and an unused silo, which produces a fantastic echo if you yell up it. The path of grass on the left is dotted with highlighter-yellow dandelions. A covered porch sags slightly in front of the house, and a charming diamond-shaped window sits at the triangle at the top of the edifice. Behind the house, a herd of cows wanders around a field, munching on grass, occasionally approaching the electric fence to assess any visitors with their characteristic blasé glares.

Connected to the big house is a smaller structure, what's known in Amish environs as a "dawdy haus": a little domicile built for grandparents when they become too old to run an entire farm and one of their descendants takes over the main building. On this farm, though, the roles are reversed: an elderly couple resides in the big house, while the dawdy haus is occupied by Christina Cortez, twenty-eight, and her two foster sons, Cairo and Brooklyn, ages two and thirteen. Cortez is, of course, not a name one often hears in a community where a vast majority of people descend from German or Swiss stock. But if you were to visit, she'd greet you at the door wearing an ankle-length, monochromatic dress and a scarf or white gauze bonnet covering her brown hair, looking every bit the Amish homemaker.

Christina was born in the flat, dry, quasi-urban expanse of Bakersfield, California, to a mother who is part white, part American Indian, and a Mexican father. ("I'd almost love to do a genealogy test to see what all comes up," she told me.) She describes her childhood as a lot of fun: biking to the local park or swimming in public pools, playing tennis and softball, and hanging out with her large, "rambunctious" network of Mexican family members who lived close by. Her paternal grandparents were devout Catholics, and as a child, she attended Mass every Sunday with the entire family; later, she went through catechism class and partook of her First Holy Communion. Before the conclusion of any gathering at her grandparents' house, all the grandchildren would be lined up in a row and Christina's grandfather would go down the line and bless them. She found the whole milieu of Catholicism "so ornate and so put together," she told me. "As a little girl, it was amazing."

Her home life was turbulent though. Her parents divorced when she was young enough that she doesn't ever remember them cohabiting. They had a decent coparenting relationship—they managed to stay out of court for anything related to custody—but aren't on good terms to this day. When Christina was seven, her mom moved across the country to the Oakland, Maryland, area. The following summer, when Christina was eight and her older sister was ten, the girls went out to stay with their mom, who by now had remarried and had baby twins with her new husband. Christina was over the moon with her new siblings, and also smitten with the rolling green pastures of Maryland, so she asked her mom if she could stay permanently. Her father agreed.

Not long after relocating, Christina noticed Amish people shopping in town or navigating their tractors or buggies down the long country roads. She'd never seen anything like them before, and wondered to herself if they might be a little like the Catholic nuns she'd seen in church as a child. ("It's not like there are any Amish in California!") In fact, Catholics are about as theologically distant as you can get from Plain Anabaptists within Christianity, the latter having been founded around 1525 in the wake of the Reformation by a group who deemed even Luther's revisions insufficiently radical, particularly on the point of infant baptism, which the Anabaptists staunchly opposed. Groups of Anabaptists sprouted up in Switzerland, Germany, the Netherlands, and France, stressing adult baptism, pacifism, and strict separation of church and state. The Amish were the last and most stringent of the Anabaptist groups to separate, falling out with the Mennonites in 1693 largely over the practice of shunning disobedient church members, which the Amish were in support of. In the early eighteenth century, Plain Anabaptists began migrating to North America; today, virtually all Amish people live in the Midwest, with a few communities scattered in parts of the American South, Plains states, and parts of rural Canada, and are best known for their "plain" clothing, broad rejection of modern technology and education, and farming and craftsmanship.

As far as Amish settlements go, the Oakland-area one is small, comprising only about seventy families (and, according to Christina, currently declining, due mostly to the young moving out of the area). It's also rather unusual in its practices. For example, one would *never* see an Amish person driving a tractor on the street in Lancaster, where it is largely verboten to use them for transportation. The Amish in Oakland are what's called New Order Amish, a sect that broke off from the larger Old Order body in 1966 over a number of issues, including the use of modern farm machinery, with the New Order advocating greater liberalization. Today, New Order Amish will drive tractors on the roads—though car driving and ownership is still prohibited—while the Old Order Amish refuse, because they view tractors as inevitable precursors to cars, and they worry that access to a car will allow people to travel further and with greater ease, thus fraying their strong, localized bonds. The Oakland New Order church is actually part of an even smaller subset of the New Order Amish often colloquially called "Electric New Order," because they hooked their homes up to the electrical grid and got landlines in the 1960s (televisions, radios, computers, and internet in the home are largely discouraged, though more by implication than by outright edict). Compared to the more rule-oriented Old Order, New Order Amish tend to be a bit more evangelistic in tone; they hold Sunday school classes after church services and speak more freely of spirituality, salvation, and personal relationships with Jesus than the Old Order Amish, who are more reticent on such matters.

Part of Christina's interest in her oddly dressed neighbors might have been related to her love of history. She'd been "enthralled" with the Little House on the Prairie series as a girl, and often daydreamed about what it would have been like if she'd been born in a different time period, traversing the country in a covered wagon or picking in the fields alongside others in the United Farm Workers movement (the American labor activist César Chávez was the subject of a school project of hers). When Christina was in the sixth grade, her older sister did a report for English class on the Amish, which piqued Christina's interest further; but for years afterward, her fascination simmered beneath the surface of her perfectly average American teenage life of softball, socializing, student council, and homework.

Not until her freshman year of high school did she decide to begin her own research, somewhat obsessively. First, she read every history book on the Amish she could get her hands on; later, she turned to the Bible, which she'd barely read on her own before, and to *Martyr's Mirror*, an epic chronicle (many editions span over a thousand pages) of the persecution of early Anabaptists, which she ordered online. Beginning in the first half of the sixteenth century and through the seventeenth, Catholic and Protestant nations outlawed Anabaptism—even going so far as to prohibit people from sheltering, feeding, or helping Anabaptists—and tortured and executed its followers. (Sample entry, for a Dutch woman named Anneken Heyndricks, executed by burning in 1571: "They did not let her speak . . . but filled her mouth with gunpowder, and carried her thus from the city hall to the fire into which they cast her alive.") Shortly after their move to Oakland, the family had switched from attending a Catholic church to a Baptist one, eventually switching again to a Methodist church. "All of these different types of Christianity had their own viewpoints on what was right and what was wrong," she told me, and she was eager to see how they all squared with one another and with the Bible itself.

Though no one had explicitly told her this was important, she, like other converts we've met so far, felt instinctively compelled to find the scriptural basis for everything she'd heard in these churches, but immediately noticed the disparities, particularly between the Catholicism of her earlier youth and Anabaptism. Why was there purgatory in Catholicism but no mention of it in the Bible? Where did the idea of infant baptism come from, or praying to an intermediary like the Virgin Mary, or using rosary beads? How could an institution she'd been taught was good and kind have so brutally persecuted the early Anabaptists? Above all, she was attracted to the fact that the latter's beliefs were so obviously manifested in their lifestyles, compared to other kinds of Christians, who filed out of church after Sunday morning services to resume lives indistinguishable from their non-Christian neighbors. "For me to see that these people *lived* a certain way, I was just so drawn to that."

Christina had heard grand stories of being saved by Christ, but for her, there was no moment of personal revelation, no white light or bursting sun in her chest, just a gradual recognition of the fact that instead of investigating these people for some abstract or academic reasons, she was, instead, grasping with an actual question about her own life: *Can I actually do this?* she began to wonder. Do *people do this?*

The answer to that question is essentially: not really. Over the course of modern Anabaptist history, seekers have come, on occasion in droves.* Sometimes they're back-to-the-landers, other times biblical fundamentalists, but rarely have they properly estimated what it takes to integrate into such a particular, demanding culture, one in which a pregnant pause could signify a thousand rebukes or the width of a hat

---

* The Amish often refer to converts and potential converts as "seekers"; I use the terms interchangeably here, though I give preference to the former, because it's the more readily understood.

brim indicate church allegiance. There are notable exceptions, of course, like a former chef at Michelin-starred restaurants who joined a small Amish church in Maine and opened a charcuterie there, or the California party girl who found God and then parlayed a conversion memoir into gigs on the Food Network and Nat Geo. But according to experts, the number of true converts in the entire Plain universe is likely just among the hundreds. One of these people, a middle-aged nurse named Curtis Duff, who'd converted as a teenager, happened to live on a farm right in Oakland, but Christina didn't know him yet. Years later, too, her shelves would feature books by some of these "successful" seekers—*Called to Be Amish* by Marlene Miller, a high school baton twirler who fell in love with a good Amish boy, and *Road to Freedom* by Sanko Waight, who struggled with addiction before becoming a Conservative Mennonite. Later, a friend gave her an ad from an Amish magazine—the Amish have a robust media ecosystem of periodicals just for them—written by a young girl named Caitlin. Caitlin was joining an Amish church in Michigan and was hoping to connect to others in similar positions, and she and Christina exchanged letters for years, even eventually adding other correspondents and circulating missives and responses around the group (a kind of analog chain mail, this is known in Amish environs as a "circle letter"). But at fourteen, Christina had no concept that such a subculture of stalwart seekers, no matter how small, existed, nor that she would end up joining them.

One day in the spring of 2010, when Christina was in eleventh grade, she was in the car with her mom, who asked her daughter offhandedly where she was thinking she might want to look at colleges.

"I don't think I want to go to college," Christina replied. "I think I want to look into the Amish."

Christina remembers her mom staring directly at her in shock as she continued to drive. (It was an unintentionally comedic moment: "I remember the car swerving a little bit," Christina said.) "You're joking, right?" her mom asked.

Looking back on it, Christina wishes she had approached the topic a little less bluntly: "I was coming into this full force." But by the end of the conversation, Christina's mom agreed that they could approach the Amish couple who owned the local bulk foods store, where the family often shopped. "I think her main thinking was, *Let's just get this over with. That way you can go on to start getting stuff prepared for college and figuring out what you're going to do in life.*" The Amish couple suggested that Christina tag along during the youth activities, so in December of that year, she joined the annual Christmas caroling around town. She still wore "normal" clothes like jeans in her daily life, but she picked out a long khaki skirt for the event, not nearly insulating enough for the chilly weather. The seventy or so youth members at the time crammed alongside hay bales in three large trailers, and tractors drove them to each of the church family's homes, where the kids would tumble out and sing a mixture of German and English holiday songs. Christina had "a lot of fun," and the Amish kids were uniformly kind and welcoming, but she got the distinct sense the girls saw her interest as a passing phase.

It wasn't. After the caroling, her mom suggested they take some time to think things over. "If you still want to pursue it," she begrudgingly offered, "you can go to church on your birthday." Come February, Christina was ready, clad in a skirt and with her hair in a bun at the nape of her neck. The sermon that day was about how people needn't become fully Amish to be true Christians. (Though she can't be sure, she told me she didn't think the sermon was directed at her specifically.) Their nonproselytizing stance struck Christina as confident and pluralistic, rather than xenophobic or haughty: "It almost made me trust them more, because they were okay with where they were," she said. From that day on, she was at church every single Sunday.

At one point, though she doesn't remember how it started, whoever was driving her would drop her off about a mile away, and she'd walk in either by herself or with a few other families she'd meet up with along the way. Little by little, she began to change the way she dressed outside church, too, opting for long skirts and always wearing her hair up in a bun or ponytail, a stark change from her previous "tomboy" get-up of shorts and sportswear. Her closest friends noticed but largely refrained from remarking on the change; it wasn't until her final semester, when she was wearing full Amish garb—including a beautiful purple dress made from Ukrainian fabric that ladies in the community had sewn her and the obligatory veil atop her hair—that kids began to tease her.* "I remember some of them mooing at me and saying, like, 'Where's the barn?' But it only made me more firm in my resolve to keep it up. Because to me, if someone is okay with being martyred for their faith, what is a little teasing compared to that?" she said. "There's no comparison with what I was going through than what others have gone through before me."

Many seekers who approach the Amish find it aggravating that they aren't immediately warmer or more conciliatory to outsiders; indeed, the Amish themselves often seem perplexed as to what to do with the fiery types who show up in their spaces, having projected all their romantic ideas of biblical primitivism onto them, with no real under-

---

* A veil is usually a scarf, more casual than the gauze pleated "coverings," worn largely on Sundays and often covered by black bonnets.

standing of how deep the cultural roots of submission and reservedness run. Unlike most other religious traditions, the Amish offer no structured path toward conversion; this, combined with the nonproselytizing stance, their "tightness" (a term from cultural psychology that describes societies that are highly ordered and have a low tolerance for deviance), and the language barrier, makes true assimilation difficult.

In Christina's case, the fact that there was another convert in the church likely worked a great deal in her favor: the leadership had seen a model of effective spiritual change, so they were more willing to help her than the bishops and ministers at other churches might have been. They decided first to give her a crash course in Anabaptist theology in advance of the standard "instruction class" Amish teens take before baptism. Beginning in the late spring of 2011, they walked her through the eighteen articles of faith, a list of core beliefs including not swearing oaths, partaking of communion (which the Amish do biannually, in conjunction with washing each other's feet), and practicing nonresistance.

At the same time, women and young girls in the church volunteered to teach Christina Pennsylvania Dutch. She had a leg up because she'd been taking German classes at school specifically to help her integrate into the community, but Pennsylvania Dutch is not a written language, so there were no textbooks or Rosetta Stone programs she could use to further supplement her learning. Instead, the group would gather during the evenings and tackle a specific topic, like the seasons: flowers blooming, snow falling, leaves changing, the clouds and the rain and the sun. "It was basically going back to school again and learning everything all over," she said. The Amish women would say a particular vocabulary word, then Christina would write it out phonetically on an index card; eventually, her collection of cards mushroomed to over a hundred. In church, one of the women would sit next to her to whisper a translation of the sermon and point out the letters in the hymnbook, written in an ornate, antiquated font. She cozied up to her church friends' children, who were unabashed in their critique of her pronunciation, which was more helpful than the politesse of the adults. She'd also arranged to live with a family from the community for the summer before her final months of high school (she graduated a semester early, in December 2012) to get a feel for the rhythms of an Amish household: rising early, tending to hydroponic tomatoes, learning to sew with the help of the family's teenage daughters, and milking cows.

On March 18, 2012, Christina Cortez arrived at church early, dressed all in black. She retreated back into the private chambers where the bishop and three ministers gather before church; the men asked her if she was feeling all right, if she had truly given her life over to Jesus, if she felt prepared for the day. The church service was standard that morning, except for the fact that all the women were clad in long black dresses, to mark the solemnity of the occasion. "I know the weight of the decision had hit me before that, but I think it really hit me on that day too," Christina said. Contrasted with the theatrical baptisms of Evangelicals, the atmosphere of Christina's re-baptism sounds borderline funereal. "It wasn't really sad. It was just kind of a heavy weight, of knowing that this is your life. [The dress code] makes you visually think about how somber and how serious this is."

Her mom and her stepdad's mother and sister were there, as well as a couple she knew from the Methodist church and a handful of friends from high school (they've almost all lost touch by now, the gulf between their worlds widening ever more over the ensuing years). On baptismal days, the ministers read through the episode in the book of Acts where Philip baptizes the Ethiopian eunuch after the latter's brief but enthusiastic spiritual awakening. And then at the end of the church service, Christina stepped up to the altar area and knelt down in front of the minister, pulling her gauze covering back slightly so as to not get it too wet. The congregation rose to their feet, and then the bishop poured water onto her head from a jug. As the water trickled through Christina's hair, the bishop's wife reached out her hand and helped her rise to her feet, to join the congregation as "a sister and as one in the church." She was the only person to be baptized that day, which feels fitting, given how singular her journey was.

Almost exactly ten years after her official entrée into the Amish church, I stood in the threshold of Christina's home. From the entryway, you can see into the small laundry room stocked with food she and her foster sons canned themselves, a common activity for Amish families. The week before I first visited, they'd made dandelion jelly, in a process that sounded satisfyingly tedious. "You have to get *all* the yellow parts off," she told me. Through a small kitchen and into the living room, I scanned the bookshelves and noticed a smattering of novels—*Redeeming Love*, a Christian romance set during the California Gold Rush, and *Unbroken* by Laura Hillenbrand—next to religious books, like one called *The Gospel in Tolstoy*, and a cassette tape story version of *Toy Story*, the movie of which, presumably, they never watched. A freestanding air-conditioning unit oscillated quietly in the background; on a small table, a digital frame cycled through family photos of when Cairo and Brooklyn first came to live with Christina, the new familial trio smiling for the camera, the boys looking very Amish in their suspenders and crisp white shirts.

Christina thought that maybe the frame could show photos that others sent directly to it via email, but she didn't have Wi-Fi in the house, so she couldn't be sure. In high school, she'd had a computer and a phone, and had gotten close to getting her driver's license, but then she got baptized before she took the test, so obviously that ended that. (Her family still made fun of her, she told me, by saying it was good she became Amish in the end, because she was a terrible driver, a distinction she rejects.) She got a smartphone in 2021 when she started working as a caregiver for her younger half brother, who has autism; when she began fostering, she was required to utilize tons of apps and have access to Zoom so she could meet virtually with social workers. But when I was there in the house, the phone mostly sat idly on a countertop, and I snuck a guilty glance at it every time Christina left the room to tend to something and I unlocked my own phone to frantically, and largely unsuccessfully, will it to get more than a single bar of service.

At one point during my visit, while Christina was sewing new black pants for Cairo—"this is time-consuming," she said, but in a way that indicated gratification, not exasperation—I launched into a diatribe against modern culture's relationship to technology. Yes, it's a cantankerous talking point, but it's basically how I feel, and I felt like she'd be a sympathetic audience. I mentioned to her that there seemed to be this default position when it came to tech usage, that people just started acting as if something was necessary, so then everyone else would assume it was and also start using it, even if they disliked it to some degree, or knew deep down that it wasn't actually as much of an imperative as its mass adoption seemed to indicate. I used the example of Twitter, as it was called then, in the media sphere: almost everyone working in media has Twitter, I told her, so everyone assumes you *need* to have Twitter to be successful—to locate sources, say, or promote your work, or just to chime in on the endless discourse—but no one had actually ever determined whether there was a direct link between professional achievement and Twitter usage. But I had no Twitter, I told her, with no shortage of pride at my clearly very brave show of resistance. And I was just *fine*.

"Yeah," she said, opening her large eyes wider and grinning in agreement. There was a pause, then slightly timidly, she asked, "Is that like a text-messaging service or something?"

※

In writing about their relationship to technology, it's become common to compare the Amish to computer hackers. Rather than reject new technology outright, the argument goes, the Amish first evaluate it carefully, then, if they feel it's useful but has some potential pitfalls, see if they can develop some creative workarounds, just like hackers do. Examples of said workarounds abound: to avoid being hooked up to the electrical grid but still use electricity, many Amish homes have solar panels. Amish farms may use machines that run on pneumatic motors powered by diesel or gas engines, so people aren't stuck milking dozens of cows by hand. I read an article recently about how, in Kentucky, some people are trying to create a weather-only radio service to get around the Amish ban on mainstream radio—all that unnecessary global news, all that salacious pop music—after five children there died in a flood when a creek overflowed.

"Amish lives are anything but antitechnological," writes Kevin Kelly, one of the founding editors of *Wired*, in his book *What Technology Wants*. "In fact, on several visits with them, I have found them to be ingenious hackers and tinkerers, the ultimate makers and do-it-yourselfers." A preeminent authority on Amish culture, academic Donald Kraybill, devoted an entire episode of his podcast series *What I Learned from the*

Amish to the idea of Amish "hacking." "Hackers take charge of technology. They mold it into the Amish moral order. And good hackers, especially, balance respect for tradition while seeking alternative ways to allow change." Books with titles like *Virtually Amish* and op-eds debunking the widely held idea that the Amish are unquestioning Luddites often suggest that we non-Amish should "emulate" their attitudes toward tech. "My challenge really for you is—you don't have to wear a bonnet, but for all of you to unlock your inner Amish," the writer Alexa Clay urged an audience during a Tedx Talk titled "The Power of Buttermilk: Confronting Techno-Optimism." "Unlock that . . . instinct inside you and bring that to the world so that we can design technology that better amplifies our humanity."

Perhaps individual modern people can and should take a more cautious approach to technology, waiting and debating before deciding whether to buy it or download it or stream it. But there are a couple of reasons to wonder about how well Amish technoskepticism could really work outside that community. The Amish, after all, aren't lone-wolf resisters; they do so in a community that largely sets those norms for them. They don't have the burden of having to make all those decisions themselves. A person can transgress, of course, but there's no inherent pressure to do so unless, like Christina, they have some specific reason to cross the metaphorical bridge onto the mainland: their kids will never be forced to Zoom into their classroom, and they'll never find themselves unwittingly put on a neighborhood WhatsApp group or faced with a restaurant menu that is just a big Magic Eye of a QR code.

Their culture, too, is a "culture of restraint," as Kraybill puts it: they place a high premium on withholding, on abstinence, on constricting growth, which comes out in all sorts of ways, from keeping their businesses and schools small to rejecting modern conveniences or regulating their usage. They often frame said rejection not only as passive adherence to religious dictates that come from on high, but as a conscious and active choice. In a paper on internet usage among Old Order Amish and Haredi Jewish women, Israeli scholar Rivka Neriya Ben-Shahar noted that many of her subjects went even beyond their communities' mandates, because they associated stringency with virtue. "Nonuse constitutes an important part of one of the most valorized aspects in those communities' value systems: isolation from mainstream society." There is little sense that the average modern American person would also associate stringency with virtue, because the character of American culture is in many ways the polar opposite of Amish culture: it's an individualistic, competitive, transient one, interested in capital growth, mesmerized by fame and public accomplishment. In other words, an Amish person refraining from using technological devices is making a broadly countercultural decision but, on a more micro level, a culturally comprehensible one; an American who attempted to do the same would be pushing back against the dominant tone of their culture, and doing so alone.

The Amish got into farming largely as a practical matter, when persecution in their European homelands forced them to be more self-sufficient; they also feel farming, which requires all members of the family to work together, within the home, is the best lifestyle for a devout person. Only as time went on did it evolve into a kind of mash-up of Christianity and proto-environmentalism, and in America today, the Amish relationship to agriculture, and to activities like canning food, making their own clothing, owning livestock, and smaller-scale gardening, has developed a strong spiritual hue. Indeed, Amish people themselves might even have a hard time disentangling it from their strictly religious beliefs. Whatever the impetus, because Amish society never really shed its valuation of manual labor, there was no vacuum to fill with technology by the time the gadgets came to steal our atten-

tion. Even if Tweeting incessantly was totally fine with the church po-
lis, it would be hard to find time to do it, what with all the domestic
chores needing to be done.

Meanwhile, mainstream society has moved in exactly the opposite
direction: as we've become more of a knowledge economy, we've
devalued—both financially and in terms of cultural cachet—jobs that
require working with your hands. In the Amish world, work is often
simultaneously social, because groups will get together for quilting
circles or barn raisings or shelling cobs to make popcorn; in the mainstream culture, we're confined to cubicles (or these days, home offices),
staring at screens. The Amish spend ample time outdoors—their lifestyles require as much—whereas we've become so nostalgic for an
agrarian past that we've resorted to watching homesteaders wrangle
wily ducks or plow fields of sorghum grass on YouTube. It wasn't really
surprising to me that when the COVID-19 pandemic began, and so
many more people were confined to their homes, there was renewed
interest in domestic hobbies and handiwork, although of course people
had to document the growth of their sourdough starter or baby chicks
on a dedicated Instagram page rather than just, say, enjoy breadmak-
ing or tending to chickens. It's not really enough to label a particular
activity as wrong or bad, as so often happens with tech; some alternative means of filling one's time, of earning one's living, or of becoming
esteemed in one's community must be available to take its place. And if
it isn't already there, it's certainly going to be difficult, if not impossible, to go back and reinfuse meaning into something we've been told,
implicitly and explicitly, is no longer valuable.

Finally, the Amish are also motivated to abstain from certain parts
of modernity because they see themselves as protecting Amish culture,
which is a specific, identifiable, and (to them) infinitely precious thing.
Their posture is wholly defensive. They know themselves to be different,

to be outside of, to be—to use a favorite descriptor from the apostle Peter—a "peculiar people"; they have a keen sense of themselves as the bearers of not only a religious lineage but also a strong historical one, living out their beliefs because people like Anneken Heyndricks were unable to. All their weird sartorial choices, all the odd little things about their homes, all the idiosyncratic rituals—the holy kiss (a ritual kiss, cited in scripture, given during church; who participates depends on the community's rules); the shunning; the High German liturgy; or rumspringa, the period of experimentation teenagers engage in before joining the church (the Oakland community, like many others these days, does not have rumspringa)—conspire to create a clear entity called the Amish, and, like other groups that the historian Arnold Toynbee would call "creative minorities"—we Orthodox Jews among them—they erect high protective ideological barriers around this thing, their culture.* A mission this grand can be galvanizing and all-consuming, and you might be inclined to make any number of choices that look befuddling to outsiders in service of it. The average twenty-first-century individual, to contrast, might not be entirely clear on what it is they would even be protecting by removing themselves from the mainstream: certainly not their cultural identity, as most aren't predicated on rejecting modern conveniences, so what?

To be clear, some Americans *do* resist of their own accord; it's just generally harder to do so, because the baseline assumption is that you'll participate, and if you don't, this choice isn't immediately recognized

---

* Arnold Toynbee coined the term "creative minority," though he theorized that all creative minorities eventually took over as the moral majority, a crucial step toward a civilization's inevitable decline. I'm using the term more in the way that Joseph Cardinal Ratzinger (today recognized as Pope Benedict XVI) and Rabbi Lord Jonathan Sacks did: as small groups on the margins of mainstream society who seek to preserve their distinctive identities and maintain a delicate symbiotic relationship with the dominant culture.

as a conscious or important one. I speak from personal experience. Facebook arrived at my college campus my sophomore year, in 2003, a year after it was launched at Harvard. For a variety of reasons, I didn't end up joining, which at first passed as unremarkable. By my senior year, though, my refusal had become more than just a random fact about me, like my hair color or my short stature, and instead was seen as an integral part of my public *identity*. Classmates would drunkenly joke that "Kelsey is too cool for Facebook!" and I and the one other kid who I knew wasn't on it, a lanky, brilliant economics major who ran in the same social circles, would inevitably high five when the topic came up. Because I, like the Amish, had experience exercising my technological resistance, and because people expected me to stay on brand, it was easier to abstain from later offerings from the Silicon Valley overlords: Twitter, Instagram, Clubhouse, TikTok, and so on. I remember an awkward meeting right before my first book came out when my agent and various employees of the publisher gently suggested that I consider joining Twitter: I was good at quipping, it would potentially be helpful promotionwise, what was the harm? Though I seriously considered it, I eventually decided I couldn't do it. And now that the momentum is in the direction of tech avoidance, I'm rarely, if ever, tempted or pressured to get the newest thing.

This all sounds quite smug, I'm sure. And I shouldn't overstate the case. Yes, being a millennial and having no social media is unusual, but there are plenty of ways tech infringes on my life. Email is my biggest Achilles' heel: I check it obsessively and I tend to be *very* responsive. I have a smartphone, even if I resist getting new ones for as long as possible and refuse to buy models with facial recognition (terrifying!). Other things are harder to get on board with. The concept of an Alexa or an Echo sends me into a panic. When I want to procrastinate, I usually consume a bit of the news from four or five websites and then immediately have this distinct feeling of having reached *the end of the internet*. If someone does send me a link to a funny video on YouTube, I'll sometimes find myself momentarily seduced by the algorithm, but that familiar scrolling nausea rises pretty quickly, which I take as a surefire sign it's time to close the tab. (Everyone has this, I think; mine just kicks in early. Perhaps I've unwittingly done as Clay suggests and harnessed my inner Amish.) I used to characterize myself as a Luddite, but this is probably a misnomer: I am sure I *could* learn how to use social media if I wanted to. In actuality, I am more like a tech conscientious objector, although this sounds rather lofty. I once interviewed the luminous Buddhist meditation teacher Susan Morgan—Morgan had considered entering a Catholic convent as a young woman, and then later underwent a four-year silent meditation retreat with her husband/teaching partner—whose emails are signed with the standardized disclaimer, "i am a digital ascetic, and only check email *intermittently*," which I wish I had the guts to steal. More provocatively, I sometimes think of myself as a digital *anorexic*: I see the bounteous feast laid out before me, and I choose not to partake of it, in hopes of preserving some kind of internal purity.

More than anything, I think my tech resistance is an attempt to recapture the intense, unblemished concentration I'd enjoyed in childhood, the way I'd lose myself for hours in at once intricate and lawless games I concocted, the way I could feel entirely, blissfully alone and yet observed and marveled at and cherished from afar. I pined for nothing in my life quite as much as that sharp focus born entirely of solitude, which for whatever reason I reminisced about frequently as I grew older. In my midtwenties, I became enamored with Simone Weil, the twentieth-century French would-be Catholic and philosopher who equated "absolutely unmixed attention" with "prayer." I sometimes felt that my eating disorder, too, had solely been about that same desire for monofocus. One night, during my first hospitalization at age fifteen, I went on one of our allotted daily walks with a handful of patients and a hospital chaperone. While traversing the looping driveway of the white colonial mansion that housed the facility, I looked up at the stars in the clear night sky and thought about how untethered from the larger world I felt, my whole life shrunk down to this ragtag group, this vista, this short list of demands (eat, sleep, speak, repeat). I felt for the first time in years wholly and ecstatically encapsulated in a single moment. It's a relief I wouldn't feel again until more than a decade later, when I began to observe Shabbat.

"Six days you shall labor and do all your work, but the seventh day is a sabbath of your God: you shall not do any work—you, your son or daughter, your male or female slave, your cattle, or the stranger who is within your settlements. For in six days God made heaven and earth and sea—and all that is in them—and then rested on the seventh day; and therefore God blessed the sabbath day and hallowed it." Thus reads the first mention of Shabbat, the Jewish day of rest, in the Book of Exodus. Like much of Jewish practice, it has been, over its history, equal parts maligned and fetishized, rejected and appropriated, seen as a rigid tool of control and a mysterious means of reaching a spiritual apex. Its holiness derives from its differentiation from other days, the Hebrew *qadosh*, meaning separate, set apart, chosen, like the Jewish people themselves. The prophet Isaiah called it a "delight"; our prayerbook calls it "the most cherished of days." In melodies and liturgy, it's anthropomorphized as a queen, dressed in her finest garb, gracing the houses of ordinary people with her presence. "Come out my Beloved, the Bride to meet," goes the chorus of Lecha Dodi, sung at every Friday evening service. "The inner light of Shabbat, let us greet." In the mystical Zohar, it is said that if you keep Shabbat, it is the equivalent of keeping the entire Torah.

So obviously, it's a pretty big deal.

As with the Amish rules on technology, the Sabbath appears, from the outside, to be simply antitech. Usually the only thing outsiders know about Shabbat (or Shabbos, in Yiddish; I use both) is that observant Jews won't go to their jobs, answer their phones, or drive their cars, so it looks like the sum total of Shabbat is not doing your job or using electricity. The actuality, however, is much more complicated. Though the Torah doesn't elaborate as to what it actually means to "work," the rabbis of the Talmud built a complex system of law based on the idea that work meant any activity done to build the tabernacle, which they divided into thirty-nine categories, things like trapping animals, dyeing, kneading, baking, tying and untying knots, writing and erasing, building, and extinguishing a fire. (Indeed, the tractate governing the laws of the Shabbat is the longest in the entire Talmud.) "Be deliberate in judgment, and establish many students, and make a fence for the Torah," as it says in *Pirkei Avot*, a book of rabbinic ethics, and so, much like the Amish, they complied, making sure to forbid the thing that isn't really forbidden but even just *looks* like the forbidden act, so as to ensure you won't come within a mile of transgressing.

Over the course of history, new technologies or questions arose that required clarification: Was killing a bug that flew into your house "trapping"? Was operating an elevator akin to lighting a fire? Could you use an Alexa device, given that you aren't manipulating it with your own hands? The reams of scholarship piled up; the fence grew, in Orthodox environs anyway, taller. For a period of time, I learned the laws of Shabbat over the phone with a very pious young mother in

Brooklyn, who used to lock herself in her parked car to speak with me, because there was no quiet space in her two-bedroom apartment, with four kids under the age of six. Though I'd observed the Sabbath for more than eight years at that point, I was astounded to learn of all the prohibited activities of the day, many of which I'd never given a second thought: filling a pitcher from a water cooler, leaving on a household surveillance camera, cutting a cake that has words written on it in icing, scraping dried mud off a shoe, wearing a watch only for the sake of telling time (if it's nice enough to be considered ornamental jewelry, it's okay), putting together a puzzle, using a bar of soap to wash your hands, using a swing connected to a tree, snapping to a beat, handling loose buttons, and on and on. A friend is fond of saying that the more you learn about the laws of keeping kosher, the more you realize you've never actually broken them, but the more you learn about the laws of Shabbat, the more you realize you've never fully kept Shabbat.

Despite its many demands, the effectiveness of Shabbat as a binding agent for the Jews cannot be overstated. In her book *The Sabbath World: Glimpses of a Different Order in Time*, Judith Shulevitz writes that if you were given the task of creating the perfect society, you might design something exactly like Shabbat: a designated period in which everyone, regardless of employment status or social standing or age, would be forced to spend time together indulging in luxuries like good meals, leisure time, and wine. "If a strong and powerfully interconnected communal life was high on your priority list," she writes, "you'd quickly realize that you had stumbled on a very good way to achieve it." The early Zionist writer Ahad Ha'am had a pithier way of getting at the same point: "More than the Jews have kept Shabbat, Shabbat has kept the Jews." It's become something of a touchstone for writers and thinkers anxious about the ways that modern society has made us all feel starved for time and aching for some kind of short-term reprieve.

"There is a rapid, dirty river of information coursing through us all day," *The New York Times'* resident nostalgist, David Brooks, wrote in an op-ed titled "Longing for an Internet Cleanse." What was one possible solution? Shabbat, of course. "On this day the Orthodox do less and in slowness can glimpse the seeds of eternity." Indeed, its charm is more readily apparent to outsiders than almost all other Jewish traditions. In a scene from the Israeli TV show *Srugim*, a young observant woman's secular boyfriend stands at a window, looking out at the hills of Jerusalem, and sighs contentedly. "I'm crazy about Sabbaths in Jerusalem," he says. "It's so peaceful, everything looks different." No one's face is transformed by longing when you talk about Sukkot or the laws of ritual purity, but very often I find secular acquaintances get misty-eyed if I bring up Sabbath observance.

Just before I started to observe Shabbat, I saw all of the magic, and little of the headache. Like many converts, Shabbat was my gateway drug, and one of the major reasons I ended up pursuing an Orthodox conversion as opposed to one under the auspices of a different denomination, where the commandment is less obsessively obeyed. As a long-standing tech skeptic, I readily understood the virtues of spending twenty-five hours without electrical devices. I could easily articulate—and did, probably too often—why it was so important for everyone to protest the wares of Mark Zuckerberg and his ilk; if pressed, I could probably even inject some spirituality into my tirades and make seeking the peace of a mind left undistracted into the equivalent of a religious act, which is obviously nice and true but also totally irrelevant (Shabbat isn't really about the ability to concentrate, after all). This was in 2014, and while "capitalism" hadn't become shorthand for everything wrong with everything, there was a lot of hemming and hawing about what we called then "work-life balance," and about how technology had made it easier than ever for our bosses to get ahold of us at all hours. This was very offensive to me, even though technically speaking at the time I had no boss. People weren't supposed to live like this! A human being couldn't be expected to be "on" 24-7! How could we be our best selves if we never rested? And therein lied my early mistake: Shabbat, I assumed, was for *me*. It was a way for me to express my resentment against our plugged-in era, a tool to help me reach my highest creative potential, a means of relaxing in a high-speed, high-stakes world. It was not for God. Not yet, anyway.

At the time, I was living with my then boyfriend, now husband—and yes, I recognize the irony of pursuing holy ritual while "living in sin"—who expressed little interest in upping his religious observance. Our cozy one-bedroom apartment was about a forty-five-minute walk from the shul I most enjoyed attending at the time, a weird little Chabad house/gallery on the campus of an art school, frequented by hipster sculpture students; ideological refugees from the very conservative Hasidic sect of Satmar, based in nearby Williamsburg; and a handful of young newly religious families from the neighborhood. Many Friday evenings would see me hosting friends for dinner, and Saturday mornings, I'd tumble out of bed and walk, usually alone, to go to services. Afterward, there was always a lively lunch filled with conversation, warm cholent (a thick meat and bean stew, designed to withstand many hours on a hot plate), shots of whisky, shouting and backslapping and impromptu sermons and armchair-reviewing the latest cultural offerings, after which I'd walk home.

By this time, it would be mid- to late afternoon, and the trouble would begin. Depending on the season, a pleasant light would be coming through the windows of our house. Hours stretched ahead of me, with nothing really pressing to do—anything pressing, in fact, I was expressly *forbidden* from doing. I was frequently by myself in this time, as my boyfriend was a first-year associate at a law firm and often worked on weekends. So I'd flop down on the couch next to my cat and spend fifteen happy minutes studying Hebrew flash cards or reading a book, thinking how *nice* it was to have this time all to myself, how special and sacred human focus was, and how much we had all collectively done to destroy it.

But soon after, I'd begin to get restless. Rudimentary Hebrew vocabulary couldn't hold my attention for quite that long, so I'd start to sift through other things. I'd feel a familiar longing, for someone to just show up and rescue me from my own boredom: a friend paying an unexpected visit, a hullabaloo on the street. As I was going through a particularly fanatical career phase at the time, I thought of all the writing I could be doing if I were allowed to use a pen, let alone a computer. My fingers practically cried out to tap-dance across the keyboard. Productivity, in my mind, was inextricably linked with literary output, and it pained me to forgo a moment's opportunity, even if I was aware that I often squandered the time in which I *was* free to produce. Any thought that popped into my head that seemed germane to what I happened to be working on at that moment felt infinitely more precious than the ones that arose when I was capable of recording them, but my elegant inner monologue disappeared in a comic book *poof* the second Shabbat was over. As a writer friend commiserated, "When the Sabbath Queen goes, she takes with her all my beautiful words."

As the light faded from its pleasant late afternoon butter yellow into its evening ashy gray, it stole my words, too, and along with it, my brief sense of peace. Sometimes, I'd think about how there's a popular idea in Judaism that after the Messiah comes, it will be Shabbat all the time—that essentially what Jews call olam haba, or "the world to come," would be an endless "relaxing" loop of big meals, schmoozing, napping, and praying—and I felt horrified. But when would you ever *do* things? I wondered. Could I really spend an *eternity* mired in this kind of self-indulgence, just eating and sleeping and making small talk? How could anyone consider what amounts to laziness as paradise? "Maybe you could think of yourself as being *spiritually* productive?" a friend, a very pious convert I knew who lived in the Hasidic enclave of Borough Park, suggested. If I could have yelled over email, I would have: *But what does that even* mean?!

During this time, I struck up a random pen pal–type relationship with a Hasidic writer, also from Borough Park. She had been raised secular—I have a vague memory of her telling me that she partied with the Rolling Stones in her halcyon days—but was now what she called a "religious fanatic," slightly wryly but with unmistakable pride. I met her in person only once, when I visited her in the narrow one-bedroom apartment she shared with her husband in a dull postwar complex in Borough Park. She absolutely radiated joy and lightness—not terribly surprising, I suppose, because she was a devotee of Rebbe Nachman, the Hasidic rabbi who insisted that being happy was a mandate. When I told her about getting antsy at the end of the day on Shabbat, she nodded thoughtfully. "It sounds like what you're doing is *enduring* Shabbos," she said, which seemed correct. She relayed another story from her mysterious past: years earlier, she had been living in a rural area of upstate New York, and in the dark of winter, when Shabbat began midafternoon on Fridays, she'd often find herself feeling so bored that she'd wander outside and stare at the dark sky and feel a vast, irritating nothingness. In her worst moments, she'd will the time to move faster. But that, she said, was all before.

"And now," she said, a beaming smile spreading across her face, "there can never be enough Shabbos." It was all I could do not to roll my eyes: it seemed lovely and all, but I doubted very much I could ever emulate her. For me, I figured, Shabbat would remain like a doctor's appointment or a juice cleanse: something I didn't hate but didn't really *enjoy* either, something I tolerated because I knew it was important for my overall well-being.

Not long after, I read Abraham Joshua Heschel's *The Sabbath*, a slim, gorgeous book in which Heschel attempts to explain the ineffable poetry of the day of rest, and all but required reading for every Shabbat neophyte. Much like Soloveitchik does in *The Lonely Man of Faith*, Heschel opens by positing that modern man is drunk on "conquest of space." We are so enamored with the trappings of technical civilization—the hunger to acquire and manipulate physical land in previous eras, leading to the hunger to acquire possessions and manipulate our personal environments, be it our front yards or our physical dwellings—that we've forgotten entirely how to simply be with time. We've developed, he theorizes, a "deeply rooted dread" of it. (The book was written in 1951; in contemporary times, we might also assume he'd see the obsession with flag-planting in digital space as similarly problematic.) Shabbat, he says, which is the sanctification of *time* rather than place or object, is the antidote to all this. "There is a realm of time where the goal is not to have but to be, not to own but to give, not to control but to share, not to subdue but to be in accord," he writes. The apex of this is Shabbat, which was the first thing ever declared *holy* in the Torah—not a monument, not a natural wonder like a mountain, not a person or group of people. It is a "palace in time," as Heschel memorably calls it, and he uses rousing language to describe what it takes to pass through the doorway:

> He who wants to enter the holiness of the day must first lay
> down the profanity of clattering commerce, of being yoked
> to toil. He must go away from the screech of dissonant days,
> from the nervousness and fury of acquisitiveness and the
> betrayal in embezzling his own life. He must say farewell to

manual work and learn to understand that the world has already been created and will survive without the help of man. Six days a week we wrestle with the world, wringing profit from the earth; on the Sabbath we especially care for the seed of eternity planted in the soul.

The book touched me deeply. Upon reading passages like the above, I felt that familiar righteous anger at a society that would encourage me to defile myself with all the little idiotic things I was required to do during weekdays. I wanted to pump my fist in agreement at so many of Heschel's statements, a move that would have been totally at odds with his often soft language.

But while the book did tell me about the emotional experience of embracing the Shabbat, it stopped just short of *showing* me how to make that lasting and holistic spiritual paradigm shift, one I still struggled to make despite my intellectual embrace of it. For a long time thereafter, I remained someone who went through the motions of Shabbat: lighting the candles, having guests for dinner, refraining from checking my phone, trudging to shul in the morning. I was a person who prided myself in my follow-through, so it was satisfying to announce I would no longer touch a light switch and actually *stick* to it, though there were some measures of observance I considered a bridge too far, like preripping toilet paper (now, Friday evenings see me creating mountains of single squares of Charmin). More often than not, I felt like I was white-knuckling the entire twenty-five hours, just waiting for the moment when I could turn my phone back on and check my email and drink in all the fascinating information that had surely accumulated in my time away from the world. (What exactly did I expect had happened in my absence? My MacArthur Genius Grant had finally arrived?) To anyone who would listen, I continued to argue vociferously and convincingly as to why Shabbat was the most valuable idea in all of history; I waxed existential about how it's the perfect response to our contemporary hell of overinformation. But spiritually, I just couldn't seem to transition from enduring Shabbat to relishing in it, from thinking of it not as an "interlude," as Heschel says, but "the climax of living."

I honestly don't remember how or why things began to shift, but over time, I noticed that the old urgency that set in on Shabbat afternoon—to get back online, to tackle that stack of dishes, to be able to freely watch the latest episode of whatever show I was currently binging, to get back to "real life"—became less prominent. Those things, indeed, began to feel less and less like my real life at all. Almost certainly, part of this was muscle memory, like riding a bike or swimming: as I got more accustomed to being away from Heschel's profanity of clattering commerce, it just became easier to withstand the nagging suspicion that big things were happening every moment that I was offline and I wasn't a part of them. There had always been a slight air of specialness, of holiness, that I felt twinkled around me on Shabbat, but now it felt like a more defined aura, less like I had to summon it and more like it was just *there*. I could walk down the busy streets of London, where I was living when this change started to unfurl, and feel like I occupied a different universe than the people with their heads fully immersed in their iPhones next to me. Undoubtedly one contributing factor was that I became more embedded in the Jewish community and was developing stronger relationships with others who were also shomer Shabbat. The more of these friends I made, the more phone-free meals I attended, the more synagogue began to feel like a community of people in my life—people I supported when loved ones died, people I worshipped with, people I ate with—the fuller and warmer that sanctified time felt. I stopped looking forward to Shabbat so I could be better rested for the work week ahead, or so that I could tap into a preexisting means of tech defiance, or so I could spend a little time away from the news. My chirruping metacognitive exploration of Shabbat faded away, and I was able, for the first time ever, to direct my worship where it belonged: above me, to God, who'd had the wisdom to give me this gift in the first place.

Like Heschel, it's hard for me to offer a clear road map from enduring to relishing. Perhaps sustained, disciplined observance in a robust community is the whole secret, or perhaps it's only a piece of the puzzle, and the remainder I can't quite verbalize. I only know that by the time my family relocated to a diverse and significant-size Orthodox community in the Bronx, which happened eight years after those first fidgety Saturdays, I had officially become a person who savored every moment of Shabbat. During the other six days of the week, it is easy for me to forget the part of me I call my soul; I'm completely mired in the responsibilities many adults in the twenty-first century have, like my children and my home and my work. I strive to connect with God in all sorts of ways at all sorts of moments, a bit like how Hasidim see any human activity as a means of channeling the divine, but usually most of my chores—shopping for breakfast cereal, refilling the tires of my car, trimming the hedges along my driveway—are not in and of themselves mystical experiences, and I perhaps lack the imagination to make them so. In the lead-up to Shabbat, I'm often running around frantically, making sure everything is prepared: is the water boiler switched on? Is the hot plate warming? Is the challah done baking? Are the kids (relatively) clean?

But the second the candles are lit, everything else falls away. My world shrinks to my house and my neighborhood, to the *techum*, the area from which you must not travel on Shabbat. ("Let everyone remain in place," Moses instructed the Jews shortly after the exodus from Egypt. "Let no one leave the vicinity on the seventh day.") We have a drink, we sing, we enjoy each other; the next day, we go to synagogue, we share meals, we nap, and all of this, every action, feels like prayer. I often make an effort to leave certain rooms in my house dark, not only for energy conservation purposes, but because I'm eager to feel what it would be like to be reliant on the sun's rays for light, as we humans once were. "[W]hat we have gained in [time-telling] precision, we may have lost in connectedness to the basic rhythms that regulate life on our planet and to the phototropism that guides plants and animals," writes Dr. Nehemia Polen in his book *Stop, Look, Listen: Celebrating Shabbos Through a Spiritual Lens.* Incorrigible email addict though I am, I never feel even the slightest bit enticed by my devices during this time, though enacting limits on my computer usage during other periods of the week has never been successful. Elsewhere in his book, Dr. Polen describes how his father, a "heavy smoker," felt no cravings for nicotine on Shabbat either. "What was it about our family's Shabbos observance that supplanted, if only for a day, his intense physiological need and psychological dependency?" (Perhaps the peace of Shabbat itself is an addictive substance.)

At a recent Saturday lunch, which took place on a temperate autumn afternoon on the back deck of a neighbor's home, the adults ate salads and steak and watched as the children played outdoors. The conversation came quickly and richly, as if we'd all known each other for much longer than we actually had, buoyed by a shared sense of our commitment to the moment and the milieu being just as essential as whatever might be happening *out there*. I thought to myself then, as I do often, that I couldn't imagine ever living without Shabbat, whatever its secret is. I thought of the things I do that undoubtedly look totally insane to outsiders—traveling hours out of my way to get proper Shabbat food if on vacation, taping down the refrigerator light to avoid it flicking on when I reach for a jar of mustard, missing one-night-only concerts or parties—all in service of touching this bit of holiness. If I had to, I'd do much more.

"There is a word that is seldom said," Heschel wrote, "a word for an emotion almost too deep to be expressed: the love of the Sabbath. The word is rarely found in our literature, yet for more than two thousand years the emotion filled our songs and moods. It was as if a whole people were in love with the seventh day."

When we say goodbye to Shabbat on Saturday evenings, we do so over a long, ornate candle, with a cup of juice and a jar of spices, which we smell as a way of savoring the last moments. Then we sing to welcome in the new week. At one point when they were both toddlers, my sons took to moaning, somewhat histrionically, as the song concluded. "Shabbos!" they'd whine, theatrically pouting. I knew they were doing it for my benefit at least in part, but I also hope that they know already, even at their tender ages, something it took me far too long to learn: There can never be enough Shabbos.

In a few ways, Christina's life can seem to have paused in 2012. She remembers reading *The Hunger Games* series and the young adult novel *The Fault in Our Stars*, and wishing she could have seen how the filmmakers chose to adapt those stories, but both films came out after her baptism, by which point she'd already sworn off movies. She read all the Twilight series books and saw the first two movies but was baptized before the third was released: for her, Edward and Bella's relationship remains chaste, their half-vampiric daughter forever unborn. At the end of the day, though, she didn't find it very difficult to give up most of the content you might lump under the heading of "media." "It didn't really matter to me. Like, I like TV. I could easily watch it, growing up," she said. "But obviously it's not necessary to have these things in my life, and if anyone can live without them, so can I. It wasn't really a martyr mentality though. I just think I was kind of like, eh, I can do without them too. It'll be okay. I'll get over it."

She'd followed Obama's two presidential campaigns because she'd taken AP Government in school, hoping to get as many college credits as she could ("not that it mattered, in the end"). Though she was always conservative on issues like abortion, she found the suave Chicagoan inspiring, and she and her sister often argued in favor of his liberal immigration policies with her then-stepfather, an ex-Navy man who vehemently disagreed with them. But Christina barely paid attention to Obama's second term, and doesn't know much about politics now, as the Amish avoid getting involved in government to the extent they can. For a while she got the print edition of *The New York Times* delivered to her house, but it became too expensive, so she now only subscribes to their daily email newsletter (she still has a few older physical copies lying around she occasionally thumbs through, just because she likes to read). When we met, she was pretty up to date on the war in Ukraine—lots of religious Christians are, because it's a popular region for missionaries, including Conservative Mennonite ones—but otherwise there were many current events she'd never heard of or had only a passing knowledge of. For example, when I mentioned something about the fact that I lived in the United Kingdom when they voted to leave the EU, her eyes widened. "Oh, I didn't know they'd done that!"

She prefers to limit her internet usage to email only, skimming the major headlines from the *Times* and liaising with the professionals assigned to her foster sons' case. It isn't that she doesn't understand the appeal of the wider web—"I'm sure it would be really handy," she said—but she tires of it quickly. Some mornings she feels like she's on the phone constantly, making appointments for the boys, who have complex medical needs, or texting their caseworkers, or calling into Zoom meetings. "It gets *annoying*. If life is going on around you, you should watch it happen." If she's on her phone checking in with one treatment team or another (as the network of caseworkers, social workers, and therapists who help her with the boys is called), then occasionally she'll look something up on the internet, but it's almost always information for the kids—recently, she was browsing sensory toys for Brooklyn—or, on occasion, the answer to a gardening question none of her local friends knew (Christina didn't grow up gardening, but taught herself through trial and error when she converted). Besides, she couldn't browse endlessly even if she wanted to, because there's no Wi-Fi in the house, and she might bump up against the limits of her data. "I'm sure if I got started with it, it would be hard to stop. I'm sure it would be *really* hard to stop."

Many people I know—and people generally, according to studies on the topic—would love to have the kind of largely indifferent relationship to the news cycle Christina has. Most of us don't want to go without the other things tech affords us, but we still wish there was a way to avoid the onslaught of depressing information we can access with the flick of a finger in any moment of downtime. ("It's to the point where I can't even read *The New York Times* anymore, it stresses me out so much," one friend told me.) Companies have come up with myriad ways to try to help people regulate their media intake, from apps that alert them they've gone over their allowed screen time to filtering programs with names like Serene and Freedom that block certain websites. A software engineer at the BBC named Alicia Grandjean developed a prototype that would allow users to blur out news stories that contained words they'd chosen as triggering or were on topics they found upsetting. There's even some evidence that the dumb phone is making a comeback, with companies that manufacture them reporting huge surges of sales in the last few years.

Religious people use these kinds of tools too, and in fact may be their original architects, though their explicit aim tends to be barring obscene (by their standards) content rather than staying focused or keeping anxiety about global affairs at bay. In the Orthodox world, some people use "kosher phones," which is an umbrella term for old-school flip phones or more sophisticated models that come with website filters or certain features predeactivated (they're called "kosher" because they are given a rabbinic stamp of approval, like kosher food). Plain Anabaptists like Christina can subscribe to the *Plain News*, run by a Mennonite man who handpicks certain major news stories and then condenses them as much as possible to the bare facts. Beginning around 2010, countless articles advising readers as to how to get better-quality sleep urged them to think of their bedrooms as sanctuary spaces and to leave their phones elsewhere, because the blue light emitted by screens had been proven to disrupt healthy sleep cycles. The truly hooked could buy a mobile phone "jail," with a tiny little lock and key, or a timer-activated lockbox, so they couldn't doomscroll at will. All these workarounds recall how, in many Amish communities, landline phones are sometimes kept in shacks at the end of driveways so as not to disturb the home, which is considered a sacred domain.

But not everyone believes we should unplug—there is also the pervasive, often-unspoken idea that there is something cowardly or corrosive about willful ignorance. Consider the curious case of Erik

Hagerman, a former executive at Nike who was so disturbed by the election of Donald Trump that he decided in 2016 to completely stop engaging with the news. His methods, chronicled in a 2018 *New York Times* profile, were extreme: he abandoned social media entirely, listened to white noise while purchasing his morning coffee (he preferred a constant stream of ambient sound to music, as nearby conversation could "creep in between songs"), and banned his friends and family from mentioning any political developments around him. Able to maintain what he called "The Blockade" by virtue of having amassed a considerable wad of cash during his corporate days, he had decamped to a pig farm in rural Ohio years earlier, where he made sculptures. Had he had a family or been poor, surely such isolation would have been less tenable. "We all would like to construct our dream worlds," the *Times* quoted his sister, Bonnie, as saying. "Erik is just more able to do it than others."

The story struck a nerve among readers; some expressed envy or admiration, but many others thought his behavior ridiculous, even cruel. One journalist at Mashable went so far as to title her follow-up piece, "'The New York Times' Profiles the Most Selfish Man in America." People name-checked the hot-button political issues of the day—the possible erosion of the Affordable Care Act; the violence that erupted during the Unite the Right rally march in Charlottesville, Virginia; the travel ban on Muslims. (On a somewhat related note, I'm always surprised when others express anxiety about the fact that I wouldn't have heard of major news events at the moment they occurred because they happened on a Saturday, like Ruth Bader Ginsburg's death, Biden's election, the Bataclan shooting in Paris, and the Tree of Life massacre in Pittsburgh. What concrete value, I wondered, would my knowing mere hours earlier have had?)

Some seemed to imply that because the stakes were higher for certain groups, like immigrants and racial minorities—who had to be aware of the threats on their rights or even their lives, both existential and literal—it was only right that Hagerman be as, if not more, aware. In the profile, even Hagerman himself alluded to feeling guilt over being an irresponsible citizen. But in none of the critiques did anyone suggest anything concrete that might come out of his reengagement with public life. Would his knowledge of the travel ban inspire him to . . . what, exactly? Go back to law school to become an immigration lawyer? A journalist based near Hagerman in Ohio wrote a lengthy Twitter thread in which he listed a litany of social welfare statistics, such as the fact that Hagerman's own county had recently been demoted from economically "at risk" to "distressed" by one state agency, in an effort to highlight the realities Hagerman was assumed to be ignoring. But of course, community engagement and online engagement are not the same thing; plenty of people are aware of the existence of poor people—certainly Hagerman, having lived most of his life outside The Blockade, was too—and yet do not magically transform into effective altruists. (Did this journalist, I wonder, give away a sizable portion of his own income to the local poor?) For what it's worth, Hagerman wasn't doing absolutely nothing up there in his little swine palace: he'd purchased a nearby plot of land on the site of a former strip mine, which he planned to transform into a sprawling public park.

I wouldn't say that I think Hagerman's path is wholly laudable; surely there has to be a way not to be completely overwhelmed by the world nor retreat quite so thoroughly. I'm sympathetic to the idea that one should educate oneself about matters of injustice, and I do recognize that there are people who are compelled to action because of things they learn about online or in the news. But the idea that modern humans should simply bear witness to horrors near and far via endless scroll—in hopes that they will spur us to action or perhaps just incite us to some contemporary form of self-flagellation for being cosseted—deserves some criticism considering how little it's questioned. Unlike Christina, I was not only aware of Brexit, but living in England when the voting occurred—and still, of course, powerless to change it. I moved back to the United States in 2017 and endured three years under Trump, during which time I did approximately nothing to stop him from being a maniac aside from griping about him to friends.

In many ways, Christina's life is more virtuous on certain key issues of the moment than mine is, despite my being more plugged in. Though likely not an eco-warrior philosophically—we didn't talk about climate change in depth, but most fundamentalist Christians are skeptical of it, at best—her habits are much more sustainable than those of many people I know. She almost never flies on a plane and rides in a car sporadically, always with others; she used to have a horse and buggy, but she had to get rid of the horse when the barn burned down, and she hopes to get another one soon. (For her, relying on a horse and buggy is about spirituality rather than carbon emissions: "Using a horse and buggy, it forces you to slow down and look around you.") There's a diffuse network of anticonsumerist individuals today who call themselves the Voluntary Simplicity movement, but the Amish come closest to perfecting the concept. Torn clothing is repaired, not thrown out; vegetables are picked whenever possible, not purchased. Christina might not use her phone to look up rates of drug addiction or poverty levels in her surrounding area, but she's taken neglected children into her own home to actually care for them. (Christina became interested in fostering when she met a foster family at Faith Mission Home, an

Anabaptist-run residential facility for children and adults with intellectual disabilities in the pastoral Blue Ridge Mountains of Virginia, where she lived and worked for two years postbaptism; fostering and adoption is also a fairly common pursuit in the Plain world, and one way for unmarried women to take part in an intensely pro-familial culture.) If one's concern is the underlying ethos that guides a person's decision-making, then one might object to Christina's life because her choices are, to her, about Christ and not politics; if, though, you were more worked up about ultimate ends rather than means, Christina's life is a much larger success than many average ones.

It's not that everything about the adjustment was smooth for her. Indeed, the thing Christina most wanted people to know about her was that she wasn't perfect, which I can't say is an anxiety that interview subjects normally express to me. The last we hear of the eunuch in Acts is that he departs from Philip "rejoicing," but Christina went through a very rough emotional patch right after her baptism, though that had far less to do with giving up creature comforts than it did about finding her place in the community. And she regrets not going further with her education, both because she always loved learning and because, as the most studious child in her family, she worries she let them down. "Mom had always felt that I would be the one to get a PhD," she told me. Even at a young age, she'd wanted to be a special education teacher—the training for which would have been enormously useful in her role as a foster parent—but she assumed she had to forgo that dream when she was baptized. (Now, given that even some of the ministers' children have their GEDs, and that the community accepted Curtis despite the fact he'd attended not only college but nursing school, she's considering taking courses online or enrolling at community college. "I think if I could keep it local, I could do it.")

When Christina was baptized, she also had to give up listening to music altogether. Amish music is peculiar indeed: entirely a cappella, nonharmonious, often threnodic or droning, and very, very slow (some of their signature hymns take up to twenty minutes to get through). All their songs are intoned in high German, and all are learned by ear, as their hymnbook contains no musical notations. Those raised on a variety of musical styles might find it dull; I find it soothing. The Amish generally discourage playing musical instruments, worrying that prowess in individual activities might lead to pride, though occasionally people will play harmonicas or accordions. Christina learned to play trumpet in third grade and was in the marching band in high school, which she loved. She'd listened to music across genres, everything from Panic! at the Disco to Linkin Park to classic rock like AC/DC and the Eagles. Her iPod was a "big, huge, random mix" of songs and bands. (Metal was the one genre she hated: "I didn't understand the concept of screaming and it being good to listen to.") Now, she does play the harmonica, but it's a pale imitation of her first musical love. "It's just not the same as a trumpet," she says, just a touch forlornly.

When I ask her if there's something else she wishes she could do but cannot, she replies, "It would be fun to take the boys to Disney World. I'd love to go again myself." But the Amish don't go to amusement parks, owing to a general distaste for what she calls "public entertainment," which includes sports outside of the occasional communal volleyball game. It isn't really that the Amish think things like learning piano or riding a roller coaster or playing soccer—or, for that matter, having Wi-Fi or driving cars or any number of other technological innovations—are inherently *evil*. They just operate using the precautionary principle: If we allow this particular thing, how might it damage our social fabric? (Or, alternatively, if we don't allow it, what potential harms could that cause?) In some ways, Christina certainly errs on the side of conservatism. At Faith Mission Home, for example, everyone had access to filtered internet, but even that she considered potentially problematic: "You're not going to be able to stop people's curiosity getting the better of them. The more that people get, the less they're satisfied." She recognizes that all this restriction could look overly joyless to an outsider, but it isn't, not to her. "It's not necessarily saying you shouldn't enjoy life. You should, but you can easily do it at home, with your family or friends or church community."

Sacrifice without a purpose, or with a paltry one, is unbearable. Surely nearly everyone on earth has experienced this. But when you are in pursuit of something meaningful, you can give away almost anything. Once I rolled over in bed on Saturday mornings and texted my friends; now I would rip my hand back from my phone, as if from a scalding pan. Years ago, Christina put on headphones and blasted the latest alt-rock hit; now the only melodies she hears regularly are the ones sung by her fellow church members on Sunday, in unison. Everything she's done and everything she is doing becomes its own creation, one she freely offers up to the power above her.

"The people that we meet in life, the things that we go through in life, make us who we are, and in some turn, make us how God has envisioned us being," Christina said to me of how she views the unexpected path she's traversed. "We see dimly through a dark glass. We see the underside of a quilt being done, and God sees the actual masterpiece that's being made."

In the waning afternoon the first Sunday I spent in Oakland, I was sitting in my friend's trailer where I was staying, watching house finches try to crowd each other out on a bird feeder just outside the window. Christina texted to tell me that some neighbor friends had invited her and the boys over for "popcorn and juice," and were wondering if I might like to come along too. This is the Amish tradition of "visiting," the preferred leisure activity for their Sunday Sabbath afternoons. When I first started writing about Plain people years ago—before I'd converted or I'd really acclimated to Shabbat—I'd sometimes get subjects who would call me just to chat, or who told me of spending time at the home of someone they'd just met because they figured out they had a distant relative in common, which I found thoroughly confusing. If you were getting together with someone, in my world, there had to be some kind of *other* focal point, like a movie or a concert or a bar atmosphere. When hanging out, didn't you also need to be *doing* something?

At Christina's friend's house, the adults sat in the living room as the light dimmed outside, while the children—Christina's two boys, plus three of the host family's older children—migrated into another area to play. The host couple's youngest, a thin baby with disproportionately fat cheeks and bright eyes, sat cooing on the floor; their eldest, a sandy-blond boy around eight years old, lay back on the couch, shyly contributing on occasion. The host couple were friendly, and the conversation was wide-ranging, covering school choices for our children to the husband's Old Order background to our respective travels.

At one point, the kids decided they wanted to take me outside to show me their lamb and baby goat, one of whom was named Jingle Bells, so we wandered out to the barn, where we giggled while the animals frolicked nervously around our feet. When we emerged, it was almost dark out, and Cairo and Brooklyn nearly disappeared into the murky light, Cairo to play on a nearby jungle gym and Brooklyn to stand chatting to himself a little bit farther into the yard, toward the road. I aspire to be free-range-ish as a parent, but I kept getting little flare-ups of panic, thinking the kids would step on a nail in the barn or wander into the street, and it disappointed me to see how much my caregiving style had been shaped by my typically upper-middle-class American fears. Right before I left, the mother of the children snapped a picture of me and her daughter—also named Kelsey—on her phone, while the eldest boy kept shyly trying to gift me two pieces of wood he'd nailed together to make into a cross and I kept awkwardly trying to rebuff it. I drove past their buggy and their barn and their tractors and zipped down the rural road, darker and lonelier but more peaceful than what I was accustomed to in the Bronx.

Was the dream of the pure Amish life alive and well, here or else-where? Christina, more than her friends, had expressed lots of concerns about the prospect of sending the boys to public school, if she ended up adopting them. The father of the host family had said he'd moved down here from Pennsylvania because he liked the church better, and while he didn't seem bothered by his own more lax relationship with modernity now, he was a little sad his children's preferred language was English rather than Dutch. I thought about a Sunday school lesson held in the basement of the church that morning, during which a group of ten or so women sat around what looked like a school cafeteria table discussing Hebrews 1. It had rained nonstop in the area for the previous forty-eight hours, but the deluge began slowing down as the church services progressed, and a gorgeous dewy luminescence filtered through the windows. Christina sat doling out snacks to Cairo in an attempt to get him to sit still—a tall order for an energetic toddler—while the women went around in a circle and expounded upon a small excerpt from the text they'd each chosen. A teenager with an aquiline nose and chestnut brown hair selected verses eleven and twelve:

They shall perish; but thou remainest; and they all shall
wax old as doth a garment;

And as a vesture shalt thou fold them up, and they shall be
changed: but thou art the same, and thy years shall not fail.

"I think what this tells us is the world is changing all the time," the young woman said, "and it changes so fast, and this just reminds us that God is always the same; He never changes." For all the time I've spent in Amish environs, for all the writing I've read reminding me that the Amish aren't cast in amber, that they feel the cultural waters getting choppier, too, and so on, I still was surprised to hear a note of anxiety in this young woman's voice. *In what way*, I wondered to myself, *does* her *world change?* I guess I'd figured that, because the party line was that the Amish were exceedingly nimble at addressing rapid technological change, that meant that each individual Amish person felt confident that they were de facto protected against the onslaught of modernity. The generations before them had gone to enormous lengths to shield the precious jewel of their culture, and now that they weren't being literally massacred, the pressure to gird themselves against destruction wasn't as intense as the type felt by people living in the mainstream, who have to scramble to make tiny atomized shelters from the world, or who have no shelter at all.

But maybe that was a naïve assumption. In my own community, there is enormous concern over making sure things like Shabbat are maintained; I know it, because I feel it. When my own children ask wearily if Shabbat is over so they can listen to an audiobook, or if I catch one of them cheekily flicking a light on and off, watching to gauge my reaction, I wonder if I'll be able to adequately communicate to them how priceless this resource is, how much others wish they could have what we have. What will it be like when they're teenagers, and they just want to spend the day posting on Instagram or TikTok or whatever is cool a decade from now? Will they treasure the long, relaxed Saturday afternoons of their childhood, the endless lunches and conversations and restorative naps? If they decide to dismantle their palaces in time, so that one day simply bleeds into the next, so that no time is sacred but rather every moment is an opportunity for the world to infringe on their consciousness or for them to project their private selves outward toward some hungry, faceless mass, will they yearn for the days we had no agenda but to be together and read and walk outside, admiring the newly blossoming bushes and the lightning bugs making their cheery debut at dusk?

The height of our fences is, in many ways, justified. Tradition has died before, after all; children have walked away, seduced by the buzzy siren song of the new and the quick and the easy. Even those who unequivocally opted for the bigger, rougher world over the simpler, smaller one seem sometimes unsure the cost of entry was worth it in the end.

Many years ago, in the course of writing a story about Amish converts, I met a woman who'd moved to rural Ohio with her young family in the 1970s. They'd gone aspiring to be homesteaders, but ended up joining a Swartzentruber Amish community. The Swartzentrubers are one of the most conservative of all Amish sects; to this day, they eschew indoor plumbing; putting accoutrements on their buggies, including yellow flashing lights for traffic safety; Velcro; and propane gas, among other things. It was clear that this woman, who'd left after fourteen years in the church, held a great deal of resentment toward her former friends and neighbors, but she also mentioned numerous times during our lengthy conversation that it would be sad if the Amish were to disappear. I asked her why, if she thought the Amish were a repressive force, their eradication would be a tragedy. Her response was one of the most poetic things I've ever heard someone say aloud, almost like an incantation. I think about it all the time. As you say it in your head, imagine a quiet, steady voice, taking ample opportunity to pause.

"Well," she began, "they would be probably the last living examples, in America, of that particular life. You know, it's adulterated. They've got maybe a phone booth at the end of the road or something. There's some concessions they've made to living in this century, but it's almost a look-back, like one of these historical farms or something, but they're actually doing it full time. The ways of doing even little things, how to put the harness on the horse, or when do you plant those corn seeds? Well, you wait 'til the oak leaf is the size of a squirrel's ear and then you go plant your corn. Then it's safe. All those things would be lost. What is the value of it? Well, I think that there is value in seeing how people who are different from the vast majority, how other people make it from one day to the next. How they conduct their lives. I think that's important. Just to look at it and see. What did somebody else do when faced with this? I think that's important."

6.

ORIANNE, TO THE EXPANSIVE SILENCE OF CATHOLICISM

Her speech is silence and her silence speech.

—SAINT JEROME ON THE LIFE OF
SAINT ASELLA OF ROME

In her youth, Orianne Dyck was what one might have called spiritually precocious. One of her earliest memories is from when she was three or four years old: she was running around the outside of her house with her brothers, and she looked up at the clear blue sky and flashed God a smile. "I just knew He was there, and I knew He was smiling back at me," she'd later say of the experience. "I can't tell you how many times I have gone back to that memory and that conviction that I had in that moment of *God is there*."

Her only dark night of the soul was more of an experiment: at around ten years old, she began to realize that many people around her didn't believe in God—indeed, they "actually scoffed at the idea of His existence"—so she wondered if maybe faith was something irrational and specific to her family, an odd superstition passed down through the generations. "And I remember very distinctly going to my room one day after wondering that for a while, and sitting on my bed and saying, okay, if God exists, that should make a really huge difference. And if He doesn't exist, then you should notice. It should *mean* something."

She sat perched on her windowsill and looked out at the world for five minutes, trying to view the landscape as though God did not exist, to see if that changed her perception. "Everything looked so *empty*," she told me, "and I realized that God's presence brings extra meaning to things and holds things in love. And that was the thing that allowed me to love the trees and to love the sky because that was coming from Him." Orianne didn't even last the entire five minutes. "As soon as I recognized that was a thing, I was like, Oh, so He exists. The end!"

Orianne was born in 1990 in Winnipeg, Manitoba, the eldest of three children; she was a "shy, but also friendly" child, "just by disposition, a cheerful person," who enjoyed reading, soccer, and friendships. Her family had a unique religious makeup (she often calls her parents a "made in Manitoba only" mix). Her father's father came from a line of assimilated liberal Mennonites—she couldn't recall any horse-and-buggy ancestors, and her paternal grandfather held a PhD in genetics, which would be unlikely in a conservative Anabaptist milieu—while his mother's family were members of the United Church of Canada, the largest mainline Protestant denomination in the country.

Her mother's parents were Lebanese Druze. The Druze are an ethnocentric, esoteric, nonproselytizing people dotted throughout the Levant region, with many today residing in Syria, Lebanon, Jordan, and Israel. The exact tenets of Druze beliefs are kept secret as the faith closed to converts around 1044. It's considered an offshoot of Islam, sharing its monotheism; its view of the major figures of the Abrahamic faiths, including Moses, Jesus, and Mohammed, as prophets; and an Arabic linguistic and cultural bent. But it also draws on Greek philosophy and Hinduism (for example, Druze believe in reincarnation). It is a tradition suspicious of ritual, asserting that the three major monotheistic faiths rely too heavily on ceremony as a foolproof means of absolution; consequently, the Druze have no holy days, no fasts, and no fixed forms of prayer, a stark contrast to the faith tradition Orianne would join later in life.

Despite the Druze taboo on intermarriage (in Israel, for example, fewer than 1 percent of Druze marry outside the faith), Orianne's grandparents allowed their thoroughly Canadian children to marry for love, causing them to be ostracized from the wider family. "I've never met my Druze family," she said. "They don't know I exist. I don't know who they are." Her grandmother didn't even know her own mother had passed away until one of her family members broke ranks and contacted her to pass along the news.

Though Orianne's mother wasn't technically considered a Druze—anyone who marries outside the faith loses their status, and there aren't really "culturally" Druze people the way there are cultural Jews and Catholics—Orianne was still deeply influenced by the faith of her maternal ancestors. For instance, Orianne's mother encouraged her children to read the Quran, one holy book according to the Druze, and she lived and breathed the Druze view of God as a being who suffuses every moment of one's life and of all experience as a form of prayer, which had a significant impact on her daughter. "I always had a very strong sense of God's presence as a child. I wouldn't say that I had a defined idea of who He *was* necessarily, but I did have a strong sense of His presence. Some of my earliest memories are of some type of natural form of prayer that just spontaneously comes out of your heart."

From the beginning, Orianne's mom was the one who made decisions about the family's faith. Somewhat ironically, considering she herself never had been baptized, she felt strongly that her children should be, and decided to have them baptized into the United Church of Canada. It was also her mother who would take the family to church every Sunday (her dad joined "sometimes"). Orianne enjoyed church: she liked sitting up straight and proper in the pews, drawing pictures of Jesus with the loaves and fishes during Sunday school, consuming the Welch's grape juice and cubes of fluffy white bread they'd have for their communion. At such a tender age, she found it amazing that the ritual of the bread and the grape juice connected her to people thousands of years ago, that "something happened so far back to a specific group of people that impacts how we live our life and see our identity now."

When Orianne was seven, her family moved to Deep River, Ontario, a small town along the banks of the Ottawa River, for her dad's job. Upon the move, her mom began looking for a new church to attend; she never explained her concerns to her daughter, so all Orianne ever knew was that her mom felt that the United Church of Canada wasn't as "biblically grounded" as she'd like it to be. As a child, Orianne's mother had once gone with a friend to a Catholic church, and she fondly recalled how "reverent" the service was and the focus on scripture, so she decided to start taking the family to Mass (her dad's attendance dwindled to only holidays, and Orianne told me she thought he might have felt a little alienated, especially as he knew he shouldn't be receiving Catholic Communion as a Protestant).

Though certain aspects were off-putting to young Orianne—the statues of Mary and Joseph were "a little bit worrisome" and strange to a child raised essentially Protestant, because of the latter's aversion to iconography—she ultimately preferred it to her previous church. "United Church is really a beautiful faith community and there's a re-

ally strong sense of God as your friend, someone you can trust, someone who's intimate," she told me. But it was during Catholic services
that Orianne first started to feel the enormity and significance of God
as not just a friend, but the creator of the universe. "There was this
beautiful understanding of His fullness," she said. "Even the physical
element of how worship was expressed, there was a fullness of how you
worship—not just with your mind and your heart, but also with your
body"—the smells of the incense, the feeling of the cold floor as you
knelt down—"and your whole self." It was that wholeness—her own,
and her God's—that eventually proved irresistible to her, and that she
would later sacrifice a great deal to pursue.

Anthony the Great—not to be confused with other saints named Anthony, like Anthony of Padua—was born to a wealthy Christian family
in Egypt in the middle of the second century CE. What little we do
know about him comes from his biographer, Athanasius, a Coptic
Christian and erstwhile pope, who describes young Anthony as equan-
imous and simpleminded (in a good way), a child who, despite the considerable resources of his family, "was content simply with what he
found nor sought anything further." Both his parents died when he
was in his late teens, leaving him executor of their estate (around three
hundred acres or so of land, plus a substantial monetary inheritance) as
well as guardian of his younger sister.

Not long after their deaths, Anthony was on his way to church, contemplating how Christians of his time would frequently abandon their
entire lives to follow Christ. When he arrived, the Gospel reading was
auspiciously on that very same topic: "If you would be perfect, go and

sell that you have and give to the poor; and come follow Me and you shall have treasure in heaven," Jesus says to a rich young man, as transcribed by the apostle Matthew. The man departs deflated, to which Jesus responds with one of his most famous dictums: "It is easier for a camel to go through the eye of a needle, than for a rich man to enter into the Kingdom of God."

Anthony was flabbergasted. Feeling as though "the passage had been read on his account," he left the church and began immediately divesting himself of his possessions (he even gave his sister to a community of virgins). Then he began a self-directed study in asceticism, visiting local hermits and learning their ways: how they eschewed anger, fasted, prayed "unceasingly," and studied. After a harrowing battle with the devil, who tried all manner of temptation to persuade Anthony to deviate from his nascent saintly ways, Anthony shut himself inside a tomb outside his village, instructing a sympathizer to intermittently throw him some bread—by then, the entirety of his diet—and continued to wage spiritual warfare.

When he later pushed himself further into the desert, seeking an even greater isolation, a curious thing began to happen: just as Anthony had sought out hermits to learn their pious ways, now others, so hungry for spiritual leadership they tried to "wrench off the door by force," began to seek his counsel. When he finally emerged, twenty years later, he looked healthy and peaceful—hardly what you'd imagine of a man who'd lived in a cave eating only bread for two decades—and gave such sage and calming advice that other seekers began to move nearby and become ascetics themselves. "And thus it happened in the end that cells arose even in the mountains," wrote Athanasius, "and the desert was colonized by monks, who came forth from their own people, and enrolled themselves for the citizenship in the heavens."

———

Anthony was not the first hermit; that distinction is usually given to Paul of Thebes, who is said to have lived alone in the desert for almost a hundred years. Men like them went to the desert because it was geographically convenient, but more importantly, because it was a place of spiritual sojourn—where the Israelites wandered after the exodus, where Jesus himself was tempted by Satan. The desert was (and is) the purest topographical metaphor for desolation; it "offered them nothing," as the Catholic monk Thomas Merton wrote. "There was nothing to attract them. There was nothing to exploit."

Anthony also wasn't the first monk to find that a community developed organically around him in his self-imposed isolation: early Christian desert spirituality is riddled with figures who sought anonymity in the harshest environs only to be hotly pursued by needy fans. My favorite has to be Simeon Stylite, a Syrian Christian ascetic born in the fourth century, whose piety was so extreme—he was too vigorous in his self-flagellation, and he refused to eat except on Sundays—that he was kicked out of a monastery as a teenager. Simeon Stylite amassed such a crowd of followers that he eventually sought refuge atop a tall pillar near Aleppo, where he lived for thirty-seven years. (Even Simeon's hermeticism had its limits, though: he implemented set times to address his legion of visitors in the afternoons, an early example of Christian monastics' desire to balance solitary contemplation with hospitality.) Other hermits would go on to found monasteries or lauras—compounds of sorts in which groups of hermits could live in separate dwellings but come together for prayer, work, or meals—when the trickle of seekers grew into a steady stream.

Gradually and organically, even the kind of rogue, DIY spirituality embodied by the Desert Fathers became more regimented and institutional. Community leaders often wrote "Rules," blueprints that provided a mixture of spiritual guidance and logistical precepts to help the monastery function smoothly and the new monks hone their religious practice. Arguably the most famous and influential rule was authored by Saint Benedict of Nursia in the sixth century. Saint Benedict preached constant personal vigilance by the monks, whom he believed should be prepared "to serve like soldiers under holy obedience"; he stressed deference to the monastery's abbot and strongly criticized "Sarabaites" (monks who lived alone or in small groups) and the "Girovagi" (who were individualistic like the Sarabaites but nomadic) for refusing to answer to any (earthly) authority. His instructions ranged from the grand—one should "love enemies" and "put one's hope in God"—to the granular, such as how many psalms should be said at night or how the monks' sleeping arrangements should be organized. To this day, orders of monasteries and convents live by a written rule, many of which have remained unchanged for hundreds of years.

Early monastics were not always men: women, too, heeded the call of God and wandered off to the desert, or found themselves ensconced in a monastery, or set up a miniature community with a group of similarly pious ladies in city dwellings. Many young women of yore insisted on becoming religious to protest certain values contemporary feminists also vociferously decry—namely, the prioritization of wealth, marriage, and procreation above the right to self-determination (although a nun might quibble with the use of "self" there: she wouldn't see her choice as made in service of her own well-being, and might not even see it as one *she* made at all, but rather one God made for her). Indeed, the women at the center of these stories would still strike us as radical or countercultural today—chopping off their hair; eschewing comfort and privilege; and indulging in behavior that looks borderline insane to outsiders.

When faced with impending marriage, for example, Clare of Assisi ran away from home and chucked her fancy outfits in favor of plain robes, joining a Benedictine monastery with the help of Saint Francis (she later wrote the rule for what would become some of the strictest orders of nuns in the Catholic Church, the Poor Clares. In certain Poor Clare monasteries, the nuns sleep on straw mattresses, wake up in the middle of the night to pray, and go barefoot much of the time). Macrina the Elder, born into a noble Cappadocian family, began adopting ascetic habits when her fiancé died, eating with the household's servants and wearing similar clothes. She eventually dispensed of her family's money, turned her estate into a monastery, and influenced her brothers to convert to Christianity (four of her nine siblings were eventually declared saints). As a child, Ida of Nivelles would beg for bread, cheese, shoes, and medicines for patients at a local hospital. Many religious women tended to the sick, indigent, or otherwise socially outcast people, beginning what would become the long Catholic history in health care; many, too, gave away enormous sums of wealth to the poor.

A Catholic woman of a certain age today might have had a childhood in which nuns or sisters loomed large (a nun generally refers to a cloistered religious woman, who lives a "hidden" life of prayer in a monastery; a sister is an "active" nun, often engaged in industries like teaching or eldercare, though many, including nuns and sisters themselves, use these terms interchangeably). They might have been their kindly aunt or the funnily dressed ladies they saw at Sunday Mass or, as with my childhood nanny, their tyrannical educator. In her memoir *Virgin Time: In Search of the Contemplative Life*, the writer Patricia Hampl recalled her friends' fascination with the somewhat aloof sisters who taught at her Saint Paul, Minnesota, high school, the way the girls would try to determine who came from one of the city's prominent families or peek behind the door to catch a glimpse of their quarters. "The life lived within these red brick walls was so clearly *something*, in distinction to the random snarl of existence littering life in general, life *out there*." (The nuns didn't ever say as much, Hampl hastened to add; they seemed too "busy" to do too much judging.)

But statistics from the late twentieth century on Catholic religious vocations show a demographic in free fall. In 2021, there were fewer than fifty thousand professed Catholic sisters in the United States, down from around one hundred eighty thousand in 1965; one study, from 2009, concluded that there were more nuns older than ninety than younger than sixty. There are lots of theories as to why this happened, most of which ring at least somewhat true: a decreased appetite for sacrifice in an increasingly secular world, the terrible PR from the sex abuse scandals that have roiled the church since the 1980s, more options for women who wish to live independent lives of intellect or service and remain unmarried.

In recent years, scholars, journalists, and people who work in vocations have suggested that religious life could be poised for a modest resurgence. In 2015 in the United Kingdom, there was a wave of media content highlighting how a number of Catholic organizations were noticing an uptick in the number of young women "discerning a vocation" (that's Catholic for "trying to figure out what God's plan is for them"). The trend made it across the pond to the United States a few years later: A 2017 survey by Georgetown University showed that 10 percent of never-married Catholic female respondents had considered becoming a sister, up slightly for millennials and particularly among nonwhite millennials, statistics some writers have noted with awe.

But it's a long road from consideration to active pursuance—"Is there a Catholic girl who has not paused, for a longer or shorter fantasy, over that possibility?" Hampl rhetorically asks—so it's still unclear how all that interest will manifest. It remains the case that, for most young women today, their most salient image of a nun is Julie Andrews twirling atop a mountain or Whoopi Goldberg chafing against Maggie Smith's prissy authoritativeness in *Sister Act*, or, in Orianne's case, the sister who walked into the Tim Horton's chain restaurant where she was working as a teenage waitress. That sister only spoke French, though, so in the end, she and Orianne could barely communicate.

※

Orianne's mom—whom I've never met but envision as a kind of spiritual savant—didn't really understand that becoming a Catholic was a little bit more complicated than just showing up to Mass. This kind of blissful religious ignorance extended to her children's education as well: because Catholic school is free and open to all in Manitoba (a holdover law from France's reign), Orianne's mother enrolled her kids there, not really pausing to consider that there might be times when their status as non-Catholics would pose an issue. Ultimately, Orianne recalled, "she really wanted me to be educated in a space where there was an allowance for prayer and a celebration of prayer."

The attitude toward prayer in her home was not as regimented as it would be in a traditional Catholic family's, nor as it was in Orianne's school. "We would pray together before bedtime. But in terms of communal prayer, that was the most we would do together as a family." She found the traditional Catholic prayer she learned at school difficult: she wasn't good at memorization, and she didn't understand why it had to be so monotonous. *Why am I repeating myself over and over and over again?* she wondered. *He heard me the first time!*

For whatever reason, everyone at Orianne's school just kind of assumed the Dyck family was already Catholic, to the point that when Orianne's second-grade class was getting ready to receive their First Communion, she was shuffled through the lessons with her classmates. One day, while a teacher was speaking about the Eucharist, Orianne—who, at eight years old, was already very well versed in her Bible, having been given a children's version to read at home—raised her hand and began to argue, albeit politely.

"Actually, miss," she said, "cannibalism is forbidden in the Old Testament and Jesus would never break his own law. If the Eucharist *is* his body and blood, we couldn't actually eat it because that would be cannibalism. So that doesn't make any sense."

The teacher was flummoxed. "It is *body and blood*," she repeated, and Orianne, taught not to disrespect her elders, didn't press the issue. She ended up taking Communion with that class, but years later, she'd admit during an interview on a podcast called *The Cordial Catholic* that she had some trepidation about the way it worked out. "I'm just going to be really honest: I should not have been given First Communion." In hindsight, though, she recognized this mistake gave her a gift: it allowed her to wrestle with her doubts in a way she wouldn't have been able to had she abstained.

In the fifth grade, Orianne transferred back to a public school; it had a French immersion program and her mom felt it was important for her to learn Canada's second official language. The school was more multicultural than others in the area because there was a medical research facility nearby and the children of scientists from all over the globe who relocated to the area attended. Though she was no longer in a Catholic milieu daily, a sense of unease regarding her sometimes-faith still plagued her. She would catch a religious debate on TV about whether Christ was really the Messiah and feel compelled to watch, though many other eleven-year-olds would have immediately changed the channel to cartoons. When on occasion she would go to church with her Protestant friends or discuss the Bible with them, she found herself struggling with the idea that Catholics and Protestants often interpreted biblical texts differently, even though only one, she knew, could be correct. She took long walks through the streets of Deep River, a diminutive figure with a mop of dark Botticelli ringlets, praying "very honestly and vulnerably" for greater insight into God, for the ability to know Him. "I also prayed the other dangerous prayer of asking the Lord to bring me where He was most fully," she recalled on *The Cordial Catholic.* "And I was like, I don't care where that is. I will go there. *I will go there.*"

Her perambulations with God were ultimately what led to her decision to get confirmed with her peers from the Catholic school (confirmation is the final of the three sacraments of initiation in Catholicism, after baptism and Holy Communion, and usually occurs around age thirteen). Compared to her First Communion, which was more perfunctory, pursuing confirmation felt like an act of true agency. But in hearing her story, it wasn't what I would pinpoint as her real road-to-Damascus moment. That would happen shortly after her confirmation.

Though she'd more or less decided to identify as Catholic and stop debating, if only internally, between Catholicism and Protestantism, Orianne still felt a deep connection with her Druze roots, and often read the Quran. In her bedroom, she'd set up a miniature altar on her dresser ("I was that kind of kid") upon which sat a crucifix made from cedar of Lebanon, a blue Bible, and a green copy of the Quran, side by side. One evening, she was reading the Quran when she noticed the following passage:

That they said (in boast), "We killed Christ Jesus the son of Mary, the Messenger of Allah"; but they killed him not, nor crucified him, but so it was made to appear to them, and those who differ therein are full of doubts, with no (certain) knowledge, but only conjecture to follow, for of a surety they killed him not.

There are a number of interpretations of this passage, including that it wasn't actually Jesus who was crucified but a lookalike, or that Jesus only *appeared* to die, and that people thinking he did was the result of mass delusion or divine hallucination. As it had in the past, it occurred to Orianne that only one of these could be true: either Jesus was crucified, or he wasn't. Since her earliest youth, she'd always known God to be the purest and most powerful expression of love. Which is the greater love, she asked herself: sacrificing your only son for the sake of humanity, or only giving the illusion of having done that? The answer was as clear as water. And so Orianne "very lovingly and affectionately" took her Quran off her dresser-altar and put it onto her bookshelf, moving her Bible directly beneath the crucifix and leaving it there. "It was a very difficult moment, I have to say, for me, and very emotional."

This isn't to say all her questions were completely answered. Throughout her teen years—she returned to Catholic school for high school—she still wrestled with some pretty fundamental aspects of the faith. Praying to the saints struck her as borderline idolatrous, and she didn't totally understand why priests needed to be men. "It irked me," she said. "I thought it was a little bit archaic." When she was a kid, her dad hadn't been terribly worked up about conventional gender roles, but her mom was quite traditional and made her do ballet even though she wanted to do karate like her two brothers, so being forced into prescribed jobs based on one's sex preemptively annoyed her.

But gradually, her questions were answered through various channels. At school, she joined a group of students who prayed the Rosary together, and they were able to elucidate some of the biblical "mysteries" Catholics meditate on while praying the Rosary and dispel the myth that it's a prayer "to" Mary. She also watched YouTube channels like Catholic Answers and the one run by Father Mike Schmitz, a priest and minor internet celebrity with all the energy but little of the creepiness of Tony Robbins (Schmitz would later become well known for his wildly popular podcast *The Bible in One Year*).

At eighteen, Orianne entered Trent University, a four-hour drive away from her home, where she studied anthropology and international development. She'd always been interested in land conservation, especially from a social justice perspective, and she planned to go abroad to study in an international development program. But before she left her parents informed their kids they were divorcing, and Orianne decided she needed to stay home to support her family through the transition. The divorce was "very hard" for her, prompting a period of intense reflection, sadness, and self-doubt.

At university, she hadn't been as diligent about going to Mass as she had been in high school—"You're young and tired and stressed and have fun things to do," as she put it—but in her moment of despair, she looked to God for comfort, as she always had. One night, unable to sleep, she found herself sobbing and pouring her heart out to God ("I literally wrote Him a six-page letter"), and when morning finally came, she knew she had to go to confession, even though it was one of those Catholic things she'd never really been able to get on board with. "I couldn't understand why for any reason you would have to go to a person, like a physical *person*, to say anything that you wanted to ask God's forgiveness for. I didn't understand why you couldn't just say it in your room, you know?" But she dragged herself to the nearest Catholic church, so nervous she felt like "puking," and told the priest there that she hadn't been to confession in years but felt like her inner turmoil wouldn't stop until she did. He walked her through the process and gave her absolution. "I walked out of there with a freedom that I didn't know I could have again. And I couldn't have told you after that all of the logical reasons why one ought to go to confession. But I knew that God had asked me to, and I knew that it was real, and I knew that it worked.

"So when I went to confession that one time, it kind of kick-started me to go back to Mass every week and to go to confession once a month," she said, a practice she carried on through changing professional tracks and attending a teaching master's program, through a stint teaching in the United Kingdom, then back home, where she got a job teaching French at the Catholic school she herself had attended. She also got involved in youth ministry.

But despite her very observant lifestyle, she still felt something was lacking. "I was just kind of realizing that even for my own happiness or my own fulfillment, I wanted to be able to give more," she told me. "I wanted to be able to receive God more, if that makes sense. And I didn't know how." This was confusing to Orianne—she was working so hard at her teaching job, which she loved, almost to the point of burnout; she was doing all the things a faithful Catholic ought to do. What else could she possibly be expected to give? "There was no reason I should be feeling this way," she said.

While working in youth ministry, she supervised a group of high school kids visiting the mission house of the Sisters of Saint Joseph in Chincha Alta, a city on the Pacific coast of Peru. With houses around the globe, the Sisters of Saint Joseph, who don't wear habits, serve the needs of whatever community they're in; in Peru, Orianne recalls them building houses and doing the legwork for poor families to enroll their children in school. (Because children couldn't go to school without shoes, families would bring them to the convent, where the sisters would measure them and buy their shoes.) It was the first time she began to wonder if maybe religious life was "a little bit less austere and a little bit more life-giving than I would have thought."

Still, when a sister looked directly at her and said something in Spanish, and another attendee translated that she'd said Orianne would make a good sister, Orianne was sort of offended. Outside *The Sound of Music* and that one sister she'd met waitressing, Orianne most closely associated nuns with the church-run Canadian residential schools for Indigenous children. The schools, which operated from 1883 to 1996, became notorious in Canada for their appalling conditions: aside from the existential wound of having their culture ripped from them, the Native children there were routinely subjected to physical and sexual abuse. When they died—from tuberculosis or Spanish flu or a fire in one of the shoddy campus buildings or somewhere out in the wilderness, trying to make their way back home—their parents sometimes weren't even informed. Indigenous communities today estimate that the total number of "missing children" could be anywhere from three thousand to thirty thousand. Indications of grave sites have been found on school grounds; some remains will, undoubtedly, never be located. Orianne was horrified by these stories, and couldn't imagine associating herself with the perpetrators of such violence. Besides, she figured the sisters were eyeing her because she was young and single, which further irritated her: she liked her life, and she wasn't worried about her ability to attract a guy in the long run!

Still, over the ensuing few months, numerous others wondered aloud to Orianne about whether she'd ever considered a religious vocation. Finally, while accompanying a group of teens to a Catholic conference in Toronto, a priest said something that pushed her over the edge. There was a public confession being offered at the conference, with about fifty priests prepared to hear from any number of anxious high schoolers, and Orianne, sensing the kids' trepidation, offered to go first. During the confession, the priest asked if she'd ever considered her vocation.

"I don't know what God wants of me right now, other than just living fully in the present moment," Orianne replied.

"I don't know, but I just feel like there's something there," he said. "Maybe you want to talk to your parish priest."

Even though she was rattled, something seemed to click into place for her. She'd wanted to give more of herself to God, but she hadn't understood this feeling: Why would she be having it if she weren't meant to make a drastic change, and what is it she could have possibly done *except* discern a religious vocation?

Orianne followed the advice and reached out to her parish priest. Twice they made an appointment, and twice it fell through. The second time the meeting was canceled, Orianne sat in her driveway, looking up at the dark August sky, furious. *This isn't meant to be after all,* she thought. She prayed too: *give me a sign, God.* It was meteor shower season, and so she asked God to send her a shooting star. But almost immediately, her error struck her: she was threatening the God she'd had such an intuitive, deep relationship with since childhood. She immediately recanted; she knew He wanted her to make that third appointment, meteor or no meteor.

Her priest was bogged down in his own work but pointed her to online directories of religious orders, like Vocations Canada (she'd wanted to stay in Canada), and described how the process of discerning was a bit like early dating: more about asking questions and considering possibilities than immediately locking yourself into one thing forever.

While browsing the listings of orders, one name caught her eye: the

Daughters of Saint Paul. Founded in 1915 by Father James Alberione and Sister Venerable Mother Thecla Merlo in northern Italy, the group's charism, or main mission, is to "evangelize through the media" using "the most modern and efficacious means." Historically, that's meant publishing religious literature and operating bookshops. While they still do those things today, they have also developed some very twenty-first-century side hustles: one sister, a former punk rock fan, had a Twitter devoted to memento mori, the practice of regularly contemplating one's own mortality; two share an Instagram dedicated to the main convent's gardens (@nunsplow); yet another started a Zoom Rosary group dedicated to Anthony Fauci during the coronavirus pandemic. Inevitably, if you come across an article about nuns on TikTok, it will feature the Daughters of Saint Paul. There are Daughters of Saint Paul houses in Canada, throughout the United States, and all over the globe, everywhere from Japan to Colombia to Spain to Pakistan. (The contraction of religious life in recent decades has affected the Daughters of Saint Paul too: in 2022, they closed four of their houses in the United States.) Originally, Orianne had assumed she'd join a teaching order, because she still loved nurturing children, but she felt immediately attracted to the quirky, joyful women she saw on the Daughters of Saint Paul's website. They looked, she thought, very much *themselves*.

In 2019, *The New York Times* published an article about a curious project called "Nuns and Nones" in which millennial "nones"—young people who don't ascribe to a religious tradition—moved into a convent for six months in a kind of spiritual take on MTV's *The Real World*. The impetus, one of the millennial organizers explained, was that the young participants had been searching for ways they could live "radical activist lives, lives of total devotion to their causes," and realized that convents were intentional communities designed to support this exact impulse.

Much to the sisters' surprise, the new occupants' first and most pressing question concerned one specific aspect of the nuns' lifestyle. "I said to the other sisters, 'You will never guess what the millennials want to talk about: the vows,'" Sister Patsy Harney told the reporter Nellie Bowles. "Everybody laughed. It was kind of like a joke, you know?"

Poverty, chastity, and obedience: they are a famous trio of bummers invoked by Catholic consecrated people, including sisters and nuns but also priests, monks, hermits, and consecrated virgins, with some tweaking here and there depending on the context (certain orders of cloistered nuns, for example, also take a vow of enclosure, while Benedictines take a vow of stability, which means they ideally remain in one monastery for their entire lives). At first glance, they seem to imply that a Catholic life—certainly of the consecrated variety but also generally—is a joyless, sexless one, filled with self-mortification of the most harrowing sort, a life in which one indiscriminately bows down to any and all ruling figures. It would probably be surprising to many that Catholics believe that all Christians—indeed, all people—are obligated in some of them, and that none are meant to be unduly onerous or torturous, despite the numerous saints with a predilection for hairshirts. What they entail isn't always as specific as Jewish or Muslim law, but neither are they as vague as (most) Protestant edicts; rather, they exist on a sort of spectrum, by which being "called to poverty" might mean anything from "eschews unnecessary consumerism" all the way through "lives as a mendicant," whereas being called to obedience could refer to recognition of the wisdom of the collective body and a refusal to center the self, as Saint Benedict himself codified in his rule.

The vows aren't always cast in obvious terms either: I've seen poverty defined by nuns not only financially, but also temporally—that part of the poverty of life in a monastery is renouncing control over one's own time—as well as in terms of the personality, meaning that one should try not to be too unusual or exceptional, lest one distinguish herself too much from her fellow women. Contrary to popular opinion, chastity isn't synonymous with celibacy and doesn't imply a hatred of sex; it's just a mandate to live a life of sexual health, even if that does mean constructing certain fences around your sexuality and treating it with due reverence.

"[T]here is nothing about chastity per se that makes it the sole preserve of consecrated religious," the writer and Dominican nun Sister Carino Hodder has written. "There is nothing in [its] definition about renouncing marriage and sexual relations. The call to chastity applies just as much to spouses and to single people looking for romance as it does to consecrated religious, for all the faithful are called to a graced integration of our sexuality with our desires and our state of life." Though living in accordance with all the vows may involve some amount of pain or difficulty, the goal isn't a simple debasement of the human spirit; rather, Catholics see them as removing obstacles that might prevent the individual from becoming as Christlike or as "perfect" as possible. (A nun once used that word when describing the end goal of the vows for me, but she did so while making air quotes with her hands and rolling her eyes: clearly, she did not see herself that way.)

Why were the millennials in this article so attracted to the vows? By their own admission, they felt their values too amorphous, their lifestyles too free; they craved a spirituality and sense of ritual so much they were able to overlook the stickier aspects—like the fact that chastity, as defined by the Church, would automatically and unequivocally preclude sex outside marriage or nonstraight sex—and latch on to the aspects that seemed more zeitgeist friendly. And they aren't alone in their attraction: though the vows seem anathema to contemporary values, chastity and poverty are on the verge of making a comeback (obedience, not so much). Squint and you'll see vows of poverty in miniature all around us, like the increasingly popular idea of giving up shopping for a stretch, or, as in the case of some effective altruists, making ruthless calculations of one's income with a mind toward giving away all but the bare minimum to charity. And though we're more celebratory of all sorts of sexual arrangements other than long-term heterosexual marriages and far more open, for better or worse, about the details of our sex lives, there's also the rather paradoxical adoption of celibacy as a wellness endeavor. The new celibacy usually looks different for men and women: for men, it's the NoFap movement, which originated on Reddit and links abstaining from masturbation with mental clarity and physical strength, whereas celibacy for women is less about physical flourishing and more about emotional self-actualization (it's also often cast as a way of protecting oneself against male boorishness and sexual violence). "My evenings at home became richer and less predictable now that I spent them alone," the writer Melissa Febos wrote in an essay on her year of celibacy, which she describes as a period of bountiful creativity and self-knowledge. "Instead of talking to lovers on the phone at night, I read and ruminated. I called friends in other cities. . . . For the first time, I got to know my own tastes, unaffected by the preferences of another."

It's deeply surprising to see this kind of attitude toward sex voiced today, but on the other hand, maybe it's obvious, given how many religious practices—Shabbat, meditation, fasting—have been appropriated for personal optimization purposes. It also makes sense that the pendulum would swing back from early aughts *Sex and the City*–style attitudes, as is the inevitable course of trend cycles. Undeniably, our culture remains deeply confused about the nature of sex. "We act as if life without sex is impossible, and entertain the thought, even if less commonly nowadays than in my youth, that sex with strangers is harmless," the philosopher Zena Hitz, a convert to Catholicism who spent three years as a lay monastic at Madonna House, wrote in her book *A Philosopher Looks at the Religious Life*. "Both cannot be true: Either sex reaches down to the core of our being, and so ought to be treated with reverence and caution . . . or it is harmless, like chewing bubble gum, and can be given up without a second thought." (Mainstream society's warped attitudes toward sex are also commonly pointed out by the asexual community: "The truth of the gender inequality in sexual freedom, and the importance of teaching women to honor their sexual desires, has distorted into the belief that female sexual liberation only looks like [promiscuity]," as Angela wrote in *Ace*. "Overcorrection doesn't solve the problem.")

The Daughters of Saint Paul don't sleep on straw mattresses like Poor Clares, and they wear shoes whenever any average person would. They don't take on extra-special penances; Alberione considered it a penance enough that they had to "accept with a joyful spirit the mortifications demanded by common life in religious observance" (in other words, it's hard enough to live with a bunch of roommates, let's not make it worse). But their life involves a level of giving up that many modern people, even millennials besotted with the notion of "ritual," would probably consider untenable. As the order provides for the needs of its sisters—medicine for the infirm or elderly, special food items for those with dietary restrictions—none of them are allowed to have a bank account or a credit card in their name. Each sister has a laptop and a smartphone designated for her use, because the order's founder stressed that they should have the best tools for the mission, but none of them actually *own* these objects. They wear uniforms daily: a white button-down shirt, a midcalf skirt, sensible dark shoes, a veil, and a Daughters emblem necklace, depending on whether they are officially professed or not. They don't shave their heads, but need to keep their hair short beneath their veils. (They cut each other's.) If an old friend is passing through town and wants to go out for coffee, they can so long as it fits with their prayer schedule and they clear it with their superiors, which doesn't sound all that different from having a job and asking your boss to go on a long lunch break, until you consider that their bosses also live with them and eat with them and pray with them. Similarly, if they want to go home to visit family, they need to ask permission; it's usually granted unless it's an inconvenient time for the mission, in which case it would give the sister a chance to practice obedience. There's also the matter of money: that Starbucks a Daughter of Saint Paul enjoyed with her friend would have to be purchased by said friend, or by some other generous benefactor, because the order lives largely off donations. They do get some income from their publishing ventures—though their earnings have plummeted over the past few decades—but for other costs, like food or building renovations, they rely on outsider support.

Personally, I don't *feel* deprived of much because of my religious beliefs. Though there are strains of it in Hasidism, Judaism isn't an overly ascetic faith; mostly, it's a belief system that exalts moderation in most things. I'm still able to live in my own house, acquire possessions, go on vacation, and so on. Because I'm "modern" Orthodox, I can partake of a wide range of cultural offerings in the form of literature, film, and art, although I try to do so judiciously. But there are some things I have had to let go of, and though many of these feel puny in comparison to what desert ascetics or contemporary nuns relinquish, I am often surprised to be reminded that others are slightly scandalized by this, until I remember that our secular contemporary culture—which largely venerates the ability to have one's desires *met*, rather than the ability to *overcome* said desires—has given people almost no framework for understanding sacrifice.

Keeping kosher seems to rankle outsiders in just this way. Though I was a New England kid, raised on the idea of lobster dipped in warm melted butter as the ultimate gustatory pleasure, I didn't find it unduly difficult to eliminate what some call glatt treif: extremely nonkosher things like pork, shellfish, and chicken parm or other dairy-meat combos. (On occasion I feel a pang of longing if I think about gulping briny oysters, but if I sit with the feeling enough, I realize it's more for the implied glamour of such a meal rather than the actual taste.) Still, though, it isn't really the area of Jewish practice I love the most. I can understand its purpose from a sociological perspective—our dietary restrictions mean we are bound to eat more often with other Jews, thus strengthening our communal bonds—but logistically speaking, it can be a nightmare: there are very few kosher restaurants in the world, and telling someone you can't eat things cooked in their oven never fails to be offensive, no matter how eloquently you explain it. You'd imagine that, given the ever-multiplying dietary restrictions people encounter these days, there'd be more understanding of mine, and yet I've not really found this to be the case. Years ago, I met a young woman in London who was considering converting via a liberal movement, although she made it abundantly clear that if she did it, it would be perfunctory. "So you wouldn't eat a BLT!?" she asked incredulously, alternating nonkosher sandwiches in various combinations. "What about a bacon and tomato?" I found the whole line of inquiry a little annoying, but I also understood the confusion: even though cheeseburgers and BLTs were kind of a zero-stakes cancel for me, given that I never really loved them, if I find it occasionally exasperating to keep kosher, certainly a secular person, for whom the language of renunciation is about as comprehensible as Swahili would be to a Hungarian, would have a hard time grasping the point.

There is no equivalent to the vow of enclosure or stability in Judaism; the closest thing is either the Shabbat techum, the concept that limits the area a Jew can walk during Shabbat, or Hillel's assertion, in *Ethics of Our Fathers*, that a Jew ought to live in a place with a critical mass of other Jews. A non-Jewish friend who visited me not long after I moved to the Bronx once reacted with surprise when I mentioned that Jews tended to live in clusters because they needed to be within walking distance of a synagogue. "I had assumed it was because they didn't like other people!" she said. While that may be true in some places—the impulse to self-ghettoize after centuries of forced ghettoization cannot be denied—it's *more* true that our spiritual needs and our practical ones, like being close to food we can eat and people we can pray with, mean that we've ended up in just a few strongholds worldwide: New York, Miami, Los Angeles, Israel, Melbourne, Antwerp. At the end of the day, even if you technically *can* live an Orthodox life on a mountaintop or in the middle of Kathmandu, it's a much more difficult experience than doing so in Brooklyn or in Israel or in another Jewish enclave: kosher food is hard to come by, children have to be sent away to school, the joys of a close-knit group of neighbors who are present for every birth and death are forgone for Shabbat meals with sojourners and solo prayer. Jewish theology is heavily group-oriented—the ideal prayer is in a quorum, the best learning is done in pairs—and there just isn't a ton of room for freelancing in there. So while you may not have to take a literal vow to live in a particular place, you end up practically doing the equivalent upon accepting the yoke of the mitzvot.

There was a time just around my conversion that this registered as a loss for me. In my youth, I'd fantasized about a life of itinerance: running off to Paris for a few years to write a novel and eat baguettes, taking a job in San Francisco to work for a dot-com millionaire who self-published novels that mostly ended with the hero self-immolating (true story!), spending a year working on an organic farm in Italy crushing grapes with my feet to make wine. Once, I stumbled across an ad in search of a person to teach the children of staffers at an eco-lodge on the Sinai Peninsula, and that occupied the better part of my imagination for *months*. I would wake early to do yoga in the Egyptian sunshine and then turn my attention to this scrappy band of youngsters! Never mind that I had zero teaching experience and hated yoga: the idea of the adventure—going somewhere *else*, to do something *else*, to become someone *else*—was what appealed. But when I became religious, my dreams of being a wandering hippie type had to shrink. The places where I could feasibly reside whittled down to just a handful; even the locations I could travel in some degree of comfort and safety narrowed. It was hard to go from seeing myself as an ever-mobile independent spirit to one bound to a particular group and its geography. Sometimes I felt like the sadness was just a misplaced nostalgia for my youth; at these times I comforted myself by remembering that most people become more limited as they age, by marriage, children, their job, or some combination thereof, and that it was a little weird to be as peripatetic and rebellious at forty as one was at twenty.

These things helped, but there remained a residual sadness about my limitations until the early pandemic lockdowns. Like many, I can't say I was immediately thrilled at the idea of being kept inside indefinitely with my two rambunctious boys and husband (who was working a lot at the time), nor would I ever say the horrors of coronavirus were worth my own personal epiphany, but the whole thing made me wonder what it would take to transform the home from a place you only prefer if you're boring and antisocial to a locus of serenity and creativity. If one could succeed in that paradigm shift, the mandate could then feel like being enclosed in the way cloistered nuns described it, as keeping the world *out*, rather than keeping me *in*; it would allow us to prioritize Soloveitchik's Adam the Second, who is instructed to "cultivate" Gan Eden, rather than always looking for new land to conquer, à la Adam the First. I thought about my younger self's wanderlust, and wondered if it was just a way to cover up for a lack of confidence; an endless desire for transformation, after all, could very well indicate the absence of sturdy core. Years earlier, I'd spent a Shabbos in New Square, a town north of New York City inhabited solely by members of the extremely conservative Skverer sect of Hasidism. At the time, I'd bristled at its provincialism, the way all the women seemed only able to talk about domestic things, the way teenagers I met at dinner all looked thoroughly confused when I asked them where they'd like to travel someday, before finally answering Israel. But maybe, I now considered, they were onto something by not considering the entire globe their giant personal playground, by focusing their energies on their own domains. "Like a sparrow wandering from its nest," Solomon writes in the Proverbs, "is a man who wanders from his home." Was it really the case that perpetual movement was an "achievement" carrying "a vast significance, an aura of virtue," as the philosopher Agnes Callard sarcastically wrote in her takedown of recreational travel? Was our societal need to equate our self-worth with the number of stamps on our passports making us fail to treasure the things we saw every day? Could something about confining one's physical reach actually *encourage* growth, like a spiritual version of Flaubert's dictum that a writer be "boring and ordinary" in one's life in order to create "violent and original" work?

——

Particularly pious Christian women in medieval Europe took this view to the extreme. Known as anchoresses, these women would apply to their local bishops for permission to be walled up in a small room, usually no more than twelve square feet, attached to a church. Once inside, they would devote their days to prayer, some amount of manual labor, like lacemaking, and penance: in a thirteenth-century guide known as *Ancrene Wisse*, the anchoress is told that to avoid keeping her hands too delicate and white, she ought to "scrape up the earth every day from the grave in which they will rot." (Talk about punk rock.) A role of some religious power at a time when women could hold no official church position, anchoresses always outnumbered anchorites, the male equivalent; in the thirteenth century, for example, there were three times as many anchoresses as anchorites. (The writer George Sand actually accused her friend Flaubert of being "something of the anchorite" in one of her fretful letters to him during his reclusive old age.) The life of the anchoress was in many ways similar to a Desert Mother's, in that via her harsh habits and unceasing prayer she sought to become dead to the world—at the ceremony walling the anchoress in, the priest would even intone the prayer recited at a person's funeral—and thus wrench herself open to the divine. And yet the difficulties of anchoress life were balanced with socialization, even levity: anchorholds often had small windows carved into the wall, so that visitors could come and ask the anchoress for practical advice, spiritual guidance, or gossip. The famous anchoress Julian of Norwich, who wrote the first work known to be authored by a woman, is even depicted with a pet cat.

Historians don't know much about the lives of anchoresses, and speculation about what would have driven them to such extremes will likely never be satisfied. No one can say for certain whether their choice was a rebellion against the Church, which denied women mystical agency, or another capitulation to it; we don't know whether their actions amounted to self-mutilation for its own sake or if they really *did* believe that such extreme isolation was the only viable pathway to God. The title "anchoress" is pregnant with obvious meaning: she served as a literal anchor for the Church, who, much as the ship's anchor keeps it rooted in place, prevents the whole enterprise from simply drifting out to sea. Sometimes I look around at contemporary secular life and I see everyone rushing around, hungry to consume, eager to be elsewhere and experience newness, to pledge new fealties and discard old ones, and I wonder what it would take for people to think of themselves as rooted to the ground, as having made a promise not to leave, not to discard, not to abandon or forsake or stray. A contemporary religious hermit I once interviewed for an article—a woman whose visage had been ravaged by cancer, a woman whose stint in a cloistered monastery proved not quiet *enough* for her—recommended I read what the great mystic poet Hermann Hesse wrote about trees to better understand the solitary life: "When we are stricken and cannot bear our lives any longer, then a tree has something to say to us: Be still! Be still! Look at me! Life is not easy, life is not difficult. Those are childish thoughts. . . . Home is neither here nor there. Home is within you, or home is nowhere at all."

In September 2017, Orianne boarded a plane to St. Louis, Missouri, to begin her postulancy with the Daughters of Saint Paul. The trip was a culmination of a long process, starting with a clandestine visit to the

Toronto house almost exactly a year prior—she'd played hooky from work and taken the train down—followed by visits to the chapters in Alexandria, Virginia, and Boston, Massachusetts, where the order is headquartered. Potential postulants (literally, candidates) are also required to write a spiritual autobiography and undergo formal interviews. She got the news that she'd been accepted on July 1, Canada Day.

She told her family and friends in stages. Her youngest brother and her mom knew first, followed by the rest of her family and her social circle. "Some of my friends were really supportive. Some of my friends were really concerned," she told me. "And some of them were sad." Of everyone, her maternal grandmother had the hardest time, because she worried that it was Orianne's way of "despairing" of marriage after experiencing her parents' divorce. Orianne was young and pretty, with her dark curls and her perfect white teeth and the sparkle in her eye; how could she throw her life away like that? But not long after Orianne had left for St. Louis, her grandmother got into a taxi and began "pouring out her woes" to the driver.

"Oh no, miss, don't discourage her!" the cab driver replied. "My sister became a nun, and she helped me through my alcoholism when no one else would. She was so happy, I would never take that happiness away from her." Deeply moved, Orianne's grandmother later apologized for not being supportive.

Like Orianne's grandmother, I found myself wondering if foreclosing the prospect of romance and traditional family life down the line was in the forefront of Orianne's mind. I kept expecting her to admit to some trepidation about this, but she always responded by acknowledging certain losses and reframing others. "It was hard for me to leave my family and my friends," she admitted. "I had roots in my community. You know, I left all the places I volunteered and my parish community." She'd always wanted to adopt children, and she still wondered whether she was being asked to give up that desire. But she didn't view postulancy as a commitment, only "a question," so she didn't feel she was staring down the barrel of a celibate lifetime just yet. "You've taken no vows. You know, you're just learning," she said. Still, she recognized that she was asking the question because she hoped it would lead to a long-term commitment. It's easy and accurate to make the comparison to dating, for her: "When you marry somebody you give up a lot, including some things that we would label as freedoms. You're tied to someone; you've bound yourself to someone. So it's kind of a similar thing. Like, yeah, I knew I was giving some stuff up, but I was excited. I was in love."

In St. Louis, the novices began adapting to a version of the sisters' schedules, modified slightly so as not to overwhelm the newcomers and to allow them time for orientation-esque activities. They prayed for two and a half hours a day, including daily Mass—no doubt longer than they'd been praying at home, no matter how pious they were. In between they fit in shifts at the bookstore, the occasional outreach trip to local parishes, trips to Boston to experience the spectrum of work done in the Daughters' publishing house—from editing manuscripts to doing social media marketing—and a series of classes on theology taken alongside novices at a nearby Carmelite monastery. Orianne began rising earlier in the morning than she was used to (now she gets up around 5:30—"It's not as early as some orders, but for me, I'm a night person"). While this is not as punishing a schedule as that of some cloistered nuns, who rise in the middle of the night to pray, it is undoubtedly a full and frenetic one. The orders' founders liked to call the Daughters of Saint Paul "contemplatives in action," which Orianne understands to mean that without the rigorous prayer requirements, they might lose sight of what it is they were evangelizing for; it also could be interpreted as a mandate to carry a contemplative spirit—one that maintains its equilibrium, is pliant yet deliberate, that remains focused on God—with you as you move throughout the world. Once, early in the order's history, some of the sisters felt they were buckling under the prayer load and decided to ask Father Alberione if they could cut it down so they could prioritize their work. At the time, they were literally printing and binding the books themselves, so they were doing much more manual labor than the sisters do today, and they were exhausted. Father Alberione listened attentively to their request, then responded by adding thirty minutes of prayer to their day. "He really believed that the more important the work we were doing was, the more we had to pray," Orianne explained.

Postulancy was two years. During the first, Orianne still wasn't sure at all that she was being called to this life—she had some issues to resolve with God, she told me, involving her family of origin—but by the second year, she felt more certain. In 2019, she moved to the Daughters of Saint Paul's motherhouse in Boston, where "novices" lived. It's a sprawling building of sandy brick—indeed, even though seventy-odd sisters live there and it includes the publishing offices, sound, video, and radio transmission studios, a chapel, a library, living areas, and more, it can feel cavernous and empty—surrounded by twenty or so acres of lawns and gardens where tomatoes grow, fat as fists. Three out of five of the postulants from St. Louis also moved to the novitiate stage at that time, and the little trio entered into what some of Orianne's superiors called their "cloister year": the young women stepped back from some of the order's more forward-facing ministry work in order to spend time really considering whether or not they would be prepared to take vows when the time came.

"During novitiate, you're living everything interiorly and prayerfully much more intensely," Orianne told me, adding that she referred to it as a "desert time." This was a welcome change: "I think I was at a time where I needed some more intensive prayer time, and I also needed to be challenged to build that foundation because I am a person who naturally tends to overwork." Though they did do some missionary work—out on the town in their dark vests and skirts, but without the veil they'd don once they were officially professed, Orianne says the novices were often mistaken for flight attendants—mostly they stayed at the motherhouse, spending time doing lectio divina (literally "divine reading," which involves reading a passage of scripture and using it as a jumping-off point for prayer and meditation), studying the specific vows of the order, and taking care of the chapel by setting up for Mass, washing and ironing the special linens, and decorating for events like holidays or funerals.

This was a time of great change. Though she hadn't yet taken vows, she became a canonical member of the community, which means she was called Sister Orianne for the first time. The community was now providing for her in the manner it would be if she decided to remain with them, and if she'd died unexpectedly, she'd have had the option to be buried in the mausoleum on the grounds, with her sisters who had passed. Though she'd lived at the St. Louis convent for two years, she still was adjusting to this vision of community, whereby she prayed, lived, ate, worked, and cooked with the same people daily, people she hadn't really chosen to exist alongside and who, in other circumstances, she recognized she might never have been friends with. (It's curious to me that Catholic religious life is in some ways highly modern, in that it reinvents the nuclear family structure around nongenetic relationships, yet also deeply regressive, because it involves very little agency in terms of selecting one's relationships, like the opposite of "chosen family.") Sister Orianne also began to feel around then that God was calling her to be more evangelistic through her Instagram page, a task that was totally in line with the Daughters' mission yet somewhat uncomfortable for a woman who, at different times, described herself to me as shy, introverted, and a "private person." After careful discussions with her superior, she changed her settings from private to public, and began posting more frequently, but never unless she felt "prompted" to. "It didn't make sense," she captioned one of the photos, of her sitting on a bench outside the Daughters' bookstore in Kirkwood, Missouri, smiling and fresh-faced. "Why did Jesus keep drawing me back to this order? I wasn't a techie, I was a teacher. I wasn't a speaker, I was a listener. I didn't study theology, I studied anthropology. I didn't get why my spirit felt like it could run with Pauline spirituality when I wasn't equipped for the mission that accompanied it . . . that's not how it was supposed to be, was it?"

Probably one of the most significant changes, though, not just during novitiate but since she'd entered, was prayer. Though she'd always loved praying, three hours of daily prayer (novices have half an hour more than postulants) is a pretty major time commitment. The breakdown went something like this: every morning, the sisters would do lectio divina together as a community. That was followed by morning prayer—either the Liturgy of the Hours, which is comprised of psalms and supplementary recitations said at particular times, or prayers from their Pauline prayerbook (a book formulated with the ministry's mission of evangelization in mind, with certain psalms and other prayers interspersed with reflections from the order's founders)—followed at some point of their choosing by an hour of adoration, which the Paulines call their "visit with Jesus." Most Catholics treat adoration as a kind of choose-your-own-adventure of contemplation, which involves sitting in the presence of the Eucharist and praying in silence (Sister Orianne told me sometimes she'd cry during adoration before entering the order), but the Daughters of Saint Paul follow a particular blueprint. First, they read scripture, then they meditate, followed by a period of "examination of conscience"; finally, they end with intercessory prayer, in which they would beseech God on behalf of someone else. "You're not locked in absolutely every single time to do that," Sister Orianne told me. "But it is the rhythm of our life. And it really did push me to go a lot deeper than was comfortable initially for me. And it also helped me stay an hour, because otherwise I would have been in and out of there in like fifteen minutes." At any given time in the chapel at the Boston house, you might find one of the sisters, whether a twentysomething or an octogenarian, sitting quietly in a pew, with her head bowed, immersed in this process.

Sister Orianne had always been "very reflective," but concentrating for that amount of time was challenging. "To be able to sit in the moment and not think of ten million other things or worry about something, or think of what I should be doing or whatever, that does *not* come naturally to me." As a child, she had an easy time with what you might call "spontaneous prayer"; sometimes she'd be reading a particular psalm, find that it spoke to her, and just run with it. The formulaic nature of Catholic prayer had been an adjustment for her upon entering the Church and, again, upon becoming a sister. "As a member of a religious community, we pray the Liturgy of the Hours, which is a compilation of set Psalms for the day," she said. "And that means sometimes you're praying with Psalms that are expressing emotions you're not feeling at the moment, right?" Sometimes (often, even!) David would be wallowing in misery when she was feeling upbeat, or feeling overwhelmed with gratitude when she was feeling irritable, and the juxtaposition was off-putting. But having to routinely tap into different emotions also meant she developed a heightened awareness of the fact that she was not only praying with all the sisters present with her, but all Catholics across the world—all those who prayed the Liturgy of the Hours, anyway—and all Catholics stretching back through centuries of time. "It helped me to pray for others in a much more universal way that was not reliant on how I was or was not feeling at a given moment. So I think that really does expand your view and your consciousness of other people," she told me.

When I set out to write about prayer—whether describing Sister Orianne's experience, or my own, or just aspiring to compose some Grand Unified Theory of Prayer—I'll admit I expected it would be pretty simple. Though I admitted earlier I find it hard to pray, I find it easy to admire, and things I find easy to admire I often find similarly easy to extol in prose. Nothing seems to me to be quite so moving as a chorus of voices expressing a primal desire to a higher power; fewer words read as poetic as ancient ones of spiritual supplication, and fewer things register as potent as holy silences woven throughout. The first time I visited the Kotel in Jerusalem, almost a decade before my conversion, I was awestruck by the sight of young women praying while weeping and stroking the sand-colored stones, connected in sentiment to events thousands of years in the past. Once, when my husband and I were living in London, we were walking through Regent's Park late one night, coming back from a holiday meal at a friend's house in a neighborhood north of where we lived, and we passed by the London Central Mosque. It was Ramadan, and there must have been thousands of Muslims in the giant, ornate space, and we watched through the windows as they knelt on their mats and rose in perfect unison, as if one organism. Recently, I watched a documentary about a young postulant at a Poor Clare monastery in Rockford, Illinois, who filmed herself within the monastery, which included a scene of her kneeling and praying silently in a darkened chapel, only a clock ticking somewhere in the distance. There is something in these images of a beauty that, if paralleled, I have never seen.

And yet, as I wrote, a sneaking sense of failure seeped in. Probably this is because I have only a vague idea of what prayer *is*. For Catholics and Jews and Muslims, among some others, there are certain phrases said at certain times, sure, but there is also a vast cosmos of communication beyond this that could feasibly count as prayer. "A lot of people will just straight up ask, 'I don't know if I'm praying or not,'" Sister Orianne said on a podcast she and a fellow Daughter of Saint Paul hosted on the subject. "'I'm saying words I was taught, or I'm thinking about God—does that count?'"

Prayer strikes me further as contradictory things: an attempt to control and determine real-world outcomes but also a recognition of our fundamental helplessness, literature that somehow transcends language, high theater and deadly serious, mental action that nevertheless neutralizes the mind, something happening in a particular time and place and something that is happening always, forever. "In truth, the soul constantly prays," Rav Avraham Isaac Kook, the first Ashkenazi chief rabbi of British Mandate of Palestine, wrote. Describing a prayer regimen results in text that is dry and dull, all scheduling and instruction, as if I'm outlining a calisthenics routine. Perhaps this is on account of some sheepishness: I spent a majority of my life in the secular world, where talking about God is often highly embarrassing, but attaining mental acuity a totally comprehensible, even laudable, goal. There is something of sentiment versus intellect here: the language of prayer is the language of infatuation, and the language of infatuation is mushy and embarrassing. Saint Teresa of Ávila called contemplative prayer "a close sharing between friends." How can one adequately convey something that happens exclusively between two entities, involving a private vernacular of the heart? How can one put words to such immaculate love?

When the Desert Fathers and Mothers left their urban centers or their estates and fled to dusty caves, they sought to escape the world and its attendant noise, specifically the din of human speech. They worried that now that Christians were no longer persecuted in the Roman Empire, they would become accustomed to comfort, wealth, and moral passivity, all of which were antithetical to Christian values. In their quest for perfect attention and "pure prayer," they became hypercautious of unnecessary chatter. "[I]n late antique and early medieval monasteries, speech was thought to be even more distracting than sight," the scholar Jamie Kreiner writes in her book *The Wandering Mind: What Medieval Monks Tell Us About Distraction.* "A talkative monk could hijack the thoughts of his companions at work, prayers, meals, or downtime. He could get them thinking about any random thing that didn't matter." (Some orders developed elaborate systems of gestures akin to sign language to circumvent actual speech, but they usually found that this, too, could become disruptive.)

Medieval monks came up with tools to pacify, control, and direct their mental energies, and their influence, particularly on the contemplative nature of prayer, is felt in Catholicism still today, from the silent awe of adoration to the caesura during lectio divina to let the heart digest the words one has just encountered. The daily life of a monk, nun, or sister in a convent or monastery is punctuated by silences—or, in the cases of some orders, the baseline of silence is punctuated by moments of speech—but these are not the silences of awkward conversation or absence of thought or withholding of love. So what makes a silence "religious"? Zena Hitz suspects it is the knowledge of what that silence represents. "The silence of a church or the silence of a monastery is not the sound of absence, but the sound of restraint," she writes. "It is the sound of the choice not to speak."

The value of silence itself—its uses, its ultimate meaning(s), the appropriate time to employ it—varies from faith tradition to faith tradition. It can be, at times, an act of protest against the buzzing inanity of human beings, the only appropriate response to tragedy, an attempt to communicate the way God does (in that still, small voice), or a means of being better attuned to the divine voice, like in Quaker worship. Some traditions, like Buddhism, value silence mainly as a way to encourage mindfulness of speech, a bit like how someone who wants to lose weight might begin with a very strict diet before reintroducing certain foods, hoping the period of extreme abstemiousness fosters an overall greater awareness of their intake. A Conservative Mennonite friend once showed me a little pamphlet that outlined the reasons that Plain people shouldn't use "bywords," which are seemingly innocent euphemisms like "gosh" or "oh dear," because people know what you really mean. *This attention to minutiae helps explain their overall reticence*, I thought to myself. But it isn't always that speech is potentially dangerous for the faithful, and silence therefore the absence of danger, but rather that silence itself is a potent form of communication, if a somewhat cryptic one. A story about Abba Pambo, a fourth-century Coptic Christian desert monk, tells of an archbishop who visits him in the Nitrian Desert. "Say something to the archbishop, so that he may be edified," Pambo's followers asked. "If he is not edified by my silence," Pambo replies, "he will not be edified by my speech."

This desire for silence at least partially explains why so many religious figures have struck out alone. In *A Book of Silence*, the British Catholic solitary Sara Maitland, who moved around in search of the appropriate level of isolation before landing in remote windswept Dumfries and Galloway, Scotland, acknowledges that the search for silence very often accompanies a search for a particular aesthetic: "My ideas about silence had a landscape as well as an interior dimension."

Indeed, though they stress that reverence in silence is something that can be nurtured no matter your environment, many solitaries find that even traditional religious milieus like monasteries don't provide sufficient isolation. Thomas Merton was perhaps the twentieth century's most famous hermit, the wild child turned writer-in-residence of the Abbey of Gethsemani in Kentucky, but only in the last years of his life did he manage to convince his superiors to move him to a small hermitage on the property (though he regularly traveled and, when in nearby Louisville for medical appointments, slipped away to enjoy local jazz concerts—as he would title one of his books, no man is an island). Like medieval nuns before him, Merton's decision to retreat can be viewed as a challenge to the status quo: "In an age when totalitarianism has striven, in every way, to devaluate and degrade the human person," he wrote in his slim volume *Thoughts in Solitude*, "we hope it is right to demand a hearing for any and every sane reaction in the favor of man's inalienable solitude and his interior freedom." (Funny for a cloistered monk who took a vow of obedience to speak of "freedom"!)

Ask any hermit—and I have, trust me—and they will tell you that they feel this age is marked by a particular hostility to silence and solitude. They will say that people make assumptions about them for wanting these things: that they must have social anxiety, that they are mentally ill in some other manner, that they are misanthropic, that they are eschewing certain essential human duties, that they are simple escapists, like Erik Hagerman of The Blockade. Think of the popular protest slogan "silence is violence," which implies that speech is inherently, on its own, positive, active, and impactful, and silence its opposite. While it's true that people might associate retreat with fanaticism—sometimes romantic and secular, à la Thoreau, and sometimes pathological, like Ted Kaczynski—it's also clear that people still crave solitude, stillness, and silence the way one might covet anything rare and precious. Silence fetishists, you might call them, the types who seek out best vacation locales for absolute quiet, just like stargazers venture to "dark sky" destinations (the top choice for a silent trip in a recent Lonely Planet guide was along the Zabalo River in Ecuador, but even that area only saw quiet "lasting several hours," which should prove how scarce a resource it's become). A famous "anechoic chamber," essentially a sensory deprivation chamber for noise, located in an unassuming neighborhood in Minneapolis, was inundated with requests for visits after its existence went semiviral online. (Sensory deprivation "therapy" and "float pods" more generally have become faddishly popular in recent years: some companies use the marketing tagline "experience nothing.") Amateur meditators desperate for a refuge from chatter sign up for brief silent retreats—Zen or Camaldolese, it hardly seems to matter.

One of these erstwhile meditators is Andrew Sullivan, an early citizen of the blogosphere, who wrote in his influential essay "My Distraction Sickness—and Yours" that his life, while "alone and silent" by virtue of being hyperonline, was akin to being caught in a "constant cacophonous crowd of words and images, sounds and ideas, emotions and tirades—a wind tunnel of deafening, deadening noise." He recalls wistfully having watched a documentary years earlier called *Into Great Silence*, which portrays Carthusian monks at their monastery in the

French Alps as they chop wood, feed kittens, garden, pray, and tend to their elders, all in an eerie, potent silence. As I write this, what sounds like a steady parade of planes traverses a flight path overhead, a drill-like humming emits from leaf blowers and lawnmowers tending to neighbors' yards, and I am remembering a dream I once had about rushing through the crowded Times Square subway station and then, grappling with some anxiety Awake Me never became privy to, slipping into a "praying room," a quiet, private, dark space the city had installed there for, presumably, overwhelmed commuters.

In the Western world, we've developed our own coping mechanisms for living in a horrendously noisy, crowded era. No coping mechanism has achieved such a rapid rising in popularity in recent years, at least in the United States, as mindfulness meditation. Drawing on Buddhist and occasionally Hindu (specifically yogic) ideas, mindfulness meditation and its offshoots usually involve sitting quietly and attempting to empty one's mind of thoughts or, if a thought does happen to pass by, noticing it without passing judgment. In the United States, the popularity of various forms of mindfulness meditation has exploded in recent years (in one study from the National Institutes of Health, the number of people who reported practicing it tripled between 2012 and 2017), and you can see evidence of this *everywhere*, from the popular meditation app HeadSpace hosted by former monk Andy Puddicombe; to director David Lynch's campaign to bring Transcendental Meditation (a version of meditation that involves repeating a mantra) into schools; to myriad books on how to eat, work, date, parent, or battle addiction mindfully; to the numerous behemoth corporations that bring mindfulness experts in to help stressed-out employees. (I once texted Angela a picture of a book cover I found wild, featuring a polished, handsome-looking former monk advising readers they could "train their minds" to find their "purpose": "Is the aim of spirituality to write CEO [byword]?" she responded.)

Google and Goldman Sachs aren't the only ones enamored of mindfulness meditation though: there are many examples of high-profile Catholic religious who have noted the theological kinship between Buddhism and Catholicism, particularly in its prayer practices, over the years, most notably among them Thomas Keating and Thomas Merton. And yet despite its robust contemplative practices, Catholicism fails to entice to the same degree because it is nearly impossible to divorce it from its ethical precepts and lifestyle demands, and the twenty-first-century individual has serious qualms about being subservient to anything, even though they might occasionally crave devotion. Like therapy, the twenty-first-century mindfulness of corporate meeting rooms has made all life's suffering something that can be fixed by simply changing one's thoughts. Not everyone approves of this pivot: the professor and Zen Priest Ronald E. Purser has vociferously argued that today's "McMindfulness" is "void of a moral compass or ethical commitments [and] unmoored from a vision of the social good," which is antithetical to true Buddhist teachings, which *require* speech and action in the face of injustice.

As it's developed, Judaism has become a faith—and a cultural force—not known for its silences or its embrace of the solitary worshipper; indeed, it verges on the logorrheic, and the bulk of its prayer requirements are communal and vocal. In many ways, this suits me just fine: I was accurately pegged as a chatterbox early on in my life, and difficult, weighty texts are basically my love language. "You have a very *fast* tempo," a friend of mine, a meditation teacher and musician, once told me, in a way that made it clear she wasn't paying me a compliment, even if I ultimately chose to interpret it as one. But I am attracted to the idea of burrowing inside, of hearing things in a vast silence, of deserts both literal and figurative, of praying without ceasing. And there are, if you look closely, pockets of quietude and stillness throughout. No less a figure than Moses, after all, retreated onto a mountaintop to gain clarity from the divine, in an archetypal monk move, and more modern Jewish history introduces us to others who sought to be alone with God, from the Kabbalist Isaac Luria, who spent seven years alone on the banks of the Nile deeply engrossed in the Zohar, to Yosef Yozel Horwitz, who fashioned his own anchorhold after his wife passed away, but with two windows instead of one—through one slot people passed him dairy meals, through the other, meat. (When he was finally forced out, he agreed to marry only if he could seclude himself during the weekdays and return to his family for Shabbat.)

What does practicing such restraint do to the mind? What is it *I* am actually after? A mental acuity, yes, but of a particular texture and aim, not solely for the sake of flourishing in the world as it is, but also simultaneously to hover above it. The other day, while reading Tehillim, I came across the perfect description of such a state: "Like a weaned child with its mother" the Psalmist calls the well-trained psyche, particularly evocative imagery for anyone who's ever had a hungry baby claw at one's skin in search of sustenance. "Like a weaned child am I in my mind."

Sister Orianne was first professed in July 2021, in the chapel of the Boston motherhouse; normally, family and friends would be able to attend, but because COVID-19 was still in full swing, fewer guests were permitted (the border to Canada was still closed too). The service consisted of a full Mass, followed by a verbal acceptance of the vows of poverty, chastity, and obedience. Sister Orianne was so nervous she said her own name wrong; the other sister being professed that day, who'd gone through both postulancy and novitiate with Sister Orianne, cried, despite having sworn she wouldn't. The two young women donned their habits for the first time and assumed new names: Sister Orianne became Orianne Pietra René, Pietra for the apostle Peter and Saint Rafqa, a nineteenth-century Lebanese nun (her full name was Rafqa Pietra Chobok), and René for the first American martyr, a layman missionary named René Goupil, who was canonized in 1930.

When we spoke in March 2023, Sister Orianne had just been transferred from the order's Boston house to Toronto, for visa-related reasons. I got the sense she wasn't enthusiastic about the move, but she unsurprisingly put up a brave front. "It'll be nice to be closer to family," she told me. A few sisters from Boston drove her up, in part to do some work in the Toronto house—one was a tech whiz, and the Toronto facility had crummy Wi-Fi—but mostly just to accompany her, like the world's most wholesome road-trip comedy. After they arrived, there was a blizzard, and Sister Orianne was pleased to be able to shovel snow, her "favorite chore," she told me. She posted a picture on Instagram of the sisters who drove with her to Toronto dislodging a mound of snow from a stretch of sidewalk. "In religious life, we talk a lot about 'detachment.' But it doesn't mean what a lot of people think it means," she captioned it. "The first time I encountered that word reading Ignatius of Loyola, it struck me as an awfully cold and lonely thing. Being 'detached' kind of seemed like it must mean not really caring, not relishing the little things around you, not bonding with people, being lofty to the point of complete inaccessibility and out-of-touchness (. . . it's a word now). But that's not what it means to us at all. . . . When our identity, purpose, and belonging are rooted in the heart of God, we don't love less. We love more."

In Toronto, Sister Orianne seemed busier than ever. She continued to post on Instagram, where her followers now numbered over one hundred thousand: meditations on dreary weather and one's "spiritual rainy seasons," screenshots of a recipe for rhubarb muffins she was making, a picture of her renewing her vows in the Toronto convent's chapel, a trio of older sisters gazing on as she knelt before a priest. (Daughters of Saint Paul renew their vows yearly until they are perpetually professed, which happens about nine to ten years after they've entered the convent.) She wrote posts for the order's blog, like prayer prompts inspired by *Star Wars: Andor* and *The Chronicles of Narnia.* (She's a fantasy buff.) One time when we spoke, she told me she was working on a children's devotional that uses a lot of ocean imagery, "so I have right now in my room a set of books about oceans and sailing," all of which were purchased using an Amazon gift card someone donated. "When I'm done with them, they will go to the community library," she said. "If there's a devotional that's been super helpful to me or a spiritual reading book, I might ask, *Can I hold on to this?*" As she said this, she moved her hands to her chest in a sweet cuddling motion, and I thought of her cherishing a little book with pictures of the sea in it.

The Daughters of Saint Paul convent in Toronto is a much more modest affair than their Boston motherhouse. A squat brick building that sits on an unlovely thoroughfare a half hour away from the city's downtown, it houses a bookstore, a handful of guest rooms, a kitchen, and a tiny chapel. Six sisters live there, of whom Sister Orianne is the youngest by more than a decade, but "people are always coming in and out," she told me. On the roof are a handful of pots in which herbs grow, and you can see a lone apple tree in the yard, leftover from when the land was an orchard. In the basement is the office where Sister Orianne does most of her work liaising with the Boston house. It's a spartan affair: only a desk with two books she uses as a computer stand, a small filing cabinet, and a few pictures on corkboard, mostly of saints. On the floor some dried rose petals are laid out on top of a cardboard box, which she'll crush and then bake into a clay to make rosary beads; in the corner is a dark little space carved out of the wall where a camera stand for her phone sits. "My recording nook," she calls it.

Five times a day, the sisters will head into the little chapel off the bookstore to pray together. From behind the golden stained-glass door emanates the soft intonations of their liturgy. They'll pray throughout the day too, from small spontaneous prayers to more formal ones. Before bed, they'll cease speaking, posting, texting, or communicating in any way, and enter their own individual fortresses of silence. "It's not the Grand Silence," Sister Orianne said, referring to the strict practice of some cloistered orders. "But we try."

Hundreds of miles away, in my bed in New York City, I whisper a prayer before I cease speaking at night too. The most fundamental of all Jewish prayers, the sh'ma—"Hear, O Israel, the Lord is God, the Lord is One"—hinges on its first word, a command that encompasses a surprising array of meanings: not only to hear, but to listen, to internalize, to accept, among other connotations. The Rabbi Lord Jonathan Sacks said that the closest English equivalents are the somewhat antiquated "to take heed" or "to hearken," and compares it to the psychological concept of "active listening." I am in these moments taking it upon myself to recognize God's oneness and His commandments, and I am asking Him to recognize my devotion. I am preparing to listen to Him, and I am asking Him to listen to me. *I am a person lost in the wilderness*, I say. *I am confused and I am vulnerable and I am afraid. The world is fraught with dangers monumental and miniscule, and I feel ill-prepared to confront them. Hear me*, I say. *Help me.*

And do you know what? He does.

7.

KELSEY, TO THE DIVINE
FEMININITY OF JUDAISM

She makes her own tapestries; her
garments are of fine linen and purple.
Her husband is well-known at the gates,
as he sits with the elders of the land.

—EISHES CHAYIL, PROVERBS 31:22–23

In autumn 2021, when we were approaching our second COVID-19 high holiday season, a lengthy message was posted on my neighborhood ladies' WhatsApp group (entirely, as far as I can tell, utilized by observant Jewish women). It was akin to other stock messages of inspiration people sometimes sent on this listserv, not dissimilar in tone to chain emails I received in my youth, which promised happiness and love if one just forwarded the note along, just with a decidedly more theological bent.

Aimed at mothers like myself who might be forgoing synagogue services because they had to take care of young children, the anonymous author of the message implored us not to worry or feel sad: citing a well-known Orthodox rabbi's teachings, she reminded us that even a short prayer said from our couches had as much impact as a prayer said by men in synagogue. She cited a short anecdote—it had the air of a folktale, but the writer didn't specify its origin—in which a king threw a grand party for his own birthday. The citizens of his nation gathered to offer him congratulations and expressions of gratitude one by one, and the king rewarded each one in kind. The king had a young son, who was taken care of by a nanny, who also stood in line waiting to express her well wishes to the monarch. "[But] before she could speak," the message continued, "the king said to her: 'If you are here, WHO is watching my son?!?'"

Reading this, I did feel somewhat grateful. As a fairly lazy person, the idea of praying on my couch, versus spending hours in shul, most of it on my feet, was inherently appealing to me. Given that childcare over the holidays could be a struggle to find, it was nice to know that what I could offer from my home was just as worthwhile. And the traditional reason invoked for women being exempt from so many "time-bound mitzvot," as they're called—that they're naturally closer to God, and thus don't need the constant reminders men do, like praying in a quorum or wearing tzitzit—had always sat well with me, so I actually *did* believe my prayers on my couch were as meaningful as a man's in shul were.

And yet, while reading, I could barely resist the sudden urge I felt to throw my phone across the room. I mean, maybe the nanny wanted to participate in the ceremony too! Did she not get a single day off all year? Did she, too, not deserve a reward?

Right around the time I began talking to those in my personal life about my desire to pursue an Orthodox conversion, my mother sent me an email in which she expressed confusion about this choice, because, among other reasons, of the way I'd always felt about women's rights, or something like that. I was perplexed, because I couldn't recall ever giving much thought to being female at all, much less feeling strongly about it. Though there was some degree of gender separation in my childhood environment—amounting mostly to different sports teams for boys and girls, from what I can remember—it never seemed that there were different *expectations* for either sex, or that boys were assumed to be better at certain things, like science, than girls were (of course, it should go without saying that this wasn't true of every place in the nineties, but I checked with my childhood friends from my hometown and they concurred).

The only thing I *can* recall is a kind of instinctive feeling I had that boys were *worse* than girls in nearly every way I could imagine, a view only solidified by the fact that I had two younger brothers, and therefore ample access to the kind of stupidity all little boys, I assumed, found mesmerizing (poop jokes, video games, beating each other up, sports, et al.). The idea that any girl would want to have male friends or feel jealous of boys was beyond my comprehension. Surely some of this assumption of total equality, if not an absolute reversal of the historical status quo, was naïveté: my mom would later tell me she felt like the odd mother out in our town because she worked and most other mothers there didn't, though that wasn't a divide I remember noticing, probably because kids just don't pay attention to interparental dynamics.

I don't remember thinking much about feminism as a political force until my midtwenties, beginning in the early 2010s. This marked the onset of fourth-wave feminism, when Sheryl Sandberg's *Lean In*, which preached the gospel of female empowerment via corporate ambition, was published, and #girlboss feminism was ascendant. It seemed that everything was finally falling into place for women, and the discourse reflected that: Hanna Rosin, in an article in *The Atlantic*, declared this

era "The End of Men," and Rebecca Solnit's essay decrying the phenomenon of "mansplaining" went viral (though she popularized the
idea, she's often falsely credited with coining the neologism).

Many early fixations of the fourth wave left me uneasy. For one, it
seemed to take for granted that all women should want to become corporate overlords—that this was, in and of itself, not just a worthy goal
but the *highest* one. Hearkening back to my crude childhood assumptions about inherent female superiority, I wondered why it would automatically be assumed progressive to ask women to behave more like
men—bolder, less apologetic, "bossier." Wasn't the underlying logic
there rather patriarchal in nature? The moral relativism baked into so
much of the feminist zeitgeist, such as the idea that anything a woman
deemed self-care could be labeled a feminist act, even a radical one,
irked me to no end (as, I'll admit, most systems based on moral relativism do). Finally, could anyone, man or woman, really "have it all"
without outsourcing the basic duties of domesticity, like childcare plus
all the trappings of bourgeois life, to a likely underpaid, immigrant
class of women, something that didn't seem like a truly equitable solve
at all? If you made choices in your life that resulted in you owning a
home or having children, wouldn't it make sense that you'd have some
responsibility to those things beyond simply financial ones?

Years later, I'd read a rather biting polemic by the Hungarian rebbetzin Esther Jungreis (dubbed by some the "Jewish Billy Graham")
that I felt pretty neatly summed up my feelings on the topic: "[T]o
those feminist friends who mock this 'slave mentality' I ask: Is caring
for children slavery? Is hassling in the world of business freedom? . . .
The American emphasis on separatism, independence, and individual-
ity [has resulted in] the new folk hero, the 'anti-mother,' a product of
Pavlovian conditioning, doomed to existential angst. . . . College graduates are conditioned to equate achievement with financial remunera-

tion, and therefore motherhood, which is a non-salaried position can accord one no status [*sic*]. The young housewife is led to believe that motherhood stifles all creative instincts and dooms one to bovine passivity."

If I sound very prescient here, given the later demise of the girlboss, who eventually became an avatar for the evils of capitalism and white supremacy, don't be too impressed. All this rather vaguely expressed conviction was little more than a luxury belief: it was easy, in other words, for me to say that it was stupid to want to be a CEO in the first place, because I myself never wanted to be a CEO. It was easy to criticize the idea that the more sexual partners you have, the more liberated you are, because I wasn't inclined to pursue casual sex anyway. It was easy, too, to value the simplicities of domestic life—caring for young children, cooking, tending to a home—because I had zero actual experience doing any of these things.

It was around this time that I began spending more time in not just Jewish spaces, but the kinds of Jewish spaces you'd probably be surprised to find an overly educated, politically liberal-leaning (more or less) Gentile woman: Orthodox synagogues, women's gatherings organized by Chabad houses, Hasidic weddings. I'd go to challah bakes, women-only Torah classes, even women-only rock concerts in which bands like the Bulletproof Stockings—a group fronted by two women Chabadniks wearing cat eyeliner and hip knee-length dresses, its name a reference to the thick, ecru-colored tights worn by female members of certain Hasidic sects—performed for crowds of only women. "Women need a space to rock out," the lead singer Perl Wolfe told me when I wrote an article on the group for Refinery29 in 2014. "So, we're trying to create that. It's about sisterhood."

Though I wouldn't by that point have classified myself as either above men, as per my childhood stance, or overly leery of them, I found the clear-cut gender separation a refreshing palate cleanser from fourth-wave mishegoss. I loved going to shul and sitting on one side of a mechitzah—the name for the divider between the men's and women's sections of the synagogue—with only the women and their fat, antsy babies disrupting the service by wiggling off laps and attempting to gum a shoe. I loved trying my hand at the surprisingly complicated circle dances done by Hasidic preteen girls at weddings, watching them peek through the dividers over at the men's side. Though I didn't observe it at the time—I had plenty of male friends from college I'd hang out with one-on-one, and a male boss I was often alone with—I loved, too, the idea of yichud, the prohibition against unmarried men and women being together without supervision in a closed room. (Nowadays, of course, this idea might immediately conjure up an image of Mike Pence, as yichud sounds similar to Pence's famous proclamation that he'd never eat out alone with a woman if his wife wasn't also present.) I wasn't particularly worried about sexual impropriety myself, but still, something about the restriction felt comforting, and rather sensible and obvious, to me. Perhaps it simply appealed because I am a person who enjoys clear boundaries, with which Judaism was rife: the sacred and the profane, the weekday and the Sabbath, meat and milk, light and dark, men and women. Or perhaps it hearkened back to my childhood desire to live a life largely free of men—their idiotic confidence; their drab corporate interests; their erratic, thoughtless sensuality; their dull rationality.

One of the earliest-known examples of a women-only society comes from the Greek myth of the Amazons, the group of fierce female warriors described by various historians as "killers of men," "those who fight like men," or "those who loathe all men." In one telling, Amazons only left their home region of Themiscyra to have sex with a nearby tribe called the Gargareans; they copulated to beget children, the males of which they gave back to the Gargareans to raise. In another version of the legend, Amazon girls had their right breast chopped off so as to more easily hold and shoot a bow and arrow. In Herodotus's account, the Amazons washed ashore on Scythia and eventually cohabitated with the Scythians, but only the Amazons were capable of learning the Scythian language—not vice versa—so they kept their upper hand, even eventually persuading Scythian men to flee their home country and start a new, egalitarian society with them. In most of the recordings, the Amazons are confused for men by outsiders, either because they dress like men and wage war, or because, in some versions, they literally *are* men, but with shaved faces and long hair as disguise.

The Amazons—strictly speaking apocryphal, though likely based on tales of actual Scythian women who fought and worked alongside Scythian men—differed from most ancient women in innumerable ways, but particularly in one crucial aspect: they enforced their own segregation. In contemporaneous cultures, it was almost always the men who determined where women could be present and under what circumstances. In ancient Israel, for example, women who were rendered ritually impure by way of uterine blood (from menstruation, miscarriage, or for another reason) were forbidden from entering the main sanctuary, though there was a simple purification process, and others were also barred: men who experienced nocturnal emissions were also subject to purification rituals, similar to contemporary mikvah rituals. (In addition to being used in conversion, mikvaot are where women go after their periods, to prepare themselves to resume conjugal relations with their husbands; men use them at their discretion, often before holidays, weddings, or other auspicious occasions.) From the skeletal rules offered in early Jewish texts regarding women's proper places unspooled a byzantine system of religious law on the subject, from which eventually emerged mechitzah (women and girls pray in a section called ezrat nashim, often translated as "courtyard of women" or sometimes "the help of women"), the codification of stricter laws concerning mikvah usage for women (with the almost wholesale elimination of such rules for men), and so on, until early 1900s Poland, where, as *Yentl* informs us, Barbra Streisand has to dress in drag just to get into school.

Christianity joined in the creation of such segregated spaces, in some cases taking the concept to greater extremes. Medieval convents could serve as dumping grounds for those with poor marriage prospects—many of these tragic bachelorettes were given baby Jesus dolls to nurture in lieu of their own offspring—or they could be safe havens for women who had no interest in married life and wanted instead to devote themselves to scholarship and self-improvement. In thirteenth-century Europe, there existed a liberal version of convents, communities called beguinages, where laywomen of faith, known as beguines, could live and worship together without men. Unlike nuns, however, beguines came and went of their own accord and were not required to hand over dowries upon entry. Also unlike nuns, beguines were economically self-sufficient, engaging in traditionally male mercantile activities and even real estate transactions so as to earn money to give away to the poor. Their communes were often sprawling complexes with homes for hundreds of female residents, featuring vegetable gardens, beehives, breweries, private chapels (their pulpits were often decorated with carvings of Catholic heroines and female martyrs rather than Gospel scribes), and charity hospitals. Male visitors to beguinages were relegated to public parlors and could never sit with a beguine without a chaperone present. As beguines ministered outside their own enclaves—they tended to the spiritual needs of aristocrats and prostitutes alike—they were often seen traveling through the cities in pairs to avoid accusations of sexual impropriety, wearing their distinctive garb, which in some renderings looks like a slightly more architectural version of the outfits worn by the heroines on Hulu's *The Handmaid's Tale*.

Depending on your perspective, these early women's spaces could be considered feminist utopias or prisons of the patriarchy. One woman's convent, in other words, is another's Themiscyra. Even beguinages, probably the most woke template on offer, were not wholly independent of men, as they usually relied on the fiscal and political protection of male bigwigs, including, in a few notable cases, King Louis IX of France. And even though beguines fought for self-determination, they did also shape their practices—traveling in pairs is just one such example—in response to what remained, writ large, a male-dominated society. Though quietly rebellious in their own way, the beguines did not advocate for reorganization of the established order, but eventually they were punished as if they had. Beginning with the Council of Vienne in 1311, the communities' freedoms were severely curtailed, and many individual beguines were burned at the stake as heretics. By the late sixteenth century, most beguinages had been decimated, writes historian Walter Simons in *Cities of Ladies: Beguine Communities in the Medieval Low Countries, 1200–1565*, and "the prevalent image of the beguine in this later age was no longer controversial or defiant, but rather that of a naïve, somewhat foolish but inoffensive kwezel [silly pious person]."

Widening the scope to include Eastern religious examples does little to help us determine with certainty whether gender segregation is more beneficial than it is harmful to women. Like Judaism, many Eastern religions, including Hinduism and Buddhism, classify the woman who is menstruating or postpartum as impure or unclean. In Hinduism, women who are menstruating are barred from entering temples and kitchens (and also from having sex, touching or watering certain plants, touching certain sacred foods, or attending religious functions). For centuries, women of menstruating age were denied entry into the Sabarimala Temple in Kerala, India, because the god to whom the temple is dedicated was celibate. The Supreme Court of India put an end to that practice in 2018, though devotees continue to protest women's entry (the one dissenting judge was female).

Though there is comparatively more ritual gender equality in Buddhism, certain orthodox strains of Japanese Buddhism have harsh conceptions of women. According to an influential late twelfth or early thirteenth century tractate known as the Menstruation or "Blood Bowl" Sutra, for example, women's menstrual blood was forever defiling the earth and its rivers, which offended the Buddha and other terrestrial gods; because they were constantly racking up negative karma as a result of their cycles, women were barred from entering Buddhist temples or sometimes even stepping onto the mountain a temple sat atop.

But what appears wholly negative can also have paradoxical benefits for women. As Geraldine Brooks outlined in her book *Nine Parts of Desire: The Hidden World of Islamic Women*, about her time as a Cairo-based reporter, the 1979 Islamic Revolution in Iran—probably no one's idea of a feminist movement—had the curious and unintended consequence of, in some ways, opening the world up to young women. Job opportunities for women exploded, because all-women's hair salons, television stations, and exercise studios were established, and all these new businesses required female employees. Young women from more conservative parts of Iran were able to convince their parents to let them go to university, now seen as safe because institutions of higher learning were Islamic, and therefore sex segregated. By 2015, more women in Iran were enrolled in college than men. (Of course, not all women approved: Brooks quotes Iranian anthropologist Fatemeh Givechian's critical paper from 1991, in which she prophesizes that "there will emerge a dual society of male and female stranger to one another and unaware of each other's anxieties.")

In twentieth-century secular milieus, too, it wasn't simply that certain women's institutions were liberating, powerful, and modern, while others were suffocating and parochial, but rather the same institution, under the auspices of a unified philosophy, might be both, just like a medieval convent. The Barbizon Hotel—not the only girls-only hotel in New York, but far and away the most mythologized—opened in 1927 to provide shelter for what it advertised as "ambitious, discriminating young women" within its pink-bricked facade. Over the years, it cosseted the likes of Grace Kelly, Sylvia Plath, Joan Didion, and countless hopeful models, actresses, and artists, most from well-to-do families who wanted their daughters educated and cultured but eventually wed in suburbia. "With mandatory teas, curfews, and chaperones, the Barbizon was like an upscale nunnery," writes Elizabeth Winder in *Pain, Parties, Work: Sylvia Plath in New York, Summer 1953*. Like at a beguinage, men were verboten except in the lobby or during evening bridge games in the lounge, a sanctioned (and supervised) time and space in which residents could flirt with suitors. Many former Barbizon girls recalled their stays as giddy and expectant; their acceptance into such a vaunted institution boosted their confidence. But as writer Gael Greene—herself a former resident—reminisced in a 1957 column for the *New York Post*, the place could engender a fear of the dangerous outside even as it assured denizens of their ambitions. "In those days, many young women and their parents were just riveted on the dangers and risks on every street corner in New York," Greene later recalled.

"For me, [the Barbizon] was a revelation of so many paralyzed, petrified, enterprising young women."

Through the second half of the twentieth century—a time of burgeoning equality and greater freedoms for women in the Western world—the creation of women-only spaces did not cease, but the questions around whether or not these places were necessary havens or promoters of naïve or backward safetyism only grew more urgent and complex. No sooner did one band of women successfully strong-arm their way into an old boys' club than did another hammer the last nail into the roof of their all-women's meeting hall. In her 1970 book *The Dialectic of Sex*, radical second-wave feminist Shulamith Firestone—herself raised in an Orthodox Jewish home—called for all sex-segregated institutions to be abolished ("if male/female . . . cultural distinctions are destroyed, we will no longer need the sexual repression that maintains these unequal classes"), around the very same time her colleague Alice Wolfson, pregnant with her son, was reeling at the announcement that male infants were "the enemy" and subsequently banned from the Women's Liberation office. (There were even more radical outfits, like Cell 16, based in Boston from 1968 to 1973, a women's collective that practiced celibacy and karate and read Valerie Solanas, the radical feminist author perhaps best known for her attempted assassination of Andy Warhol, at the beginning of their gatherings.) Just three years before the 1992 opening of the first all-women's Curves gym in Texas, the New York Athletic Club—the self-proclaimed oldest male social club in the world—begrudgingly agreed to admit its first female members.

This parallel-track trend continued through the turn of the twenty-first century through the present day. The famously testosterone-laden Deep Springs College, a very small, tuition-free, historically male school on a cattle ranch in rural California, decided to go co-ed just as the Arete Project, an all-women's educational summer program modeled on Deep Springs, was founded. While *The New York Times* lambasted a Brooklyn YMCA for its women-only swimming hours, across the pond the *Evening Standard* was publishing paeans to the ladies-only bathing pond in London's Hampstead Heath, a public park. The Boy Scouts announced they'd admit girls, and the Girl Scouts doubled down on their separatism. "We've had one hundred and five years of supporting girls and a girl-only safe space," a spokeswoman said in response to the news. Creating a sort of double-bind for themselves, many twenty-first-century women-only spaces—like the much-fretted-over and now defunct the Wing, a members-only coworking space designed as a pastel paradise of girlboss feminism—had the express goal of changing the society at large to make it more hospitable to women and other marginalized people (though how the revolution would be achieved through private members' clubs, no one was quite able to pinpoint).

Religious women's organizations more often leaned into the safe-haven vibe; nuns and Orthodox women usually attempted to change the world through mystical means, like prayer, rather than public, political ones. And while it's easy for an outsider to assume religious women simply accept their creed's core belief in the inherent supremacy of men and the patriarchal structure erected on that foundation, it turned out that they didn't always see it that way. In the 1991 book *Rachel's Daughters: Newly Orthodox Jewish Women*, sociologist Debra Renee Kaufman interviewed one hundred fifty *ba'alot teshuva*, or "mistresses of return," a term used to describe women who embrace Orthodoxy after a secular upbringing or a long period away from religious practice. A vast majority of Kaufman's subjects had college degrees, and many continued to work outside the home after they adopted the stringencies of Orthodox life. A number had been involved in the radical social experiments of the 1960s and '70s but eventually came to see feminism and sexual liberation as too focused on individual grievances over communal well-being. (Some also came to fear that the "free love" ethos of the 1960s was a convenient way for men to sexually exploit liberated sisters.) A desire for something more doggedly pursued Kaufman's interviewees, until they located it in Orthodox Judaism, a theology that, with its rigid codes of behavior and its lack of roles for women in the public sphere, was perhaps as far from second-wave feminism as they could get.

In her book, Kaufman describes being surprised by how often her interviewees spoke of their faith as female-centric, despite the fact that, within some Orthodox communities, women are either legally prohibited or culturally discouraged from studying certain sacred texts or becoming rabbis. Only men have the power to grant women a divorce, and in some particularly toxic situations, husbands have refused, leaving their exes unable to remarry, sometimes for years or even decades. In some especially conservative sects of Hasidism, women shave their heads just before marriage, like political traitors. But the women Kaufman interviewed claimed that Orthodox Judaism supported them as women both in its theology and in its practice. How could this be the case?

These women drew on disparate sources to construct a picture of Orthodoxy that was strongly feminine in orientation. They cited the fact that the Kabbalistic concept of *shechinah*, the earthly dwelling place of the divine, is distinctly feminine. They pointed out that Shabbat is often called a "bride" or "queen." The quintessential Jewish woman, found in Eishes Chayil, an excerpt of Proverbs sung on Friday nights before the Sabbath meal, isn't a stereotypically passive wife; in fact, she sounds pretty darn entrepreneurial. "She seeks out wool and flax, and works willingly with her hands," one translation reads. "She is like the merchant ships; she brings her food from afar." While the women interviewees didn't mention this, other feminist faithful might have pointed to the fact that Jewish women historically had their own crucial ritual leadership roles in many communities, personified by the *firzogerin*, a learned woman—often the daughter or spouse of a rabbi—who would translate the Hebrew prayers into the local vernacular during services, sometimes with her own personal extemporaneous insertions (the term is Yiddish, but similar female figures existed outside Ashkenazic Eastern Europe as well). Firzogerins often wrote prayer-poems for menstruation, marriage, and women-led sabbath rituals like lighting candles and kneading dough, events that were largely left unremarked upon in traditional, male-oriented prayer.

More important to the interviewed Orthodox women was that they felt their society was structured to give them literal rooms of their own. One gushed to Kaufman about her weekly women's group, much like those I began attending in my late twenties, which featured "music, meditation, [and] group exercise." Other interviewees spoke of what Kaufman called the "heightened air of sensuousness and intimacy" that pervades the mikvah, as strictly female-centric as a space can get, and certainly one of the most difficult rituals to "pitch" to secular women (not that I walk around trying to get women to go to the mikvah). Everyone understands the appeal of Shabbat, but tell someone they can't touch, let alone be intimate with their spouses for roughly two weeks out of the month, until they submerge themselves in a pool of water and become "pure"? That's a pretty hard sell.

Once, in an email to a friend who was interested in Orthodox life but skeptical of the gendered aspects, I managed to eke out a somewhat eloquent response about how maybe ancient peoples understood the momentousness of bodily functions—sex as it segues naturally into pregnancy, which holds the power for both life and death—and while maybe we've outgrown some of our squeamishness around such things, what we've lost in the interim is our *reverence* for them. We walk around today imagining we've conquered the body (sex doesn't have to result in pregnancy, illness in death, and so on) and yet, really, we're still more physically fragile than we readily admit, and maybe being reminded of this helps to ward off hubris, not unlike the way a memento mori puts us in touch with our own mortality.

Though that justification makes sense to me, it isn't the one I hear most often. Far and away the most common pro-mikvah narrative in the modern day is that it is a spiritually elevating form of self-care. It makes women more aware of their hormonal cycles and gives them access to a private space in which they attend scrupulously to every inch of their bodies—clipping, scrubbing, soaking—not unlike a spa or hammam. There's also the idea that it can strengthen marriages because it can heighten eroticism: spending time without touching, the logic goes, inevitably leads to a magical spousal reunion, like a honeymoon once a month instead of once in a lifetime. (There are some who doubt this though: "Mikvah is a chok, the kind of commandment that defies understanding," a Chabad woman told the journalist Sue Fishkoff, of her resistance to ascribing any greater value to mikvah rituals. "We have no idea why God doesn't want us to eat pig, or wear a garment of linen and wool. Mikvah is the same.")

By the 2000s, the mikvah had become shrouded in secrecy not because women's bodies were shamefully mysterious but *beautifully* so. In the olden days, women were said to hack into frozen lakes with icepicks or tiptoe through moldy Lower East Side basements to perform their ritual dunk. Far from being punitive, modern mikvahs featured sample-size lotions, whirlpool baths, and heated floors. An observant woman could luxuriate in a warm tub and file her nails in the blissful quiet away from her spouse and children. The one in my former neighborhood had waffle-knit robes and designer-brand shampoo; Oprah toured it for an episode on Hasidism. (It's also named in honor of a man.) Over time, the mikvah even became fashionable for untraditional uses: women went in the wake of a trauma, such as a divorce or a surgery, as a sign of emotional healing. Lesbian Jewish couples opted to use it, despite not being obligated to. The transformation of ancient ideas about sexual separation from archaic infliction to new-age indulgence, à la celibacy and meditation, seemed near complete.

It was not just Kaufman's ba'alot teshuvot fleeing secular life and its purported gender parity. In 2015, Britain was abuzz with the news that the number of Catholic women taking religious vows had hit a twenty-five-year high. Sister Cathy Jones, of the National Office of Vocations, characterized her new recruits as similar to Kaufman's subjects: "The vast majority are graduates from prestigious universities with opportunities ahead of them, or those in their late twenties or thirties who discover that a career is not enough." A spate of articles published described the bemused reporters visiting these new brides of Christ and finding something rather paradisiacal: convents in the rolling hills of the New Forest or quaint side streets of North London with bands of merry spinsters praying, eating communal dinners, or doing crafts, even updating their own Twitter accounts (nuns on social media became such a phenomenon that in 2018 Pope Francis issued a statement urging them to use such tools with "sobriety and discretion"). Replace "praying" with, say, "mindfulness meditation"—not such a stretch, really—and this might not sound so far off from an avowed millennial dream lifestyle, as the Nones in the *New York Times* piece professed.

In a convent, one British novice said, you can be free of society's obsession with "the games people play with money, sex and power"—

games, many feminists and their celibate sisters might argue, created, dominated, and perpetuated by men. The numbers in the United States took longer to reflect the trend, but the American press still seized on the story and sought out young nuns. A number of publications ran the same series of pictures from a coffee-table book about the life of a novice: her fresh, dewy face beatific during prayer, her joyful smile as she played guitar with another young nun, her limbs akimbo as she passed a soccer ball to a fellow nun during recreation time. "Why Would a Millennial Become a Priest or a Nun?" one breathless headline asked in *The Atlantic*. The answer seemed obvious.

Back to the early 2010s: so, I'm spending more time in Jewish settings and flirting with the idea of conversion, though I hadn't chosen a denomination yet. I assumed that, between my family, my Reform-raised boyfriend, and my own lack of knowledge, becoming Orthodox would be impossible, even though I found myself most drawn to Orthodox life and practice. The crux of this attraction was that, like Christina and the Amish, I admired that their theology and their lifestyles aligned. It bothered me that in the face of something Jewish that didn't jive with modern sensibilities, many liberal leaders seemed to always and automatically cast the Jewish stuff aside in favor of modernity, in a way that struck me as lacking in reflection and kowtowing to presentism.

The conversion processes of the less observant movements, which I initially looked into, had all the spiritual sustenance of being a product on a conveyor belt: in one particularly disastrous meeting, a Conservative rabbi sadly smiled at me and informed me I wouldn't be able to have a Christmas tree again (I was insulted that he would have thought I'd assumed I could) and trumpeted his own open-mindedness, before cautioning me to stay away from Orthodox people because they would never accept me as a Jew. (I knew he was possibly right about this—I was just irritated because he assumed that *I* didn't understand the nuances involved.) When he followed up with me by email, I simply deleted the message and figured that this debacle confirmed that I wanted to convert Orthodox or not at all, which probably meant I'd just remain an unfulfilled philosemite forever.

But while I felt that I probably would never *be* Orthodox, I could console myself by sneaking into various Orthodox spaces. I'd recently begun to publish work in various online outlets, and I found that saying I was working on a story was a ticket into almost any environment, no matter how closed it seemed from the outside. One day, when I was twenty-seven years old, I was flipping through *New York* magazine at my day job when I came across a very brief mention of a story out of Borough Park, Brooklyn: a group of women in this heavily Hasidic neighborhood were starting their own ambulance service, which would rival the robust and established Hatzolah EMT service staffed only by men. I immediately knew I had to cover the story, so I tracked down the woman spearheading the project, a lawyer and mother of six named Ruchie Freier, who agreed to meet me in Brooklyn one afternoon. (Freier's fame has grown since we met: The EMT service was later the subject of a documentary film, *93 Queen*, that streams on HBO. If you look closely, you'll see me looking slightly amused and out of place in an early scene. In 2016, she was elected civil court judge in Brooklyn, becoming the first Hasidic female elected official in the country.) Fortunately for me, my boss was out of town, so I slipped out early, rode the Q train for thirty minutes, and emerged from the depths of the subway system into a small foreign country in the middle of New York City: men in black hats and long black coats on a balmy July day, women in short wigs pushing baby carriages determinedly down city sidewalks, storefronts lined with silver candelabras and volumes upon volumes of religious writings in dense arcane-looking script.

In Freier's office, she and I spoke for a while about her involvement with the new EMT service, the way that Hatzolah had, under the guise of "modesty"—in Yiddish tznius, or in Hebrew tzniut, which often refers to modest clothing but can also imply dignified conduct—excluded women from joining, and about her views on feminism. "Feminist is a bad word in my community. I don't want to be a rabbi, but I think outside religious obligations, I should be able to do whatever a man can do," she said, which sounded a lot like feminism to me. I told her that I was considering converting to Judaism, though I didn't mention that I was still unsure how I would accomplish this. Before I got up to leave, she had one more thing to say: the women in her organization would probably be more inclined to speak with me if I dressed modestly, she said. I knew what this meant: elbows, knees, and collarbone covered. It didn't sound exactly like a rebuke, but I had to stop my hand from instinctively reaching up to cover a triangle of my bare chest. More than ten years later, I still remember exactly what I was wearing that day: a navy J.Crew dress, gifted to me by my mother, with a wide v-neck and short sleeves with decorative circular holes in the upper arms and shoulder area, revealing pockets of skin. Tasteful, yes; modest by Hasidic standards, no.

I've told that story often since then, and each time I've noted that plenty of other women reporters would likely have been offended by her request, and perhaps just refused to comply. But I was excited. I immediately began rifling through my wardrobe to find anything long-sleeved and knee-length (I had very little of the latter). I got a friend who grew up not far away from Borough Park to accompany me on a trip to Junee, a frum women's store that catered mostly to tweens and teens, where I bought a knee-length dark-gray skirt fit for a Hasidic high schooler, and a shell, the name for the supremely uncomfortable, tight, polyester-spandex-blend shirts that women often threw under short-sleeved shirts or tank tops to make the sinful miraculously modest. When I'd go south from my apartment in hip, brownstone Brooklyn to attend a meeting of EMTs, I'd dip into the modest section of my closest, pick out the evening's garment, and jump on the subway in my best Hasidic LARPing gear. While I never felt like I truly blended in— Hasidic women always looked polished and largely monochromatic, while I retained the odd piece of Olsen twin–inspired dumpster-chic flair, my blond hair always slightly mangy—I must have done a decently good job, because the EMTs regularly mistook me for one of them. "Oh look at you, you're so good, saying your tehillim!" a young woman gushed over me one evening, upon finding me hunched over a tiny notebook. I was too embarrassed to tell her it was my notes for the piece, not a little book of psalms, and that I was prying, not praying.

Unlike almost every other decision I've made in my life, I had great timing here. After years of mainstream women's fashion favoring skinny jeans and short skirts and otherwise revealing apparel, modesty was improbably back in. In Brooklyn, a handful of actually cool modest brands popped up, most run by young Chabad women who favored oversize dresses in jewel tones—even the odd red frock, typically verboten in Hasidic spheres as it's historically associated with prostitution—and ran Instagram accounts with photos of them in getups that would have been chic by secular standards. A few modest Instagram influencers developed cult followings, like Adi Heyman, a whippet-thin convert whose blog showcased her (very expensive) long sheath dresses and midcalf fringed skirts. In 2016, the ba'alat teshuva and "restless" Orthodox housewife Batsheva Hay began designing Laura Ashley–style dresses for grown-ups in her New York City apartment, which *The New Yorker* described as visually drawing on the looks of the Amish, American homesteaders, Orthodox Jews, and the judiciary; within a few years, her dresses would retail for hundreds of dollars and be sold at numerous high-end boutiques. (The *New Yorker* profile writer portrays Hay as ambivalent about her observance, describing her as engaged "in a complex kind of role-play.") In that somewhat mysterious yet definably cyclical way fashion moves, the runways, red carpets, and magazine pages were soon filled not with bare shoulders or plunging necklines, but ankle-grazing dresses and long sleeves and Elizabethan high collars.

It took a few years to anoint modest dressing the official look of the 2010s, though; perhaps it was finally settled when venerable fashion reporter Vanessa Friedman declared the 2010s "the end of the naked look" in a 2017 article in the *Times*. It was unclear exactly how much the burgeoning micro-market of Orthodox fashion in New York played a role here, although at least one article in *Vogue* suggested that "Orthodox Jewish Style" had inspired "Fall 2015's Sexiest Trend" (that would be the slip dress). It was at least somewhat geographically determined too. When I moved to London in 2015, where there is a large Arab population, a parallel conversation was happening, except with Muslim women at its center: major endorsements from big-name sports brands for hijabi athletes, Muslim convert Hana Tajima's collection for Uniqlo, Dolce & Gabbana releasing its first line of headscarves and abayas (the latter cost upwards of two thousand dollars), the founding of *Vogue Arabia* in 2017.

Though you'd soon find regular New York gals wearing Chabad-made gowns and Orthodox influencers in just-happen-to-be-modest outfits from Chloe or Galliano, the rationale behind why each woman would choose to cover their bodies so thoroughly was usually—but not always—different. Secular modest fashionistas and the writers who chronicled them wondered if maybe the hostile political climate after the 2016 election had made women more protective of themselves, their long sheaths representative of a newfound antiestablishment zeal. In this, there was an echo of the surprising role modest dress has sometimes played in global revolutions, where radicals framed a return to older values—and modest dress—as actually liberating. Recall the pictures of Iranian women in full chador, brandishing machine guns, during the 1979 revolution, prepared to fight against the evils of Western imperialism (and then, decades later, the images of the descendants of these women removing their headscarves in defiance of the Islamist government. Revolutionary values, like fashion, can swing like a pendulum.) Some hypothesized that maybe the resurgence of high-fashion modesty was because we were all tired of knowing *too* much about others. The rise of reality TV and the online first-person industrial complex that resulted in essays in which writers would bare way more than they arguably should have (perhaps no one can forget the rather unfortunate revelation by one internet confessor that she found a ball of her pet's fur in a *very* surprising bodily orifice) had left us craving a little decorum, a little privacy. "Once we've seen it all—from Emily Ratajkowski's fabulous breasts to Kim Kardashian's monumental butt—it now seems as if the most radical gesture could only involve donning a baggy jumpsuit or a generously cut midi-skirt," Naomi Fry wrote in *T Magazine* in 2017, in an article ("Modest Dressing, as a Virtue") accompanied by pictures of Mennonite girls in calf-length skirts, Chloe Sevigny depicting a Mormon fundamentalist housewife in *Big Love*, and a model, facing away from the camera, wearing a bulky designer suit and top, which cost over six thousand dollars.

Though both groups nodded to the idea that dressing modestly somehow protected women from men and lookism generally, à la Hana's niqab as her suit of armor, the secular explained this in terms of ideas like "the patriarchy" and "the male gaze," while the religious slightly deemphasized the role of men, perhaps worried they'd be accused—as they often were—of simply operating from a "false consciousness," a term coined by Engels that has been borrowed by feminist theorists to denote having internalized the logic of one's oppressors. "When cloaking elbows and knees, we aim to emphasize the person, not the body," Adi Heyman wrote on her blog. "By covering up what is superficial, we reveal what is more important: personality and character." Ruchie Freier told me that she felt modesty placed all the burdens on men: she could saunter through a room of men wearing whatever she wanted and she wouldn't have done anything wrong— rather, it was the *men* who didn't avert their eyes who would have sinned.

Technically, Freier was correct. The original texts often put the onus on the man to control his own urges—the Talmud demands that a man avoid staring even at a woman's "smallest finger" or her clothing, hanging on a line to dry, though a woman could stare at a man's finger all the livelong day. And yet while I did *believe* these covertly feminist ideas, it was hard to square them with the then-recent story of Na'ama Margolese, a young girl who was stoned on her way to school in Israel by a group of men who found her clothing unsatisfactorily demure, or the Iranian and Haredi women's magazines who blurred out images of women, deeming even their *faces* immodest. (To this day, I've never heard of an instance where a religious man has had rocks thrown at *him* for ogling a woman.) "To women and girls who pass through our neighborhood," a large sign outside the Haredi enclave of Meah Shearim in Jerusalem reads, "we beg you with all our hearts, please do not pass through our neighborhood in immodest clothes. Modest clothes include: closed blouse with long sleeves, long skirt—no trousers, no tight-fitting clothes. Please do not disturb the sanctity of our neighborhood and our way of life as Jews committed to G-d and his Torah." The subtext is obvious: the man would be distracted by the woman's uncovered body, and the man's piety is paramount.

Distinct from secular modesty, an appeal of modest religious dress—or what we might call "pious fashion," to borrow from Liz Bucar—is that it marks the devotee as distinct from the mainstream. It signals to outsiders that they have identifiable values, gives them an opportunity to "witness" (i.e., testify to their beliefs simply via their appearance), encourages a cultural homogeneity and/or a simplicity of spirit, and reminds the person wearing the garments of their commitment to certain conduct. (When my husband first started wearing a kippah—his own spiritual progression being a story for another time—he told me he started straightening his shoulders a bit when he went out in public. "Now I really need to be on my best behavior!" he would think.)

This is a remarkably consistent theme across religious traditions, and it is not one that only applies to female adherents to a faith. Latter-day Saints have "Temple garments"—the subject of much mockery as "magical underwear"—which look like skimpier versions of long johns, to be worn under clothing at all times. (Kate didn't start wearing hers until two years after her conversion; she told me she doesn't think they're "weird," as many religions have clothing requirements, but finds them somewhat uncomfortable, and she thinks sometimes other Mormons can be too "nosy" about it.) Hindu holy men, called sadhus, often wear saffron-colored robes, as they equate fire with purity. The Conservative Anabaptist world relies heavily on tiny sartorial details to signal church affiliation; an academic I know who became Plain even wrote an entire book on the variety of head coverings for women, called *Ornament of the Spirit*. Jewish men wear tzitzit, ritual fringes, with "each corner of the garment a thread of blue wool to remind them of the blue sky and of the miraculous acts of the Eternal Who is above the heavens." Even Quakers, who, of the religions I've written about, are arguably the least separatist today, have a Plain-dressing background— "The men wear neither lace, frills, ruffles, swords, nor any of the ornaments used by the fashionable world," wrote the English abolitionist Thomas Clarkson, "[and] the women wear neither lace, flounces, lappets, rings, bracelets, necklaces, ear-rings, nor any thing belonging to this class." They still have a small subset of adherents who dress Plain today. "It's so easy to just look like everybody else and maybe interact with people or do things that you know you really shouldn't be doing," a Plain-dressing Quaker told the YouTube video series QuakerSpeak in 2020. "But for me, I really wanted something that would call my attention to how I was interacting in the world, and looking different is a helpful tool for me." (It's ironic that so much pious fashion signals conformity only so long as you remain within the group itself: a Plain-dressed Amish or Quaker person outside the confines of a Plain environment suddenly becomes very conspicuous indeed.) When my oldest child was a baby, I even bought him a charming little board book called *Hats of Faith*, featuring colorful illustrations of various pious headgear options: "This is a Chunni (Choon-ee), which many Sikh women wear. And this is a Topi, (Tou-pi) which many South Asian Muslim men wear." It's an oft-repeated Jewish trope that the Israelites were able to survive in Egypt because they retained three things: their names, their language, and their dress. Though the provenance of this idea is sketchy, it's beloved because it's an idea Jews take so seriously: you should dress to ensure other people know you are *not like them*.

There was so much about modest dressing I felt compelled by. I loved, for example, thinking of it as a counterargument to a culture of oversharing and self-centeredness; I loved that it seemed to preserve a little mystique about you. "I'm always happiest when dressed almost like a nun," Miuccia Prada told *New Yorker* writer Judith Thurman in 2012. "It makes you feel so relaxed." The idea of having a more limited set of choices in my wardrobe (as in my life!), what some people call a "capsule wardrobe," seemed like a healthy corrective to the me of years prior: the *Vogue* intern, who briefly thought she might pursue a career in fashion and shopped *voraciously*, trying on new outfits in a way that was clear to me was more about trying to become different people entirely than about simply experimenting with different styles. (I cured myself of my compulsive shopping habit by taking a year off buying anything new—save for underwear and books—when I was twenty-five; I now find it difficult to buy even necessary things.) Around this time, voluntary uniforms even had a moment in the sun: a New York–based creative director named Matilda Kahl wrote a widely read essay in 2015 about how she decided to adopt a "work uniform" à la Steve Jobs's ubiquitous turtleneck—Kahl's was a white-collared shirt and black pants every day—in order to free up time to focus on actual work. And what was a religious outfit, really, but a sort of spiritual uniform?

I relished in the stories I heard about women rebelling by covering up. The wife of the Plain academic I knew, also a convert to a Plain church, used to sew herself Amish-style dresses while in college and sneak out wearing them—to go where, exactly, she didn't say—knowing her family wouldn't approve, which I found hilarious. One day, I hung out with a member of the EMT corps Ruchie Freier introduced me to, a young woman my own age I'll call Esther. Esther was a convert who lived alone in a room she rented from an old single Hasidic woman in Borough Park. I envisioned (and felt oddly envious of) a thoroughly

Victorian arrangement: the two safeguarding their little pious women's idyll, playing cards or praying or baking bread or engaging in some other exceedingly quaint activity. Esther ran at breakneck speed into observant life, in a way that I both admired and found a little disquieting. She told me that although her rabbis had advised her to take things slowly, she took on many obligations all at once, including dressing modestly (she openly longed for the day she could marry, so she could start wearing a wig). "When I first looked at myself in the mirror wearing my tznius clothes, I felt like a princess," she told me.

On occasion, I worried that my attraction had less to do with fledging spirituality and more to do with my general distaste for bodies full stop, particularly my own. In a way not dissimilar to how I thought about women CEOs, it occurred to me that being told to cover my upper arms was actually not only unoffensive, but a massive relief, because I'd always hated them for being bulky—miniature weight lifter's arms, when I really wanted to be ballerina shaped. Though I'd always denied that my interest in fashion had a deleterious effect on my body image, I had to admit that I'd felt slightly more pressure to be slimmer in the revealing clothing of my *Vogue* days. Once I began wearing things that generously billowed around my waistline, I exhaled a little easier, unafraid to reveal to bystanders that my stomach was, in fact, not flat. And when it came to the idea of distinguishing oneself from the secular masses, the modest fashion boom actually didn't work in my ideological favor at all. Don't get me wrong, I never planned to shop at Junee forever, or to adopt a Kahlesque uniform of monochromatic skirts and shells and bulletproof stockings; I was happy to have access to modest style in an array of price points and styles and colors (even, yes, red). And by the time I was dressing more modestly—a slow development that happened over the course of around two years, so that by late 2015 I probably dressed modestly a good 90 percent of the time—I was for all intents and purposes recovered from my anorexia, so I wasn't hiding hatred of my form beneath mounds of fabric. But the other qualm remained: If my look was now more similar to that of the average New York City millennial, the kind of girl you might see photographed on the Sartorialist, and if I could get tznius clothing everywhere from Goodwill to Bergdorf, then how was I projecting my religious affiliation? How did I *show* people that something seismic was happening in my soul?

There was perhaps one way to make myself more readily distinctive, and this was by covering my hair. In many faiths, women's hair is a symbol of sexuality, and thus deemed inappropriate for men to view. In the Orthodox world, many women customarily cover their hair when they marry, and there are a plethora of options depending on what community you affiliate with. The more liberal modern Orthodox women might wear headbands, small hats, or bandannas, their real hair visible on their foreheads or backs (some don't cover at all); in centrist modern Orthodox spheres and some Hasidic communities, wigs that closely resemble real hair are common, some of them wildly expensive and leaving the wearer significantly better coiffed on a daily basis than they would be otherwise, or at least so I assumed. In Israel generally and specifically in Sephardi communities, wigs are less common than elaborate tichels, scarves that wrap around the head, or snoods, droopy bags of fabric that hold the hair inside. In more conservative Hasidic spheres, women wear short wigs, often with small hats or headbands on top, to serve as a kind of double covering. These not-hair signifiers are symbolic of a debate that has raged in the Orthodox world for ages: if your replacement hair is a mane that cascades down your back more luxuriously and sexily than your *actual* hair, how exactly does that dissuade men from gawking at you? There's even a snarky epithet for the kind of woman whose wig does her appearance a great favor: a Hot Chani, whose existence I was introduced to after attending a Shabbat in upstate New York where all the women wore figure-hugging dresses that only just skimmed their kneecaps and wigs made of thick, heavily layered hair that reached their butts. Years later, I heard of a similar concept in Islam, the bad hijab: maybe there's a slit up the woman's manteau, something is too tight, the fabric around the head lets too much hair peek out of the veil. The letter of the law is technically maintained; the spirit of it, not so much.

In Judaism, the obligation to cover one's hair derives from the passage in Numbers regarding the sotah, a married woman suspected of adultery, who is brought before the high priests at the Temple. There, God's name is written on a scroll, which is ground up and put into a liquid the woman must drink. If she's innocent, she receives a blessing; if she's guilty, she and her paramour die. Before she drinks, though, the high priests are said to "stand the woman up before God and uncover the woman's head." Thus, the rabbis inferred the obligation of hair covering in public: because the text specifies that the woman's head was uncovered by the priests, that must mean it was covered before, and that being uncovered marks her loss of dignity. Almost all Orthodox rabbinic authorities accept this as law, albeit with some wiggle room: they debate, for example, as to whether it qualifies as a Torah-level (read: more serious) prohibition, or whether this applies only in public or everywhere. (And from there: Does one's backyard qualify as "public," for example? The courtyard of one's building? A space where no men are present?) In some cases, like in 1950s Morocco, hair covering among local women became so uncommon that their community rabbis suggested the custom be considered essentially negated: if hair was essentially no longer associated with erva, or nakedness, then men wouldn't view it as seductive, so it was no longer immodest to go about bareheaded, an argument that would certainly hold water in the West today, where it isn't gauche anymore to go about hatless in mainstream society.

If you applied such logic to many issues in Orthodoxy, much of the behaviors could crumple, yet the practice of hair covering remains alive and well, somewhat to my discomfort. I told myself that the issue with covering my hair was that it was not something that was modeled for me; surely had I grown up in an environment where every woman did it, I'd segue into it easily! The truth, however, was less flattering: I couldn't justify spending thousands of dollars on a nice wig, and I thought many of the other options looked hideous on me. My hair has always been extremely fine, which, on most days, especially as I age, means thin and lifeless. You'd think that would mean I'd jump at the chance to obscure it, but headbands or little hats only seemed to draw attention to the limp ends of my locks; scarves—awkwardly tied, always—make me appear nearly bald beneath them, although there are workarounds, like special foam padding some women use to give the impression of a full head of hair. A friend of mine, also a convert, told me her rebbetzin had said that whatever you chose as a head covering should feel like a crown, but everything I put on my head looked like a stupid shmatta covering my six hairs and casting gnarly shadows on my dumb face. I lamented that the Jewish market seemed to be slightly behind in terms of cute headgear: I mean, there are some truly *adorable* turbans made by Muslim-centric companies out there, even though the few of those I own, too, only look good on me from certain angles. Proponents of hair covering were wont to say that, like having a uniform, it made life easier for them—Never worry about blow-drying! Every day is a great hair day!—but for me, the choices seemed *more* numerous than they had been precovering, when I just let my hair hang down until it annoyed me enough to wrap it into a tiny bun and ignore it. When my husband and I were in Israel for an extended period of time years ago, I weirdly found all my self-consciousness about hair covering evaporated instantly, simply because it was so socially acceptable, but in New York, even though many women do it, I usually feel too conspicuous, like everyone can tell I am just trying on a costume, one I'll take off as soon as I get home. Imagine the paroxysms of self-consciousness I felt when tasked with taking a new author photo. Even though by that point I was covering my hair somewhat more frequently—which is to say, probably about 50 percent of the time—when the photographer arrived, I found myself clumsily brandishing a thick black-velvet headband, unsure of how or when to suggest a few snaps with it: if I didn't wear it, people might write me off as an improper authority on religion, as a faker, but if I *did* put it on, wouldn't that be, in many ways, a lie?

When I lived in London, I had a friend there, a fellow American expat, with stellar frum credentials: she grew up in a largely Orthodox enclave, went to the women's college affiliated with Yeshiva University (the academic center of the modern Orthodox world), and had been observant her entire life. She managed to cultivate an ambience of worldly, chic woman and traditional balaboosta all at once. She did not, however, cover her hair. When asked about it, she would shrug—with a hint of defiance—and say, "I know the source texts, and I just don't think it's a strong enough argument." She wore a selection of cute hats in shul, but most of the time, her short brown hair was left bare, in a tiny ponytail or curled up by her shoulders, and sometimes I'd look over at her and spontaneously think something corny about freedom being symbolized by hair blowing in the breeze, preferably as the woman sits in the driver's seat of a convertible, zipping down a picturesque highway. There was something about being so firmly *of* something that allowed one to flout its rules with less anxiety, some sense of knowing that even if you didn't do everything by the book, nobody could take your identity away from you.

Though I agreed with her on principle that sotah alone seemed a flimsy justification for sexualizing hair, and though my personal custom at the time was quite close to hers—covering it at synagogue, but almost nowhere else—I didn't feel like I'd ever be confident enough to emulate her. My dissension was born not of genuine, educated conviction, but of cowardice: fear that I'd further alienate the friends and family who'd already had to take so much change in stride, fear that I wouldn't do it correctly, fear that I'd simply look unattractive. When I ran my fingers through my own naked locks in public, I didn't feel the rush of liberation or the thrill of transgression or even the nothingness I'd felt for the majority of my life, when having an uncovered head was my default state. I felt the sting of embarrassment: there was something *more* I could be doing to show my fealty, but that I just couldn't bring myself to do.

The night my first child was born, I lay in my hospital bed as he slept soundly in a bassinet nearby, and wept. They weren't tears of joy: I was happy in the abstract, but that happiness was subsumed by the shell shock of a long and difficult labor and the eerie and unmistakable knowledge that my life had changed in a way that I had failed, despite all my anticipation of this day, to truly grasp.

But I wasn't really crying because of that either. My husband, sleeping on a cot oddly low to the ground next to my bed, had made a sweet, offhand comment about how he'd still be there to take care of me, and I burst into tears. I knew that, while that might be true in a practical sense, I was sure I'd ultimately been dethroned as the member of the family unit who would ever be first priority in terms of care again. I knew this was necessarily correct: there was a more vulnerable creature with us now, and we'd be channeling our energies toward him and away from ourselves for the foreseeable future, which stretched on as far as my myopic thirty-two-year-old self could see. And though I knew it was good and right and true that this should be the case, deep inside, I mourned my demotion from heroine of a story to supporting cast member.

This was confusing, as a person who'd once dreamed of having ten children (although I suspect now that this was more a writerly fantasy than a maternal one—so many characters to name!). Almost all the girls I knew growing up in the eighties and nineties daydreamed about future children: the outfits they'd dress them in, the pristine house they'd maintain, the places they'd take their brood on vacation. None of us thought this automatically meant we'd stay at home though; we all equally wondered what kind of careers we'd have as adults, because it was assumed you could do both without conflict.

By 2017, though, when my first child was born, the zeitgeist had shifted so thoroughly that the bulk of the conversation around motherhood seemed to center around how horrible it was. Countless articles lamented the unfair division of household labor between women and their spouses; as the years went on, the complaints morphed and grew to include the pressure women felt to breastfeed, to live up to the "momfluencer" aesthetic, to be hyperinvolved in their children's lives. Books on the topic, with titles like *And Now We Have Everything: On Motherhood Before I Was Ready* (at twenty-nine!), *All Joy and No Fun: The Paradox of Modern Parenting*, and *How Not to Hate Your Husband After You Have Kids*, ran the gamut from the humorous and pessimistic to the bleak and pessimistic; a subgenre of fiction coalesced, in which moms always seemed to be turning into wild animals and eating raw meat.

Solutions were proffered, on occasion, to the problem of Motherhood Being Hell: better paid parental leave in the United States (definitely good), cultivating an atmosphere of lower pressure on moms overall (probably good, possibly hard to achieve), parenting like the French or the Danes or the Chinese (understandably appealing, probably impossible, possibly unethical). People were always vaguely and positively gesturing at societies with communal parenting cultures—usually some monolithically defined "Indigenous," occasionally actual communes—without ever looking to the truly long-lived and successful ones under their very noses. Why, I often wondered, did no one recognize that secular cooperative endeavors—kibbutzim, sixties ersatz utopias—had largely failed, and that who they should actually be looking to was the Amish?

I noticed pretty quickly that there wasn't quite the same cry of despair emanating en masse from the Jewish world. I don't want to make sweeping generalizations here: there are surely lots of religious women who find themselves equally unmoored by motherhood, or who pursue it because they have to be fruitful and multiply and all that, but secretly, deep down, don't really want to be a parent at all. But overall, the observant Jewish moms I knew seemed much more sanguine about finding themselves attached to a shrieking barnacle than my non-Jewish friends or the writers whose laments I encountered did. "Enjoy it," the rebbetzin of a London shul I attended, herself the mother of five children, told me of the early baby days. "It's the most *delicious* time—you just sit around and do nothing all day." To me, such idleness sounded like hell; to her, maybe, like a taste of Sabbath, that state of *be*-ing and not *do*-ing that I was only just then at the cusp of understanding. I guessed to myself their transition was easier because they were part of a more explicitly pronatalist culture, one that assumes and encourages family growth—and that insists that children are, in the end, both a foregone conclusion and a blessing. (Similar, but not identical, arguments can be made about the other patriarchal pro-familial faith systems I've written about in this book, which is all of them save Quakerism.) If something was simply not a choice, after all, why agonize over it?

There was also, I suspected, some modeling at work here: my secular peers and I, having rarely been asked to consider what role sacrifice might play in our own lives, found ourselves much more anguished when asked to curtail our own freedoms, whereas observant Jews were raised with a keen awareness of the ways they are beholden to others. In her book *The Obligated Self: Maternal Subjectivity and Jewish Thought*, the scholar Mara Benjamin argues that motherhood is uniquely analogous to the Jewish experience. To be born a Jew, Benjamin writes, is "to have entered a social world already encumbered with tasks, duties, and relationships"; to become a mother is the same. Both these roles involve submitting to an external law—the "Law of the Baby," as she calls the fickle, immovable demands of an infant, and the mitzvot—that you might not have fully comprehended or consented to beforehand. She quotes Rashi, who states unsentimentally that the mitzvot are not for Israel's "enjoyment" but exist to serve as a "yoke around their necks," and, later, the profoundly disturbing midrash that depicts God as *threatening* the Jews at Sinai by holding the mountain over their heads. "If you accept the Torah, it is good. And if not, here shall be your grave." (This is a stark contrast to the ecstatic consent vision of na'aseh v'nishma.) Benjamin inverts the familiar image of God as paternal figure and instead suggests that He is, in episodes like this, closer to a petulant, demanding infant. "If the rabbinic notion of obligation comes into felt experience most viscerally in caring for young

children, then God is not an overlord but a vulnerable, dependent being who needs virtually constant attention."

In its way, Judaism recognizes that you cannot, in fact, have it all;
this is why women, assumed to be the ones managing the children and
household, are exempt from "positive time-bound mitzvot," though
this technically cuts out only 8 ritual obligations from 613. A close
read of certain texts, though, almost makes the argument that husbands bear an even *heavier* load, obligated as they are in all the mitzvot
and in the creation and sustenance—material, anyway—of a family.
(Technically speaking, men are required to have children and women
aren't.) Only men with children can lead certain prayer services or
serve as judges, presumably because it's assumed such a man will have
a greater stake in society's long-term health, and because, having
known what it is to love an offspring, he will be more "merciful" when
doling out punishment. In multiple texts, it specifies that men who
have families are still obligated to study Torah, something that women
weren't expected or even allowed to do anyway, depending on whom
you asked.

There is a recognition that these two things could be somewhat in
conflict: the Talmud says that when a man is older than twenty and
unmarried, he can delay his nuptials further only if he's "involved in
Torah and engrossed in it," though it is the rare man whose complete
failure to engage in family life would be absolved. In the Talmud, the
sages openly criticize Ben Azzai for neglecting his procreative duty:
"There is a type of scholar who expounds well and fulfills his own
teachings well, and another who fulfills well and does not expound
well," they say. "But you, who have never married, expound well on the
importance of procreation, and yet you do not fulfill well your own
teachings." Ben Azzai responds, with a hint of melancholy (maybe I'm

projecting), "What shall I do, as my soul yearns for Torah, and I do not wish to deal with anything else."

This whole setup can look somewhat feminist, from a certain angle: men must stay within and provide for their families unless a singular scholar like Ben Azzai, while single, childless women should not be stigmatized. But because the sexes need each other to have children, and because there are so many places in Jewish texts where specifically female infertility is linked to sorrow—Rachel, who said she preferred death to never having children, or Isaiah's characterization of exiled Jerusalem as the bereft barren woman—it's hard to see that loophole as truly salutary. And much like the male gaze and modesty, no matter how much onus the text puts on men, in practice, childrearing somehow mysteriously becomes mostly, if not solely, the women's job. After all, men have the countervailing force of study: what else are women going to do, if *not* take care of the house and the children and deal with all the drudgery? Women whose souls did yearn to study at higher levels than they would have been encouraged or allowed to had no convent within which to ensconce themselves; they had to squeeze it in between breastfeeding, cleaning, baking the challah, and whatever other household duties they had to get through (unless of course they were rich enough to bring maids into the marital home, thus exempting them from certain chores, though still at the husband's discretion, since, as the Talmud says, "idleness leads to idiocy"). "Such was her way, to sit always near the winter oven . . . with all sorts [of religious books] spread before her on the table," writes the early twentieth-century Lithuanian rabbi Barukh ha-levi Epstein of his formidable aunt Rayna Batya Berlin, a woman of "bitter mood and with bitter soul" over her sex's position in traditional Judaism. "All of her focus and concentration were on the books—her hand hardly moved from them! But of all that concerned the maintenance of the household, she knew little, almost nothing."

I'm not as impressive a scholar as Berlin, and besides, nowadays, there are infinitely more opportunities for women to study Torah than there were in her time, opportunities I take advantage of whenever I can. But I relate to her in that, if I'm being honest, what I really want is to do *zero* household work and instead just sit by a little stove, reading and thinking and debating, as Berlin did with her nephew. Because I'm suspicious of this brain-in-a-jar instinct ("You just want to be a plant that sits there and soaks up the sun," a therapist once told me), I try to view the embodied religious woman's role as pushing back against it in a healthy way. In my twenties, I rarely if ever thought about the food I ate—where it came from, how it was made, how it worked on my body once consumed. I'm not talking about periods of disordered eating; I'm talking about me as a typical single city dweller, who procured most of the food she ate mere moments before she ate it, and almost never prepared anything in toto for herself, preferring takeout and restaurants and random packaged food to an iota of preplanning or effort. Now, because I became part of a relatively intense hospitality culture, because I have young children, and because I am mandated to say blessings over the food I eat—specific ones depending on how the food I'm ingesting is made or grown—I am forced to purchase food, cook it, and consider its provenance as I pause to consider the words I'll intone. I tried to learn to sew once but it was sort of a disaster, so I don't make my own tapestries, but I try to take care of my household in the manner of Eishes Chayil, for—as my twentysomething self would say—what is the point of having these things if you aren't going to make some kind of temporal investment in them?

In the same email chain in which I argued for the continuing value of the mikvah with my friend, I told her I felt there was something truthful in an approach that didn't pretend true equity could ever be reached: from the moment of conception, mothers worked harder than fathers in family units, and that was just simply never going to change, unless you were okay with taking advantage of the capitalist promise that you could outsource anything unpleasant. Of course, we should strive to make our societal structures as fair as possible, but what many actually want, I suspect, is to have their cake (the family system) and eat it too (not have to make unpleasant sacrifices to maintain it), and that just isn't how nearly anything works, ever. Harsh, I know, especially because it's not like I don't regularly wrestle with the indignities of it all myself: in fact, I told my friend that one of the oddest things for me when I had moved to a more religious neighborhood was how infrequently my immediate female neighbors asked me what I did for a living, and how that simultaneously registered as both a relief and an offense. But ultimately, it felt better to be in a space, I concluded, that praised and valued domestic contributions at *all*, rather than seeing them as pesky obstacles to career success, or retrograde activities best left to the likes of June Cleaver or the hired help, that saw the home as a place of value and the rearing of children as a crucial act, and that refused to succumb to the near constant pessimism that seemed to color the overall discourse.

But from a certain vantage point, I sometimes wonder if being an Orthodox woman isn't actually the *worst* of both worlds. The great promise of the Evangelical tradwife is being able to do one thing only: in exchange for being responsible for 100 percent of the drudgery of childcare and domestic work, you get a free pass to avoid any traditionally male concerns, like finances or, I don't know, woodworking. "Our job used to be *no job*," the comedian Ali Wong says. "We had it so good!" But as is evidenced by Eishes Chayil, Judaism never offered this bargain. In addition to being expected to have children—and we comply, by having nearly double the number secular women do—Orthodox women still usually work outside the home. This holds true even in more conservative Jewish communities, where people often wrongly assume that a religious ethic of wifely submission and homemaking prevail. In fact, because the ideal in many Haredi communities is for the men to learn Torah full time, wives are often the sole breadwinners for very large families.

In my community, I'm surrounded by mothers who are doctors, lawyers, academics, psychologists, and teachers, and most of them have at least three children, regardless of their economic status. Almost all the families I know employ household help of some kind or another, but the women still bear the brunt of the domestic burden, and it can be a heavy one, particularly in the realm of food and cooking. ("Thanksgiving dinner with all the fixings?" a funny e-card I once saw read. "No problem! I'm Jewish—I do this every Friday.") I would be lying if I didn't find myself occasionally ranting in my head pre-Shabbat, while monitoring a roasting chicken and chopping vegetables and setting out a tablecloth and filling up a hot water boiler and tearing toilet paper and nagging my kids to put away their electronic toys and wondering how on earth I was going to get everyone squeaky clean and in their Shabbos best—we are greeting the queen, after all!—in such a short time, that this is SO UNFAIR and actually I REALLY AM NOT INTO THE DOMESTIC ARTS AND I'D LIKE TO REVERT TO THE WHOLE BRAIN-IN-A-JAR THING AND NOT BE RESPONSIBLE FOR NURTURING ANYTHING, EVER. I mumble angrily to myself that sure, fine, the Eishes Chayil gets her own song, just as the king's nanny is made into a parable of righteousness, but are those things really worth the exhaustion she feels from keeping her entire house afloat while her husband schmoozes with the elders at the gates? Of course she seems like the perfect woman: she literally does *everything*.

All of this dyspepsia falls away, however, when I'm tending to my challah. I've been making it weekly for more than seven years now—I first learned at a group bake hosted by the London rebbetzin with the five kids, and have used the same recipe since then—so the process has become formulaic to the point of being meditative: washing the dishes to *wash the dishes*, as the Buddhist sage Thich Nhat Hanh says, doing the thing itself, rather than treating it as a means to an end. The warm water is poured into the bowl, the yeast drizzled in and then sprinkled with sugar; occasionally, I wait and watch the yeast as it sinks into the water, and then blooms upward again toward the surface, a series of tiny bomb detonations. (It's fantastic visual ASMR.) The egg, oil, sugar, flour, salt, and then, the pleasant sensation of combining all these elements into one by kneading them together.

In these moments, I think of the words of Matthew B. Crawford, the philosopher and motorcycle mechanic: "Both as workers and as consumers, we feel we move in channels that have been projected from afar by vast impersonal forces . . . [we] begin to wonder if getting an adequate grasp on the world, intellectually, depends on getting a handle on it in some literal and active sense." I think of something Leah Libresco Sargeant once said in an interview, that to counter her instinctual gnosticism—its "attendant hatred/suspicion of the body"—she bought a sourdough starter and began to bake bread (this was way before COVID-19). I think, too, of the other Jewish women out there doing the same, the ones stretching all the way back into history who kneaded their dough, too, whispering a little tkhine as they place it into the hot oven. "So, I make this holy blessing / as You blessed the dough of / Our mothers, Sarah and Rebecca. / God, my God, / Hear my voice. / You are God / Who hears the voices / Of those who call out to You / With all their hearts."

⁎

As of this writing, it's been almost eight years since I officially converted, and over a decade since I walked into that tiny basement office in Borough Park in my short-sleeve dress. I still usually appreciate the opportunities for gender-specific events and spaces in my life, although I have definitely been in situations where such segregation felt awkward or even insulting. I once prayed at a gorgeous historic synagogue in Budapest, although I barely got to see it because the women—all two of us at the service, for a holiday nonetheless—were relegated to a cubicle-size space cordoned off by very high screens; and at my former synagogue in Brooklyn, women sat in the back of the room, behind a mechitzah that was high enough that we could rarely, if ever, hear the sermon or see what was happening at the altar—a very obvious physical manifestation, in my view, of how the synagogue leadership felt about us.

I now live in a modern Orthodox community in the greater New York City area, where the synagogues have a wide variety of customs with respect to gender segregation; the two shuls I attend most often have low mechitzahs, where women and men are still separated by a wall but are readily able to see each other over it, and, crucially, have an equally good view of the altar. There are plenty of opportunities for women-specific learning, but at the same time, no real taboo against chatting with a member of the opposite sex at meals or social gatherings or during some learning initiatives. The attitudes toward tznius are similarly varied: at morning drop-off at my kids' school, I see women wearing sheitels, others in beanies or baseball caps, and many with nothing on their head at all. I have friends who cover their hair daily while wearing short-sleeves or jeans. Though I will wear pants maybe a handful of times a year—in a fit of impulsivity, I bought a floral, paja-malike pair with cheap feathers lining the ankles right after my first child was born, and I like to break those out when I'm feeling festive— I actually often feel like an outlier here for maintaining such a conser-vative wardrobe. When out to drinks with a group of friends, one of the women present, whose hair is usually immaculately wrapped up in the same golden-yellow tichel, turned to me and lamented her inability to find the right boots to pair with her Levi's, and when I told her I wasn't able to advise because I don't wear jeans, I briefly felt extremely unhip—and not in a cool, beat-of-my-own-drummer way, but in an undeniably dowdy one.

For much of my observant life, I've gone to the mikvah without any particular tumult: like challah baking, it became rote, in a way I would characterize as neutral to good. But that changed somewhat at the be-ginning of the pandemic, when I wrote an article about what various mikvahs were doing to safeguard users against illness. Over and over again, I heard that while accommodations could be made for various other aspects of Jewish life—men could pray alone, far-flung family members could Zoom into a seder if they were lonely or depressed— mikvah attendance was nonnegotiable (unless you were okay with tem-porary celibacy). Those with skin in the game repeatedly insisted that mikvahs were perfectly safe and fine, thank you very much, even though that seemed ludicrous to me, because at the very least, we didn't know what it meant for *anything* to be "safe and fine" in March 2020. I was infuriated by this party line and rejoiced when watching the livestreams produced and reading the papers written by female leaders—teachers, rabbanits, mivkah educators called yoetzet, and others—who were actively trying to figure out workable solutions for women who were (understandably) too afraid to venture out or whose communities were completely locked down. My feminist rage at the situation dissipated a bit when I saw firsthand just how thoroughly contemporary Jewish women *do* rule the mikvahs today: for some of us, the era of passing your underwear to a man to inspect its stain is over, because you can get all the help you need from a qualified, learned, and sympathetic woman. But when I began grappling with secondary infertility, the mikvah became for me an unavoidable reminder of failure and heartbreak and resentment, something I'd heard was the case for others but never truly internalized. Many nights, I'd rush out of the hidden mikvah door, my hair still dripping wet, and sit in my car weeping, feeling about as far from a blushing young bride on honeymoon as one could get.

So why still go? Why still do any of this at all, if I recognize some inherent imbalance there? Why spend days cooking huge meals, dusting the tiniest motes of bread from my cabinets before Pesach, pushing my body and mind in pursuit of having children? The responses are myriad: Because I believe in the value of sacrifice. Because I believe in the entire enterprise of Judaism. Because I feel strongly that just because I'm going through a difficult time with a particular thing doesn't mean the thing ceases to have worth or should be discarded immediately. (Would you divorce your spouse after a single rough patch?) Because I believe the benefits outweigh the costs. Because I feel like a whole person now, one who knows how to take care of things, who knows how it feels to have obligations and meet them, who knows how to play a long game, who understands that inextricable interplay between love and pain, between fulfillment and abstinence, between creation and death, and because I believe Judaism taught me all this in a way nothing else ever could. Because I do actually believe that God literally told us to utilize a mikvah, and also that we'll never quite understand why that is, and there is value in just doing it regardless. Because I'm pretty sure I would have wanted all this anyway—a husband, a family, a house— and odds look good that, had I pursued it outside a supportive framework, I'd have been left very angry and lonely indeed. Because I do want to be like the Eishes Chayil, at the end of the day: I want my lamp to never go out at night, and I want to feel cloaked in strength and dignity, and to laugh in the face of the future, just like she does.

Afterword

I was given a generous two years to write this book, and during that time I often wondered what would change in my subjects' lives by the time it went to press. In February 2022, Angela submitted a letter to the Brooklyn Monthly Meeting in which she requested to be made a member. "The fear remains that perhaps this is the wrong decision," she admitted. "But I have gained enough self-knowledge to discern that my trepidation is a constant within me and not necessarily a sign that I do not know enough. . . . Somehow, even imperceptibly, Quakerism had become a part of my life. The decision had been made within me, without my conscious awareness. My role is to call it what it is." She was formally made a member that summer.

A few months after I visited her, Sara began dating a man (they met "on the apps") named Hank. Hank was raised in the Middle East in a Christian Indian family that had relocated to California when he was in high school. When we caught up in April 2024, she was about to head out to inspect a 3-D printout of her engagement ring, although Hank was leaving the actual proposal date a surprise. They were also planning to buy property in Los Angeles, which they'd decided to make a higher priority than paying for a big wedding (they hadn't lived together yet). The news wasn't all rosy though: the summer after she met Hank, Sara had come down with mono while working as a counselor at a Christian summer camp for teens, and she continued to struggle with the symptoms of it, mainly debilitating fatigue, for longer than the average patient, which led to some disappointing experiences with the health-care system and a lot of reflection on the idea of rest in scripture, like the angel providing for the prophet Elijah as he sleeps. When we spoke, she was coming off a medical leave from her job and returning to school, looking down the line toward a permanent career shift. "I think more and more I realize I want to be a chaplain or a pastor," she told me. Before she went to look at her engagement ring, she was having a Zoom meeting with the leadership team at her new church—she'd left Reality for a smaller non-denominational church, in part to become more involved at the professional level—to talk about the possibility of becoming a pastoral intern.

By spring 2024, Kate was also engaged, to a young man named Jesse, who worked as a city planner in the Salt Lake area. They were organizing a small ceremony in the Grand Tetons in the summertime and a traditional Temple marriage in December, near Jesse's family in Texas (one motivation for not combining the two, as many Latter-day Saints do, is that Kate's father initially said he'd refuse to attend an LDS service, though he'd abruptly and without explanation changed his mind about that a few weeks into wedding planning). Like Sara and Hank, Kate and Jesse weren't living together yet—Kate had moved since I saw her in Salt Lake, to the downtown area—and were planning to start looking for a new place shortly after they tied the knot, but, in an echo of our conversations before she'd graduated college, she told me that they weren't expecting to stay in Utah in the long term. Jesse's parents are Mexican Latter-day Saints (his father is a devout convert, and his parents are divorced), and Kate didn't think they'd want to raise kids in the overwhelmingly white, culturally homogenous milieu of Utah (she'd since changed jobs and now worked in insurance, which she could do remotely). Part of the reason she felt she and Jesse connected so well is that he'd been raised outside the Utah bubble and had a wider worldview than some other Latter-day Saint men she'd met since moving there, and she wanted that for her children. She told me she still missed the more diverse church she'd attended in New Jersey.

In the fall of 2023, I managed to travel to Riyadh to see Hana in her adopted home. Everywhere I looked in Riyadh, there was some new, dazzling project under way: a pile of rubble that would become luxury apartments; the façade of a building designed to look like two spooning crescent moons, which would eventually contain the world's largest botanical gardens; a desert Six Flags, the future home of the world's longest roller coaster. I'd meet her midday for coffee near her office at Starbucks, next to the on-site mosque, which resembled a mini geodesic dome. Even though the little icon near the women's bathroom still sported a hijab, lots of the women I saw lining up for lattes wore their hair uncovered and wore fully Western garb. At night Hana drove me to spots across the city in her tiny red Porsche, some hidden and some designed to attract attention: a giant outdoor mall with huge electronic billboards like a pedestrian-only Times Square; a run-down souk where they sold huge selections of abayas and heavy gold necklaces; the Diplomatic Quarter, where expats could legally drink alcohol and fancy California-style vegan restaurants sold exotic fruit bowls and rice paper vegetable rolls, which Hana ordered in flawless Arabic. I was shocked by how easy it was to navigate the country as a Westerner—every street sign was written in both Arabic and English, and Uber made it easy to get to malls filled with Victoria's Secrets and Zaras—and even found myself wondering if Hana ever worried that the place she'd fallen in love with years earlier was at risk of flattening into the cultural sameness globalization had wrought everywhere. Eight months after my visit, she texted to tell me she was dating a guy, and though it was relatively new, she was optimistic. "He's Saudi, of course," she said, but not from the conservative region where past flames came from. Nothing much was new faithwise, she told me, but there was other big news: she'd gotten a job with a company backed by the Public Investment Fund, the powerful sovereign wealth fund of Saudi Arabia, an indicator of her increasing insider status. In her Instagram announcement about the new posting, her hair was completely uncovered.

Christina bought a small, cheerful yellow house nearby in Oakland in August 2023 and was working on renovating it to prepare for a summer 2024 move. She had no long-term foster children in her home by then: the two I'd met, plus another who'd arrived after I visited, had all gone back to live with their birth parents, but Christina often babysat and she wanted more room for those kids and any potential future foster children. The house sat on nearly twenty acres of land and came with a small shack that she was planning to open as a market, where she'd sell eggs from her ducks, drinks, and various sundries, so that members of the community didn't have to go all the way into town for everything. She planned to name the market in honor of a well-known symbol for autism, as her half brother will be helping her with it. She told me the community in Oakland continued to shrink somewhat, but that in a way, it made them more intimate and more reliant upon one another, which could be lovely.

Sister Orianne remained in Canada, but was hoping to be able to return to the States for the order's annual silent retreat in rural Massachusetts soon. She started a master's program in theology at a seminary in Toronto, and took on a new role: her order's local vocationist, which means she's the first point of contact for a woman who might be discerning a vocation in the area (I cannot think of someone better suited to this job). She also had two books about to be published, the ocean-related devotional she'd told me about in an earlier conversation, and a guide to the sacrament of confession, aimed at young-adult readers, that she coauthored with another sister. Over email, we bonded about the trepidation an introvert can feel on the precipice of a book's publication and promised to do a Zoom tea toast to celebrate each other as the dates approached.

Over the time I spent writing this, the fear over what experts called "the loneliness epidemic" only grew, despite our slow postpandemic return to basically normal life. Leaving aside thorny questions about methodology—such as whether we're really sure that when different researchers from different countries try to measure concepts like loneliness and happiness, they're talking about the same things—it was clear that the fraying of our social fabric was a real concern for many people. In April 2023, no less a figure than the surgeon general of the United States, Vivek H. Murthy, wrote about his own struggle with loneliness in *The New York Times*, in an attempt to show it could affect anyone, no matter how accomplished, and to bring a sense of urgency to the issue. "We need to acknowledge the loneliness and isolation that millions are experiencing and the grave consequences for our mental health, physical health and collective well-being," Murthy wrote. He suggested a three-pronged approach: first, rebuilding our social systems to foster connections between people; second, renegotiating our relationships with technology; and third, making smaller, personal efforts to spend true quality time with our friends and loved ones.

Afterword

It didn't escape some that traditional religions offer all these things in a ready-made package: no "rebuilding" required! "Can Religion Make You Happy?" was the title of an episode of *Good on Paper*, an *Atlantic* podcast hosted by Jerusalem Demsas. Her guest, Arthur Brooks, a professor at Harvard Business School and a columnist at the magazine, sat firmly in the "yes" camp. "People who do have a strong sense of religious practice in their life—they just tend to be happier. They have a greater sense of organization in their life. They have a better sense of community," he said. "And life is complicated. There are things that are going to pull you in every direction all the time. And it's nice to have something that you can actually count on, whether you agree with every single part of it or not."

The idea of religion as completely instrumental, though, rankled both sides. The secular to "none" contingent didn't accept the sole solution to their woes was submitting to an authority who might issue edicts they disagree with (this authority being human religious figures or, of course, God). Still, some openly longed for the kind of deep social bonds forged in religious life, the kind that come not just from sharing interests or living in close proximity, but also from educating your children together, worshipping together, being with one another in times of loss. Sometimes it felt like witnessing a kind of mourning process, watching people struggle with the fact that no institution or ideology aside from the ones they'd sworn off completely could meet what even they acknowledged were fairly gaping holes. "I asked every sociologist I interviewed whether communities created around secular activities outside of houses of worship could give the same level of wraparound support that churches, temples and mosques are able to offer," Jessica Grose, a *New York Times* columnist who wrote five newsletters on the subject in early 2023, wrote in her final installment. You can tell she is dying for them to say something actionable, but "nearly across the board, the answer was no."

Religious people, sometimes, balked at the instrumentalization as well. Such a Jamesian framing was incompatible with how they viewed their belief system: as implacably True, in a way that had absolutely nothing to do with how happy people were or whether they felt optimized or really even what they thought at all. These objections didn't come up that often, but when they did, they exploded. When Ayaan Hirsi Ali, a former member of the Dutch parliament and previously part of the "New Atheist" crowd, announced she was becoming a Christian because she felt Christianity was the most effective weapon for fighting the various forces set on destroying Western civilization, some Christian readers were outraged: where was her mention of the Crucifixion, or her absolute belief in the Resurrection? Indeed, where was Jesus at all, in all this talk of the clash of civilizations? Was religion just politics dressed up as transcendence? Shouldn't we be aiming somewhat higher here?

Personally I've never felt the ideas of Religion as Great Solution to Quotidian Problems and Religion as Ultimate Truth to be really at odds with one another. Humans are complex: there is no reason to think they can't both be true believers and recognize the sociological benefits of faith simultaneously. Besides, if God were the ultimate good, and God created a blueprint by which humans should live, then it makes sense that at least some of its outcome would be human flourishing (but not all the outcome: in His infinite wisdom, He'd also probably recognize that being happy all the time has its drawbacks). But it also seemed obvious to me that instrumentalization alone would not afford the benefits of both complete belief and sociological structure. My subjects weren't doing well simply because they'd joined a church or a mosque; they truly *believed*, and it was that interplay of belief and behavior, I feel, that has helped them in the end. What is the secret sauce, then, that allows you to get both? I wish I could say for sure, but God works, as they say, mysteriously. One thing I can say is that I suspect some of it lies in abandoning the idea that belief is the thing that ought to *pre-cede* the behavior. A white-light moment may help because it's such an obvious and instantaneous motivator, but exploring one's own relationship to God and religion shouldn't and doesn't require you to be free of doubt or immediately transformed; it just requires curiosity, a lack of preconceived judgment, and a quelling of fear.

It would be corny and simplistic to say that my time writing this book made me feel a stronger connection to people across the religious spectrum, but it would also be true. Some of the conversations I had with my subjects were of the most invigorating and fascinating of my life, not only because of the surprising points of convergence but because of the dexterity we all called upon when we had to navigate the moments when we naturally disagreed. In some cases, we would have been thought of as mortal enemies—Jew and Catholic, Jew and Muslim—but the fact that we were able to interact in such an intimate, friendly, long-term context meant I came to value them (and maybe them, me!) not only as avatars for their respective groups but as individuals too. I don't want to end by saying personal connection of this sort is the answer to the world's religious—and political, and cultural, and whatever other major categories of demographics come to mind—tensions, because it seems a totally unscalable suggestion. So maybe I'll just say that I felt really fortunate to do it, and I think if the opportunity to do the same ever arises for you, you should take it.

It's long been interesting to me that, of the seven subjects of this book, only I was married with children when I began writing. Obviously, this isn't surprising in every case—Sister Orianne, for example, and

Angela, because Liberal Quakers don't have the same expectations as the other faiths do in this department; Kate was also a bit young to be married when we first connected, even for a Latter-day Saint—but the others have joined very pro-familial faiths, and so their status as single makes them a little anomalous.

I am the outlier of this little group. I now have three sons who are growing up in a culture I often feel I still only superficially understand, an experience that is akin in many ways to being an expat parent. My kids are still deep in the first naivete, the eldest being only seven: their minds are porous, the world is enchanted, Hashem is a friendly entity who is always near, and religious ritual is a source of easy joy, particularly as it's so often accompanied by candy. They know little about anti-Semitism and zero about the Holocaust, though they will find out soon enough, I fear. It's surreal and terrifying and exciting to watch my sons rapidly develop a fluency in a language and a tradition that I hold so close to my heart, and I both yearn for and dread the day their knowledge will surpass my own, which is rapidly approaching.

I used to think that my own background would afford me some benefits in terms of raising religious children in that I might be more adept at dealing with the doubts that will inevitably arise as they age. I went on my own journey, the thought process went, so I would have a greater tolerance for my children's. The truth is, though, that this live-and-let-live attitude was something I assumed before my kids were actually born. Now that I'm a Jewish mother, the thought of them having a crisis of faith fills me with anxiety. There is both a meta reason for this—as a Jew, I'm explicitly charged with passing down my faith and practice to them—and a micro one—*I fought really hard to give you the resources that, in retrospect, I wish I could have had, so you'll love it whether you like it or not!* I have no idea whether a seeker personality is inheritable, and neither does anyone else (mine was anomalous in my nuclear family), but when I see glimmers of this impulse in them, I worry. It's ironic, that a thing that so defines my own sense of self is something I'd explicitly *not* want for them, even if I cherish it in me as much as I loathe it. It might even be unforgivable.

It's also far from the only thing I worry about in terms of being a religious parent. I worry of course about the dangers they'll face as Jews in the world, and I worry that they'll hate me for having inflicted this on them. I also worry that the burdens of Jewish practice exclude them too much from the thoughtless comforts of suburban child-hoods, but also that they don't exclude them *enough*; I worry that I am too harsh in forcing this way of life on them, and that I am not stringent enough. I worry that they will be unable to resist the purported freedoms of an irreligious life, or alternatively (less so, but still) the perceived clarities of a more fundamentalist one. In other words, I fear that by trying to give them both a modern life and a religious one, I am, in the end, not giving them enough of either. Though the worries are there all the time—more than a secular parent, I cannot say, for I've never been one—they dissipate when, in the soft light of Shabbat, my eldest sings, in a loud clear voice, the songs he learns in school. Kol ha'olam kulo / gesher tzar me'od / veha'ikar lo lifached k'lal: The whole world is a narrow bridge, and the important thing is to not be afraid.

I cannot teach my children Hebrew, to make matzoh balls the way my grandmother did, even to pray; I cannot draw on my own experiences of having learned about the Shoah or seen the Kotel for the first time, because I was not Jewish when I did these things, and it will undoubtedly register differently for them. But I believe that humans need newness, and they need to feel that they are discovering things for themselves, even things they've been bequeathed. So perhaps one day, when they are old enough, they can read this book and be shown what it's like to meet God for the first time and to fall in love.

Acknowledgments

Thank you, first and foremost, to my subjects. I couldn't have dreamed up more thoughtful, open, lovely people to get to know over the course of these past years. There is a saying in *Pirkei Avot*, credited to Rabbi Hanina ben Dosa: "One with whom men are pleased, God is pleased." I've seen alternative translations that use "delights," and after years of time getting to know each other in this very unique way, I imagine God delights in you all very much indeed.

Thanks also to those who shared their conversion stories with me in less protracted and formal ways. This includes Nemira Gasiunas, Leah Libresco Sargeant, Allegra Marino Shmulevsky, Isis Leslie, Amanda Malek, and Chloe Nash Rosen.

Several experts—academics, theologians, historians, and others—have helped fill in the many gaps in my knowledge. These include Matthew Wickman at Brigham Young University, Jana Riess of Religion News Service, Cory Anderson of the Amish and Plain Anabaptist Studies Association, Karen Johnson-Weiner, Steve Nolt of the Young Center for Anabaptist and Pietist Studies at Elizabethtown College,

Acknowledgments

Patrice Tuohy of Vocation Match, Sister Laurel M. O'Neal, Er Dio, Sister Mary Catharine Perry of the Bronx Dominicans, Sister Regina Frances Dick, Jenna Marie Cooper, Rabbi Steven Exler, and Dr. Rachel Rosenthal of the Jewish Theological Seminary and Maharat. I was lucky enough to learn with Rachel for a year on the subject of conversion, and I owe any of my knowledge and erudition to her (any mistakes are my own)! She also translated the beautiful midrash about the convert-as-gazelle, which I then paraphrased.

For helping me track down footage from Hana's episode of *Living Different*, thanks to Allison C. Deger.

Portions of this book appeared in or otherwise influenced work of mine that was published in *The Smart Set* and *Plough*. The latter's become something of a literary home over the past few years, a place where, as editor Peter Mommsen once told me, you can write about serious things unreservedly, a great joy for me, as a person who often finds the serious very exciting indeed.

If I needed more proof for God's existence, the fact that He saw fit to connect me with my wonderful agent Katie Cacouris would be enough. She inherited me in a time of interagency shuffling, and though I wasn't sure how auspicious such a chance beginning was, she's been the absolute best steward for my work I could have asked for. Thanks to everyone else at the Wylie Agency, an agency I'm so proud to have represent me. Allie Merola at Viking took a real chance on a book that didn't have (to my mind) an obvious selling point, and I am so grateful for her faith in the project. She's been such a clear-eyed, insightful, and supportive reader since day one, and this book wouldn't be worth the paper it's printed on were it not for her gentle, probing edits. Thanks also to the other folks at Viking who nurtured this project as it made its way out into the world, including but not limited to Julia Falkner, Sonia Gadre, Lynn Buckley, and Alex Cruz-Jimenez.

Acknowledgments

For being bottomless wells of writerly support, thanks to Stephanie Gorton Murphy, Avital Chizhik-Goldschmidt, Frimet Goldberger, Angela Chen, Anna O'Donoghue, Karen Karper Fredette, Laura Delano, Hannah Dylan Pasternak, and Elyse Pitock. Lucinda J. Kinsinger belongs in this category, too, but deserves a special shout-out for her fantastic Anabaptist detective skills and unparalleled hospitality.

For being my forever first and ideal reader, Hannah Sheldon-Dean. May we share in many more manuscripts to come.

Many people aided in my spiritual development over these many years, including but not limited to Rabbis Avrom Chakoff, Simcha Weinstein (though I can feel him cringing at this sentimentality even as I write), Steven Exler, and Barry Marcus MBE. To my community in the Bronx, with which I am completely in love, thank you for embracing my family. "דַחֲיֵ־סַג סִיחָא תֵּבְשׁ סִיעֶ־נ־הָמוּ בֹּט־הָמ הָנֵּה."

Finally, thanks to my children, Isaiah and Solomon, and to my miracle baby born during the writing of this book, Caleb. We gave you all strong names belonging to strong men of faith, in hopes you'd grow to be like them, and you've already exceeded our expectations. And to my husband, Matt: you always say that I'm the spiritual engine of the family, but you've long since surpassed me in that role. Seeing your dedication to your faith and to the Jewish people is nothing short of awe-inspiring. I think you're right that Hashem must have sent me to you, not solely for me to change our lives, as you've often said, but so that one of us could always be the push forward when the other needed it. I'll strive to repay your good all the days of my life.

100 YEARS of PUBLISHING

Harold K. Guinzburg and George S. Oppenheimer founded Viking in 1925 with the intention of publishing books "with some claim to permanent importance rather than ephemeral popular interest." After merging with B. W. Huebsch, a small publisher with a distinguished catalog, Viking enjoyed almost fifty years of literary and commercial success before merging with Penguin Books in 1975.

Now an imprint of Penguin Random House, Viking specializes in bringing extraordinary works of fiction and nonfiction to a vast readership. In 2025, we celebrate one hundred years of excellence in publishing. Our centennial colophon features the original logo for Viking, created by the renowned American illustrator Rockwell Kent: a Viking ship that evokes enterprise, adventure, and exploration, ideas that inspired the imprint's name at its founding and continue to inspire us.

For more information on Viking's history, authors, and books, please visit penguin.com/viking.